Comhairle Contae Fhine Gall

Fingal County Council

Items should be returned on or before the last date shown below. Items may be renewed by personal application, writing, telephone or by accessing the online Catalogue Service on Fingal Libraries' website. To renew give date due, borrower ticket number and PIN number if using online catalogue. Fines are charged on overdue items and will include postage incurred in recovery. Damage to, or loss of items will be charged to the borrower.

Date Due	Date Due	Date Due
20/3/18		

Doctor Barnardo

Doctor Barnardo

Champion of Victorian Children

MARTIN LEVY

AMBERLEY

First published 2013

Amberley Publishing
The Hill, Stroud
Gloucestershire, GL5 4EP

www.amberley-books.com

British Library Cataloguing in Publication Data.
A catalogue record for this book is available from the British Library.

ISBN 978 1 4456 0923 2

Typeset in 10pt on 12pt Sabon.
Typesetting and Origination by Amberley Publishing.
Printed in the UK.

Contents

Introduction

Empire is murdering populations in order to steal countries, and is not the proper occupation of a gentleman. By and large the Victorians were not gentlemen, and this is especially true of those who made a lot of money. The condition of the poor, best shown by those in the East End of London, was appalling. It was an utter disgrace that a country which was imposing its British way of life on others at the end of a rifle and a bayonet should have such a beastly British way of life in its great cities. We think of London as our example, because that was where young Barnardo started banging on the Victorian world's door to get things changed, but all great cities had the same shameful set of conditions.

Thomas John (T. J.) Barnardo was a Dublin-born workaholic Irishman whose non-stop efforts in the cause of children's welfare landed him in an early grave at the age of sixty. However, in his own area of work it's fair to say that he changed Britain forever, as much as any one man can. Much of modern child welfare started with him.

This isn't just a biography, it's also a social story which happens to have T. J. as its storyteller, digging into the filth and rot of what was then the world's biggest empire. A few conscience-stricken men, such as the 7th Earl of Shaftesbury, were stirring things up and getting limited changes for the better, against the opposition of the greed and entrenched selfishness of the so-called middle and upper classes of the day. If Shaftesbury was the captain of the reform movement, then people like Thomas John Barnardo were down in the engine room stoking the boiler to get things moving.

Because of the 'Irish Troubles' of 1916–22, when a great many archives went up in flames in a fire which destroyed the Dublin Central Records Office, some sources have been a bit stretched. However I have had access to the Barnardo family archives courtesy of Dr David Barnardo and his sister Patricia, who are great-grandchildren of T. J.'s brother George. Some other archives have also been consulted. Our hero seems to have been one of ten children of John Michaelis Barnardo, his mother being John's second wife.

Barnardo died in 1905. The basis of this book is the official biography, *Memoirs of the Late Dr Barnardo*, published by Hodder & Stoughton in 1907. It was written by James Marchant, in full co-operation with the widowed Mrs Barnardo, as well as the people running what was then and still is the large Barnardo organisation.

The reason for writing this update is partly, but not entirely, to translate the terribly stuffy and syrupy Edwardian English that Marchant used, and which imprisons a good story in the style of the day. It is also in several places wildly inaccurate, as my own researches on behalf of the family have confirmed. I have a personal interest as I grew up in the East End of London and know Whitechapel and Aldgate, what we could call the Barnardo manor.

There have been a number of biographies written since 1907 and there is a bibliography at the end of the book. My aim is to discuss what this man was up to, what he was up against, and despite his somewhat difficult character at times, how wonderfully well he succeeded. In the cause of the children he went banging on the door of the Victorian world and refused to stop until the day he died.

ONE

Origins and Beginnings: 1823–1866

There had to be a lot of poor for Thomas to be their champion. Equally obviously, if there were so many destitute people around, such system as existed must have gone pear-shaped. It needed changing morally, socially and physically. In Victorian Britain poverty was thought of as normal. The wealthy thought that destitution was the fault of the paupers, some sort of crime they were committing by being so poor.

Laws were brutal and brutally applied. In 1834 half a dozen men were transported to Australia for the crime, give or take a technicality or two, of wanting to form a trade union. They were famous as the Tolpuddle Martyrs, and in fact they were returned back home six years later. Also in 1834 there was a seminal Poor Law Act which had far-reaching consequences that can only be described as absolutely appalling in both its intentions and its effects.

Victorian poverty wasn't just a London thing, it was a national social attitude. Our emphasis will be on the East End of London, but it was everywhere, in the countryside as well as in the towns and cities. There was something radically wrong with society, and in mid-Victorian Britain we were very lucky we weren't hit by the disruption that had hit France at the end of the previous century. Mrs Elizabeth Gaskell was the wife of a Unitarian minister in Manchester. Known as Cottonopolis, Manchester was the centre of the Lancashire cotton industry, controlling the grim mills and grinding conditions of places like Oldham, Blackburn and Bolton. She was middle-class and well educated, though the family was not wealthy. Between 1845 and her death in 1865 Mrs Gaskell wrote several novels with an 'in your face' forthright honesty about the appalling social state of the area. These notably included *Mary Barton* and the barely less aggressive *North and South*. She was a redoubtable campaigner on the side of the oppressed working class. Hers was a baton being carried by a writer. The situation needed far more than epic and graphic stories, it needed decisive action. That's where T. J. comes into the story. His was action with its sleeves rolled up.

*

The *Memoirs*, published a couple of years after our hero died, gives the maiden name of his mother as Drinkwater. It wasn't, that was his maternal grandmother. I have been given a copy of the 1837 marriage certificate, where his mother spells her name as Bryan. Family fables tell the romantic tale of the elopement of Elizabeth Drinkwater with a broth of a boy, Philip O'Brien, very much a Catholic from County Clare. Shock! Horror! Darkening the very Quaker Protestant Drinkwater threshold was now forever forbidden. This marriage produced two girls, another Elizabeth and her younger sister Abigail, who is the one on the certificate.

Enter now John Michaelis Barnardo. The *Memoirs* give us a complete farrago about the family's origins which I won't repeat here. The family archives and other research show that John Michaelis, on his 1860 application to become a British citizen, gave Havelburg as his place of origin. He appears to have been born there some time in the year 1800. This is a modest-sized town north-west of Berlin where the River Havel joins the much larger

Elbe, in what was then the Brandenburg region of Prussia. On arrival in Dublin, probably in 1823, he was Jewish. He changed his religion to Anglican, and documents exist showing his adult baptism on 31 December 1826, to allow him to wed Elizabeth, his first wife, on New Year's Day 1827. Yes, his two wives were sisters.

A family member researched in Havelburg in 2005, trying to pick up a back-trail, but they failed. There may be many very good reasons for this; the history of the region is highly complex. In this context ignore 1933–45, which was a century and a half later. However, with the expansion of Prussia in the mid-eighteenth century there was a great deal of upheaval, people moving or being moved. At the beginning of the nineteenth century there were the Napoleonic Wars and even more upheaval.

All of which might cause difficulties for a researcher. There is another problem, which is that the family were Jewish. Even as late as this, patronymics were still in use, as they are still in use these days in the Middle East. Let us say Abraham son of Terah, son of Nahor. The next generation might show Isaac son of Abraham son of Terah, with Nahor dropped off the end. The prefix Bar is used very like the Scottish Mac in this respect, so the son of Nathan would be Bar Nathan, and very quickly in a society which doesn't speak either Hebrew or Yiddish and doesn't use the patronymic system, it emerges after a generation or two as Barnett.

It is presented as educated guesswork, but established in Dublin in 1812 was a paper-making business run by a family called Barnett, which is a very Jewish name. John Michaelis arrived in Dublin, when surely, coming from an unexceptional town like Havelburg, you would have expected him to head for London. We have no documentation to support it, but one feels the Barnetts were cousins and that he is in Dublin at their invitation. Quite what the Jewish family Barnett would have thought of him, only four years later, converting to Christianity we cannot discuss. But shades of the Drinkwaters, in their attitude when their daughter married a Catholic.

John Michaelis was a furrier at this period in his twenties, following what appears to have been the family trade. Again we have to use educated guesswork; the family have decided to set up an outpost in Dublin. It would give him an established source, if a bit slow and cumbersome, for his materials back in Prussia until he could set up locally. It might also have provided some items ready-made back in Havelburg. The fur trade is more exotic than paper-making, so why not invent a more exotic name? Barnardo has a touch of Latin about it, sounds much more impressive than Barnett in such a high end of the clothing trade enterprise.

The paperwork for his 1860 naturalisation application has him arriving in Britain in 1823, without exactly stating his port of arrival, but it gives us a starting point. How he finally arrived in Dublin offers a variety of scenarios. One is that he had a through ticket, which meant he wouldn't have spent a great length of time in London, where he may very well have transshipped. But we must remember that this is still the age of sail. In 1823 Stevenson's *Rocket* locomotive was six years in the future.

Which lets us tell the story of what happened in the year 1806 to the Revd J. G. F. Shultze. An ordained missionary, he was on his way from Germany, exact province not known, to some far land in Africa where he was intending to convert the local population to Lutheran Christianity. Instead he pitched up on the Irish Coast near Wexford, having been shipwrecked. Ships out of Germany simply wouldn't be in the Irish Sea other than with intent. That means they were heading for Dublin or had just left it, which strongly suggests that there was some degree of trade between the Prussians in the Baltic and Ireland. It also gives us clues to the movements of our friend John Michaelis seventeen years later. The shipwreck led to other things. Shultze managed to get from Wexford to Dublin. There he found that there was a vacancy for a pastor at the church serving the German community. Deciding to quit while he was winning he gave up all ideas of Africa and accepted the job. We will meet him again a little later.

So we have to set up a scenario. John Michaelis is a German-speaking Prussian. There was a German-speaking community in what was an English-speaking country. In that sort of situation religion didn't come top of the list. This is particularly so in the case of John Michaelis, who as we already realise wasn't powerfully moved by it. He is now in Dublin and there are two priorities: learn English and start earning a living. In those days large cities had street directories. The Dublin directory for 1827 shows him trading as a furrier at 13 Castle Street. Later directories show a couple of moves until in 1841 he makes his final move to 4 Dame Street, from which he traded for the rest of his life. Family archives have a poignant entry written by his son Henry in the shop daybook, dated 23 May 1874, recording his father's death.

Papa Barnardo was no longer living over the shop, but at 4 Upper Gardiner Street, in those days a very prosperous address. He left about £1,500, which would translate to something over £100,000 in the year 2000. At one time he had been worth more, but he lost a large sum on a railway venture that failed. Son Henry Lionel had become a partner a couple of years earlier and now took over the business. He moved it to Grafton Street, Dublin, from which in the year 2007 it was still being traded by his descendants.

Dame Street is one of the best trading streets in Dublin, just along from Trinity College, so where all the great and the good could be expected to pass the door. Papa Barnardo counted the Irish Viceroy and his lady among his customers, and they don't come higher up the social ladder than that. He was doing very nicely, thank you.

But tragedy struck when Elizabeth died in her seventh pregnancy and so did the baby. Of the seven only four reached full adulthood. Papa Barnardo had motherless children and a business to run, so would Aunt Abigail please help. She was delighted to do so and the children loved her. As the saying goes, one thing led to another, and they agreed to get married.

According to the law as it then stood, such close in-laws were forbidden to marry. This was clearly nonsense in cases like this, but it took until 1907 for the law to change. It had a lot to do with something called consanguinity, which involved ancient royal succession and the inheritance of vast estates; it shouldn't have affected the affairs of a Dublin shopkeeper.

Let's recall that Papa Barnardo started out Jewish. There is an ancient Jewish law which says that if a married man who has died has an unmarried brother, he should offer to marry the widow. This would protect her and her children, and it is by no means incidental that it keeps the dead man's property in the family. There is also the fact that Catherine of Aragon was the widow of Henry VIII's elder brother Arthur, who died young. So the man who founded the Church of England was married for twenty years to the lady who had originally been his sister-in-law. Therefore what we see here is nothing new. The way out of the dilemma was that Papa Barnardo was still a Prussian citizen. He was able to claim that the legal impediment didn't apply to him. The couple seem to have got away with the fact, which no one noticed, that of course it still applied to Abigail.

I am indebted to Dr David Barnardo for a photocopy of the 1837 marriage certificate. It is a wonderful example of how original documents like this can open a window on the age they come from. We resist the temptation to be confused, and instead embark on a little social study. The document is dated 23 June 1837, Queen Victoria had been on the throne three days. What we see has suffered from the ravages of time and damp, but is still readable. It may well have been written with a quill pen.

Abigail is shown with the first name Amical. This has been written by the elderly pastor, and yes, it's our friend J. G. F. Shultze. He has been the incumbent for over thirty years and is getting a little hard of hearing. Abigail's surname is now spelled Bryan. This might be a very Irish thing; O'Brien would have indicated Catholic origins and she and her family definitely wanted to present themselves to the world as Protestants. John Michaelis has his surname spelled Bernardo, so there is a vowel change there as well. Those personal details of the happy couple we get from the crabbed and shaky hand of Pastor Shultze.

There are of course witnesses. We see that Fanny Connell has a crisp and well-formed signature. For the daughter of the house to have the leisure and the encouragement which her handwriting suggests has to mean that the Connell household had some money. James Connell on the other hand has the signature of a demented drunken spider, it is dreadful and barely readable. What his exact relationship to Fanny was is not known. Another witness, easy to read but clearly not educated, is Mary Bryan, relationship not definite. We then have a signature some sources say is Ellen Bryan. Having had a professional enlargement done, this is definitely Ellisa J. Bryan, relationship again not definitely known. This signature is hesitant, starts well but trails off badly.

Women in that era rarely signed legal documents, many women could only sign a 'mark' that someone else had to certify was theirs. Both Bryan witnesses signed in full, but there is about their signatures a question of how well they would have done had they tried to write a complete letter.

Both have an air of nervousness about them. Abigail and the two Bryan witnesses having the same surname, it is generally assumed they were her unmarried sisters.

The last witness has a strong, confident signature, nothing shaky about him. Not totally clear, but very probably Jos A. Calvert. Whoever he was, that he had success comes off the page. Modern forms usually ask for signatures and your name in block capitals. Until now I have often thought that was tiresome bureaucracy, but in the case of this last signature it would have been useful.

Shultze styles himself as Minister of the German Church. It's a pity that the bride and groom didn't sign themselves, to give us a view of Abigail's writing; there are several of John's in the archives. The records show that the amiable pastor died eighteen months later in February 1839. What a lot of social comment, having something of these people come off this little piece of paper, just by reading their signatures. The modern Barnardo family, until these most recent researches, had been under the impression that the 1837 wedding probably took place in London. It has been possible to find the Shultze register of marriages and actually find the entry, one of several that day. No question now that it was in Dublin.

Shultze was what at the time was known as a 'couple beggar'. He was one of several clergymen who were prepared to oblige couples who wanted to marry despite family opposition. Many objections were across the religious divide, others involved legal entanglements. We could possibly refer to consanguinity in this case. He was a sort of Friar Lawrence figure, who was prepared to join these Romeos to their Juliets despite the Montagues and Capulets who may have objected. Between his arrival in 1806 and his demise in 1839 he appears to have presided over about 6,000 marriages. Most of them could not possibly have been German, from his own small Lutheran congregation in Poolbeg Street, Dublin. They must mainly have been from the general community. One might say that our friend the pastor was onto a nice little earner.

The Family Records Centre in London advises that the printed marriage certificate which comes down to us from the first marriage between John Michaelis and Elizabeth is an officially recognised document. The second one, involving Abigail, which includes the printed phrase, 'joined in Holy Matrimony', was not. What we have the second time appears to be a form being produced by an enterprising firm in the printing trade, for the use of Nonconformist churches such as Poolbeg Street. In fact it is quite small and at first glance might be a receipt from a shop. The phrase Shultze uses, 'Minister of the German Church', would have been better if it had been amplified to read 'Minister according to the rites of the German Lutheran Church'. This would have clarified the very Irish hang-up over religion, that it was Protestant, not Catholic. Importantly for those concerned, the impression that comes down to us is that it would have been regarded as legal under Prussian law, so would have been recognised in Ireland.

Nature took its course and Abigail started to have children. Things must have been cramped and crowded; they were still living over the shop. Family records show that Abigail had eight pregnancies and raised six children to adulthood. Adolphus went to America, Dr David's ancestor George became an engineer and worked for the British Raj in India, Celia went back to Havelburg and became Frau Markau, Frederick became a doctor. Next was our hero Thomas John, and the youngest was Henry Lionel, who took over the shop. Of Elizabeth's family two became furriers, Theo in Cork and Bernard in Glasgow.

When T. J. was born Abigail was too weak to nurse him so a wet nurse was employed, and she looked after him in her own home. Sophie, seventeen years older than her half-brother, popped round one day to find the baby unattended and dangerously close to an open window. She grabbed him and took him home. When the wet nurse found him missing she rushed round to the Barnardo house, there to get a right roasting from an irate Sophie. She was told that if she wanted to keep the job she would have to move into Dame Street. For several months this is what the woman did.

When those who had survived childhood were old enough, John Michaelis was able to send them to school. The fact that another of his sons apart from T. J. became a doctor, something not cheap today and even more expensive in the values of those days, endorses the idea that Papa Barnardo was a prosperous man. Abigail had a very important influence on all the children, her sister's as well as her own. She was a very Christian lady, much into good works among the poor. Later in life T. J. was to say that in childhood he didn't feel any great pull towards religion, but like most kids he went with the flow.

Thomas John Barnardo arrived on 4 July 1845. As an adult he never got past 160 centimetres, or 5 feet 3 inches, and he was short-sighted from an early age. Not surprisingly he was never good at sports, but he read a lot and it rapidly became obvious that he was highly intelligent. Like most kids he could be plain bloody obstinate, not averse to getting into mischief, lively, good-natured, and generally his behaviour was quite normal. By the middle of the nineteenth century photography had been invented and there are some good, sharp pictures of him. We see him at eleven, fourteen and twenty-one. All show him dressed as prosperous middle-class, stiff starched collar and a floppy bow-tie. In the one as an adult he is wearing tinted spectacles.

What T. J. didn't like was the school he attended as a teenager, which had one of those dreadful 'beat 'em and flog 'em' headmasters. He leaves us a quote about the principal, inevitably a Doctor of Divinity, that he 'seemed to take a savage delight in beating his boys'. That was in the days of the Victorian Empire, and when one reads Dickens describing Dotheboys Hall in *Nicholas Nickleby* one realises he was quoting from life. We tend to forget that Dickens was not only a good storyteller, he was also an active social reformer. This explains why T. J. vowed never to beat any child, and deliberately, at least to begin with, never carried that necessary fashion accessory for men, a walking-stick, when he went out.

The poor had the reality of life and earning a living land on their shoulders at a very early age. With the middle-class Barnardo family, T. J. was allowed more time, and it wasn't until about sixteen or seventeen that he started to think about what he wanted to do in life. Having gone with the flow, dutifully going to church every Sunday, it was at this age that he caught the Christianity bug big time. This delighted his mum, who along with Fred and George was wholly committed. Fred was already studying medicine, but for T. J. choices weren't that simple. Plenty of people who study medicine find out after a time that either they don't have the brains, or they don't have the application. As our story unfolds we find out that while the brains were there, applying himself to the long hard slog of study was something our hero wasn't very good at.

*

Why don't we take a look at what was going on in the great big wide world? The year 1848 was a very important one in European politics. There was revolution afoot in several places. In France a smooth-talking but not very competent nephew of Napoleon Bonaparte got himself elected as president of an uneasy republic.

This he somehow managed to convert into a monarchy a couple of years later, calling himself Emperor Napoleon III. There had been a Napoleon II who never ruled and died young. In the Austrian Empire, with more revolution in the air, the unsteady ship of state came under the guidance of eighteen-year-old Archduke Franz Joseph. In Britain there were the first moves to give married women some legal control over their possessions, until then under the control of their husbands.

Not reported on the world stage but important to our story, there was a rather pleasant event that year in the English county of Surrey. The Elmlies had a daughter, who they named Sarah Louise, but who was very soon being called Syrie. This young lady will eventually have a central role in our story. In 1848 the baby's father was perilously impecunious, the family fortune gathered in by her grandfather having suffered badly. Elmslie's financial standing improved sufficiently for him to be employed at Lloyd's, but not as a full member. We can allow ourselves to call him middle-class, but he was never significantly wealthy.

When T. J. was six Britain staged the 1851 Great Exhibition in Hyde Park. It had Queen Victoria's husband as its driving force and proved an enormous success. It was housed in the Crystal Palace, a huge but elegant greenhouse designed by Joseph Paxton, whose day job was being head gardener to the Duke of Devonshire. Imagine a prefabricated building of cast iron frames and glass panels over 400 metres long and about 120 wide, built high enough to roof over several fully grown trees, which therefore didn't have to be cut down. From the first spade in the ground to completion was six months. Any builders reading this may have just had heart attacks from disbelief. In today's world it would take over two years just to get the planning permission, and heaven alone knows what health and safety would make of all that glass. Six million people paid to see all the newly invented wonders of the industrial world. Its most frequent visitor, Queen Victoria herself, was said to have visited over forty times. The considerable profits bought 50 acres of land on which were built the Kensington Museums and the Royal Albert Hall. Paxton received a knighthood for his simple genius of design and its construction on time and on budget.

That great success was followed three years later by the appalling disaster of the Crimean War, when 20,000 British soldiers died of disease and neglect, and only 1,600 from the wounds of war. At least one of the results was a revolution in hospital nursing, driven forward by the redoubtable Florence Nightingale. This in turn showed up the bad habits of many doctors, and drove up standards all round. Hard on the heels of that came the Indian Mutiny, which Britain won at great cost in lives at the time, but inevitably lost about ninety years later, when independence for India led the way to the breakup of the British Empire.

Historically hard on the heels of that was the death of Victoria's husband Albert, on whom she absolutely doted. Having had nine children in seventeen years, one would have thought the woman would have welcomed the rest. Instead she took to wearing black, went to Windsor Castle and stayed there for most of the next forty years.

Not much noticed at the time, but increasingly so as the century progressed, was Karl Marx, the middle-class son of a German family and the influential socialist. His opinions being increasingly unpopular in other countries he had lived in, he came to Britain, the one place where those who ruled were so supremely confident of their place in the world that they could tolerate dissent. There is no doubt that his heart was in the right place. It was a pity that his ideas were to prove so controversial and cost so many lives when people tried to convert what looked so good on paper into practice in the real world of real people. These days T. J. may not be as famous as Marx, but in his own day he was a charismatic champion of destitute children, shaming his contemporaries into changing their attitudes towards children in general and the poor in particular.

*

In recollections many years later T. J. wrote that while he was still sixteen, on 26 May 1862, he made his most significant decision. After what had been a long period of thinking about it, he decided that he was going to be a totally committed Christian. This was also the time when he was having trouble passing exams at school. He never was a good scholar in formal education, however brilliant he turned out to be in other things. Faced with a son who was never going to shine as an academic, Papa Barnardo arranged for him to be apprenticed to a wine merchant. It was an ironic turn of fate that it should have been that trade, given the total temperance stance he adopted only a couple of years later, as he became aware of the mess people made of their lives due to excess of drink.

I realise that I keep mentioning the social classes, but they were hugely important at the time. 'The poor are always with us' is a statement of fact at least 2,000 years old. The Barnardo family were middle-class, prosperous and Protestant. In Ireland religion had even more significance than social class. The largely Catholic peasantry was ruled by the ostentatiously Protestant elite. There was, especially in the south and west, very considerable poverty and the subliminal ethos among Protestants was that it was the religion which caused the poverty.

Very oddly, and to our own generation it seems really peculiar, the Atlantic Coast peasantry had adopted the potato as food almost to the exclusion of anything else; there were families who ate virtually nothing else. Inevitably the soil became exhausted of the necessary nutrients for healthy crops, and the stage was set for disaster. There had been warning signs over the previous two decades, as in the mid-1820s there had been considerable hunger. Then came the big one, when for three years in a row, 1847–49, potato blight struck and wiped out the crop. What followed is writ large in Irish history.

It shouldn't have been the problem it became, because in the north and east of Ireland there was extensive crop rotation and mixed farming. While it can be agreed that some of the land is difficult to farm, people made a living from it for thousands of years before the potato arrived. With sensible management, and one might say a willingness by those who governed to educate the Irish in the crop-rotation system that had been ancient when the Romans arrived, it could all have been dealt with. The government in Westminster and officials in Whitehall had the morals of hungry hyenas. At the heart of this was their deliberately anti-Catholic stance. Food was even being exported to England from the east while families starved in the west and south.

The Protestant government in Westminster could have stepped in and sorted out the Catholic destitution and starvation if it had wanted to. History tells us that it didn't, when clearly there was food available. Not least it's an island, in a sea that in those days was full of fish. This was an ignoble religious war that cost well over a million lives. It is estimated that about 2 million managed to emigrate, a lot of them to America, where an amazing number of them became policemen. Several American Presidents have claimed descent from these emigrants. The diametrically anti-Catholic – and one must say by definition also anti-Christian – attitude which produced that vast stain on the frock-coat of British imperial tyranny still vibrates in modern Anglo–Irish relations.

Returning to the ancient remark that the poor are always with us, T. J. was about three at the height of the famine, and as he grew up there was a plentiful supply of poor to be always with him. His working career with the wine merchant started in the office. Whether he enjoyed the work or not, it instilled in him good working practices which stayed with him and proved useful in later life. Despite the offer of promotion his temperance attitudes won out, and he left.

This period of his life in Dublin seems to have been very busy. He kept a haphazard journal where we find an entry for Saturday 18 October 1862, which includes the remark 'getting home from business', which we can assume was from the wine merchants. Later that day he visited Dr Hunt, a friend who had recently been unwell, but was now on the mend. Hunt was a Doctor of Divinity and this was early in the days of his great enthusiasm for matters spiritual.

The date tells us that he was now over seventeen years old. If ever a young man was taken over and absorbed by Christianity is was young Barnardo. He was heavily involved in Christian evangelism with a sect called the Open Brethren, who worked out of a place called Merrion Hall. He went about with teams from this group in an area of Dublin known as 'the Liberties', about the poorest of several poor areas of the city. Indeed, if there was a Christian organisation of this type in Dublin T. J. hadn't joined it would have been the exception. He had become a Sunday school teacher, was helping at a 'ragged school', worked with the YMCA and with Christian workers all over the city. This involved a great deal of evangelism and prayers for the sick, which we can agree didn't leave him a great deal of time for his day job.

*

And what was a ragged school? State-funded education didn't arrive until the reforms of 1870, and initially only catered for children between the ages of five and ten. It took several decades to develop, it didn't arrive fully organised and ready to go. Up to 1870 the desperately poor usually had little or no choice. There were however dame-schools for those who could find a small weekly payment. These tended to be run by respectable lower-middle-class ladies, often with the backing of the local gentry. Charlotte Brontë has her heroine *Jane Eyre* working in one for a short time. All was not entirely lost for the poorest children, because there were a number of ragged schools. These were funded by charitable donations, and were usually supported by the churches around the area. They supplied some sort of education for those children prepared to make the enormous effort it took, given their poverty, just to turn up. Standards varied, but they taught the basics of reading, writing and arithmetic, plus usually a grounding in the Christian religion.

There had been a printer in Gloucester at the end of the eighteenth century called Robert Raikes, who had set up a school, mostly at his own expense, for some of the poorest children in his area. Yet another Christian, his original purpose was to help reduce crime in the area around his home by getting young roughs and scruffs off the streets. He hoped that he might be able to get some morals and ethics into them. In practice, with the simple thinking of an honest man, get them reading the Bible. That was all very well, so long as he first taught them to read, and not only the children, but their parents as well. Up to then very few among the poor could do more than read their own name, and many couldn't even do that.

There was at that time no free education, and these poor people didn't have the money to buy any. He persuaded church folk to give it their support and they of course saw it as a way of enlarging their congregations. Emerging as the Sunday School Union in 1804, there developed a countrywide network of church-run schools, which over the next generation greatly improved national literacy and numeracy. The bonus for the churches was more money in the collection plates, albeit much of it in farthings and halfpennies. The more the poor working class learned, the more they wanted to learn. Once the genie of education was out of the bottle, there was no way of putting it back.

*

Let's progress to the decade of the 1860s. The China Inland Mission had been founded in England by one of these typical evangelical Victorians, the Reverend Hudson Taylor. The idea was to try and convert China's teeming millions to Christianity. China was at the time trying to absorb the indignity of having lost the Opium Wars, which allowed British traders to bring in opium by the ton, diametrically against the very sensible wishes of the Emperor and his government, who had been going to enormous lengths to try and keep it out. More greasy stains on the frock-coat of the British Empire! Whatever the British upper classes and the political parties they controlled claimed were the aims of their Pax Britannica, their actions made it clear again and again that no one with the least vestige of an education could have called them Christians.

By 1865 T. J. was doing some serious Bible study in a class run by Grattan Guinness, a name which suggests he was surely connected with the brewing family. In February 1866 Guinness was in Liverpool on business and he heard Taylor speak at a meeting. He persuaded him to come to Dublin and talk about his mission and his travels to his students. At the subsequent meeting T. J. was one of those present. He was immediately caught by a young man's enthusiasm for something that sounded new and exciting. Taylor was looking for recruits and several of them showed an interest. With his work in the Dublin slums T. J. already had powerful experience of what it was like to work among the poor.

It appears that Taylor encouraged those who were interested, and just as important could find the fare, to travel to London where they could all meet up again. The idea was to sort out the enthusiasts of the moment from those with a long-term determination. He perhaps didn't make it clear enough that he would only take on those he thought were suitable for missionary work, and those he didn't would find it a long way back to Dublin and he hoped they had the fare. Papa Barnardo was by no means amused and refused to encourage the venture, but many of the young man's Christian friends in the YMCA and Open Brethren gave him their support.

We therefore find him in London in April 1866, technically still a minor; he wasn't an adult until 4 July that year. If Papa Barnardo had wanted to push it he could have stopped him leaving Dublin until then. Some time in May 1866 a party of men, which did not include T. J., left London Docks on the good ship *Lammamuir*. Taylor sensed that the young Irishman wouldn't take to the discipline that he as leader of the Mission thought necessary. There was too much energy, and most importantly too much independence and personal initiative, which would make him difficult to control and just do as he was told.

Taylor had for a short time studied medicine but had given up. He softened the disappointment by suggesting to T. J. that it would be most useful to the Mission and its work if he took up medical studies. This was the key to his decision to apply to the London Hospital for a place as a medical student and it was to totally change the direction of his life. It was an ironic turn of fortune when, decades later, Taylor invited the then nationally famous Dr Thomas John Barnardo to join the China Inland Mission Board.

TWO

Early Days in London: 1866–1876

Initially under the auspices of Taylor, in April 1866 Thomas John Barnardo had arrived in London. We find ourselves in the East End. The main thoroughfare we are interested in hereabouts is Whitechapel Road, and the area is Stepney, now part of the borough of Tower Hamlets. This road goes past what was then known as the London Hospital, which still exists under its more modern title of the Royal London, and is one of the main trauma centres in the capital.

He was found lodgings at 30 Coburn Street, the home of Mrs Mary Parsons, a widow of impeccable Christian credentials. It wasn't until October that he applied to study for the entrance exam for the nearby London Hospital Medical School. That leaves us with six months to fill. We can look for help by dipping into his rather haphazard diary, possibly journal would be a better word. This suffers at times from rather long gaps, but we can paraphrase a relevant and interesting entry. Written in the past tense, it may well be a recollection written some years later: 'For four or five years the missionary work I wanted to do would have to be put on hold. This means I was being expected to use all that time to do my preparation. It wasn't how things necessarily had to work out. Whilst I hadn't gone to China, I was in the field. And the field is the world.'

Fortunately for all of us several generations later he explains what he means by this very Victorian turn of phrase.

> Although I was only in East London, unknown, comparatively friendless and without influence, yet all around me there were people I could help to evangelise for Christianity. I looked around to see where evangelistic work could be done in my spare hours. There were numerous opportunities for evangelising in the open air, for right opposite the hospital was a great wide space called the Mile End Waste, where crowds gathered and passed the long evenings of summer, listening and disputing on all manner of subjects, political, social or religious. Accordingly, on my way home after a hard day's work, I acquired the habit of turning towards the Waste and taking part.

Having grown up in London and gone to school 100 yards away from the London Hospital with sons and grandsons of Barnardo boys, I am well acquainted with what it looked like in the middle of the twentieth century, about forty years after our hero died. In the years immediately after the Second World War Barnardo was still a well-known and respected name in the area. A mile or so from the school gate is a little street named after him.

When I knew it then, the great Mile End Waste had been overtaken by development, including Whitechapel Road Underground station. There still remained a wide strip on which there was a daily market of stalls selling fruit and vegetables, clothes, and a whole range of things open-air traders sell. The market as I knew it stretched over a quarter of a mile, say nearly half a kilometre, from the Blind Beggar pub on the corner of Brady Street to Vallance Road near the school. Much reduced in size from Victorian times, and no longer called Mile End Waste, it was still a colourful bustle of robust, but usually good-humoured language. Every woman was 'Darlin' and every man was 'Guv'.

The women wanted the fruit 'orf the front, none of that rubbish rahnd the back!' Round the back was where they had the dodgy stuff they could offload onto an unsuspecting visitor. Don't lose yourself in the romance of a Cockney idyll, like most romances such a thing never existed. It was busy, vibrant and usually cheerful, they saved up their miseries until they got home. Things change, times change, nothing in society stands still. It was into this area, in among the grandparents and great-grandparents of the boys I knew and grew up with, that our twenty-one-year-old Irish immigrant arrived. As you would suspect, it would take some time for him to make an impact.

There was a little something he had to get on with: his entrance exam to the Medical School. The hard work he mentions in his journal was probably his studying. However enthusiastic he may have appeared to have been, it took him until late 1867 to gain admission and be registered as a student. Some of this delay can be laid at the door of a trip he made to Paris in the spring of that year. Hardly the sort of thing we would expect from an impecunious student who did not at that time have the full support of his father back in Dublin. It seems obvious however that he was getting a little funding from somewhere.

What does seep through to us is that he lacked full application for the course of study. He was always acknowledged as being very intelligent, and sometimes people like T. J. find study a weary flog, too restricting for them. We have to realise that medicine wasn't what he wanted to do with his life, it was only a key to a gate he wanted to open. Reading the journal extract above, it's clear that what he really wanted to do was to be a Christian evangelist, he had stumbled on medicine rather by accident. At the risk of mixing metaphors, he was opening the gate, but in a very haphazard way. Using his own words from the journal, he was getting into the field. That done he would have to get busy ploughing his first furrows.

We have the benefit of a note from a fellow student, William Mayer, who did have application to study and at the time T. J. died was a doctor in Devon. This is a good-humoured letter written to the biographer James Marchant when he was researching for the *Memoirs*. When his hopes of an immediate journey to China were dashed, T. J. left Mrs Parsons and moved to nearby Dempsey Street where Mayer and a couple of other students also lodged. Dr Mayer recalls some generally complimentary things about him, but then the cloak slips a bit.

> Gradually it became obvious that his heart was not wholly in his work at the college and hospital. Although he went along with the student life, joined in a game of football occasionally, did his professional work, none of it seems to be done with any great enthusiasm. As time went by it became clear that such things weren't his first concern, he had other things on his mind. The rest of us began to wonder what it was that our friend was really interested in.

Mayer then treats us to a little dialogue, in which T. J. is the subject of humorous gossip among his first-year student friends, Mayer being one of them. A couple of Victorian-style idioms have been gently reworded for clarity.

> 'Odd fellow, Barnardo.'
> 'Yes! What's wrong with the man?'
> 'Seems to me he's got something on his mind.'
> 'I wonder what his little game is?'
> 'He's up to something we don't know about.'
> 'He's a dark horse.'
> 'He has brains, you know. Shouldn't wonder if he's reading on the sly.'
> 'Not him! The other day he didn't know what the brachial plexus was.'
> 'Does he bet?'
> 'Doesn't look like it.'
> 'Is there a woman?'
> 'Nonsense!'
> 'Someone told me they saw him in the street yesterday. He was preaching!'

Mayer then gives us the entire group chorusing, 'Preaching!' in shocked and horrified tones.

> 'Who said that?'
> 'Smith Senior. He was positive it was Barnardo.'
> 'Good heavens!'
> 'A religious crank!'
> 'I won't believe it until I see it.'
> 'Ranter, I suppose.'
> 'Could be Christian Mission?'
> 'Hypocrite.'
> 'No wonder we don't like him.'
> 'He'll be getting up prayer meetings next.'
> 'I bet he doesn't.'
> 'It's a disgrace to the Hospital.'
> 'Wonder if the house committee knows?'
> 'Let's drop his acquaintance.'

What we have here is a group of middle-class Victorian young men – no working-class lads could have afforded the fees – reacting to T. J.'s consuming passion for evangelical Christianity. Though they would all have called themselves Christians and in outlook would have been more or less telling the truth, most of them would have summed up religion by saying, 'Church, my dear chap, is for Sundays.' They all wanted to be doctors, they were the caring and concerned sort, very decent and reasonably upright in their conduct. They could sleep through a fifty-minute sermon with the best of them. But to actually know someone who went out on to the highways and byways to preach shook them to the points of their starched white collars. Yet it is worth repeating that they were all decent young men, ready to work in a hospital in one of the poorest areas of the capital.

'But street preaching! One just doesn't do that sort of thing, my dear chap! Not cricket, don't you know!'

Simply put, T. J. didn't know, so he went on doing it. And to save you looking it up, the brachial plexus refers to a system of nerves in the arm.

If Whitechapel Road could be said to go past the front of the hospital, the newly established Commercial Road could be said to go past the back. Dr Mayer continues his letter by recalling that he once found his friend addressing a small gathering in Commercial Road. He was obviously being treated by them as a regular and was being listened to with respect. The roughs and scruffs of the labouring poor, to use the English phrase, were the ones that Karl Marx called the masses. They were often too ashamed of their dirt to go into the gleaming brass and polished oak of a church on a Sunday. The Victorian churches dispensed their middle-class version of spiritual medicine with dedicated condescension to the working-class soul. If the poor found a man whose style they liked they often preferred a street preacher, and T. J. was becoming a good one and gaining in popularity. Vertically challenged at 5 foot 3, he was a threat to no one, but all reports are that he was a dynamic speaker once he got going.

In a magazine article in later years, T. J. recalled an incident from these early days. By then an experienced writer of children's stories, we accept what he writes as basically true, but, shall we say, a little imaginatively embellished. In my own turn I have had to disinter this tale from his convoluted Victorian style of writing. He thought nothing of producing sentences of over 100 words, far too long for our modern world, but I hope in my version his humour comes across.

His various good works in the area had begun to get him recognised and the East Enders were beginning to take to him. He tells us that one evening he visited a penny gaff, which was a cross between a music hall and a boozer. It went much further than a modern pub having a band in; some of these places could hold 700 or 800 people. He writes that he asked the landlord if he could go up on the stage in the interval to say a few words. The landlord didn't really take to the idea but said he would allow it if T. J. paid him £5. Our hero said he would pay half in advance, but keep the other half back for afterwards, which proved to be a very shrewd move. When the interval duly arrived T. J. climbed up onto the stage, to be greeted by a rousing cheer. Half the clientèle knew who he was, what he was likely to get up to, and they were expecting some excitement. He now moves into the action of his tale.

'Obtaining silence at last I offered, if they would be quiet, to sing them a solo.' From this and other references it would appear that T. J. had quite a good singing voice.

Having sung the song he then quickly got into his main theme, which was to harangue them about the dangers of the demon drink. The sheer nerve of the man is breathtaking. Here he was in a great big gaff, in a rough area of London where the crowd had turned boozing into an art form, and he was preaching a temperance sermon. As we can well imagine, he is only a couple of minutes into his talk when the landlord rushes up.

'Stop! Stop! Stop! You'll ruin my business!'

'But I've paid you to let me give my talk,' says T. J. with beautifully played innocent indignation.

'I don't care what you've paid me!' shouts the landlord. 'I don't care if you've paid me twice as much, you can't preach temperance in my gaff!'

The uproar this produced in the crowd we can well imagine, it must have been the best comedy act they had seen that year. Clearly mine host hadn't realised who T. J. was, but half the regulars had known from the start and were cheering him on for the fun of it.

'I'll leave if you insist,' says T. J. when he could get himself heard. 'However you have broken our agreement. I paid you to let me come up on the stage. If you are stopping me from going on with my talk I shall want my money back.'

In the middle of a great deal of cheering and applause the landlord reluctant returned it.

'Right lads!' says our hero briskly, 'Anyone who wants to finish off our little chat, I shall be waiting for you just outside.'

With that he gave them a bow and left, he reports to rousing cheers and the rhythmic applause known as Kentish Fire. He was followed out of the gaff by a number of the regulars and proceeded to hold his meeting in the street, standing on a fruit barrow. There, so he tells us the story, he gave them a thoroughgoing harangue on the dangers of the demon drink, which he claims was well received. Having given them the best of his strong views on the subject, he went home feeling that he'd had a thoroughly enjoyable evening.

There is little difference between water off a duck's back and booze down a drinker's throat in the real world, but this incident shows us that T. J. was beginning to get himself known. He might be a bit of an oddball with his temperance ideas, but at heart the locals thought he was a good bloke. He might give forth with some stormy views, but they listened to it all with their East End humour. The idea that many of them took what he was saying seriously is a non-starter; it was a bit of fun, he meant well and it brightened up the evening. There was always going to be a vast chasm between them listening to him, which cost nothing, and the serious boozers among them actually doing anything about changing their habits. Clearly by now he wasn't just preaching a plain Christian message, he had found a theme. He saw drink as one of the root causes of poverty and domestic violence. For these reasons he was trying to get them out of the pubs and the gaffs.

When I mentioned that our hero might sometimes embellish his recollections, this is an example. He tells us that the landlord asked him for £5 before he would let him go up on the stage. One way of looking at it is that he thought of a number and multiplied it, coming up with a number so enormous no one in his right mind would pay it. Even more important, no one in his right mind would walk into an East End penny gaff with that much on him. In those days and in that area, £5 was a huge amount of money. A housemaid in service with the gentry in a much more respectable area of the capital might get no more than that in a year in actual cash, though she would get her bed, board and clothes as well. Even a butler in some less than aristocratic households was doing well on £25 a year, in actual cash, plus the same extras. In the poverty-stricken west of Ireland £5 was more than some entire families saw in a year. It was the price of the fare from Cork to America. Yet T. J. tells us he was walking around the East End with that much in his pocket and happy to spend it as described.

The Office of National Statistics emphasises that a lot of their nineteenth-century figures are only educated guesses, but they suggest that between 1866 and 2000 the value of money in the United Kingdom changed by a factor of seventy-one. In other words T. J. was offering the landlord £355 in 2000 values, just to be allowed to go up on the stage. When we give it further thought, that might not have been all the money T. J. had in his purse. We have established already that he was a young man who needed to count his pennies, because his father back in Dublin was not yet backing his adventure. His sources of income at this very early stage of his life in London are hazy. It is clearly much more likely that he was using artistic license and the amount involved may not have been more than a couple of shillings. A shilling converts to 5 pence in decimal money, so in 2000 values a couple of shillings would be about £14. And we've had some more inflation since 2000 of course!

Life wasn't always so simple. He reports that on another of his street-corner meetings he was pelted with mud held together with horse dung. Going into another gaff he wasn't so well received, but was knocked to the floor and thumped. After he was rescued and managed to get home he was visited by a policeman who wanted to know if he intended to prosecute anyone. Very wisely he said no, despite having discovered that he had come away from the incident with two broken ribs. Again the sheer nerve of the man comes out. Tightly bandaged up around his ribs, he went back to the same gaff the following evening. This won him a far better reception. Over the course of the next week he reports that he had several visitors checking on how he was. He tells us that this bit of rough treatment and his broken ribs opened more doors to him than anything he'd done up to then. When we think about it, the sheer nerve of this tiny man with the big heart was enormous. In the opinion of much of the community he was a well-meaning oddball, but he certainly proved to them he wasn't a quitter.

In another article we have a story from the 1890s, when T. J. had become a famous man, especially in the East End. He tells us that he was visiting lodging houses that his organisation ran in the area of Spitalfields, which means he wasn't far from where my grandparents lived at the time. While he was making his calls he was attacked by a gang of Victorian muggers, who stole his purse, his hat and his pocket-watch. Being the sort of character he was, he dusted himself down and got on with his house calls. Coming out onto the street ten minutes later he was approached by the gang leader, who returned his property.

''ad we a know'd you wus Doctor Barnardo, we wouldn't a touched yer, Guvnor, an' we begs yer pardon.'

This suggests that somewhere on his property, engraved on his watch or a card in his purse perhaps, was an identification of some sort. It reminds us of an incident involving the great clown Grimaldi, a much-loved character of the 1820s, to whom a remarkably similar thing happened. The story that comes down to us from what was then about sixty years earlier was that that the gang took the loot to their 'Fagin' and it was only because he could read that they found out who their victim was. They are said to have gone to his house and returned the property the next day, whereas T. J. got his back in ten minutes. We will shortly come to the fact that he had started his working life in London as a ragged school teacher about a mile away. It would seem that there were beginning to be results from his efforts. The muggers of the 1890s were just as poor and just as dishonest, but at least they could read.

*

The idea that the cockney is the absolutely typical example of an Englishman is about as far off the mark as Texas is from Timbuktu. I grew up in the area many decades after all this was happening, when the horses had gone and they were beginning to pull down the bombed-out debris of the Blitz and replace it with the treeless brick jungle of fifties flats. The determined cheerfulness of the East Ender emerged from the noise and the explosions and the awful shaking undaunted. It was shabby, some of it was still poor and some of it always will be.

Brick Lane, just off Whitechapel Road, had a Huguenot church in the eighteenth century, a synagogue in the nineteenth century, and it's now a main centre for Asian restaurants. You are more likely to find a curry than sausage and chips. People have been living by the first reasonable ford across the Thames, as marked by London Bridge, for at least 4,000 years. The East End was where the Romans moored their ships and Latinised the local Celtic name to Londinium. By the end of the nineteenth century ocean-going ships were getting too big for the old upstream docks, and trade gradually went downriver, though smaller draught vessels such as barges and river buses still ply a good trade. In the 1860s when T. J. was just starting out, the Pool of London was a huge port which attracted sailors from all nations to its wharves and jetties, bringing cargoes from all the known world and sending out a torrent of manufactured goods from the country which liked to call itself the workshop of the world.

Every race and every creed that has ever sought the bloody-minded idea that people hereabouts think of as normal, that we can have our own opinions and can express them, has found itself at one time or another in the East End. It isn't an accident that the most famous building in the East End is the Tower of London, built by the tyrant William the Conqueror. The City only borrows it, really it's ours! Built to terrify, nine centuries later it's a much-loved tourist attraction. Within 30 miles of its shadow there are people speaking 300 different languages. But the English, the English, who are the English? Nowhere will it be proved more clearly than in the East End that the English are really a load of bloody foreigners.

And all this applies to our hero, a Dublin-born Irish son of a Prussian Jewish creator of finest-quality fur coats for the ladies of the gentry. Just as there was a German community in Dublin, so there was one in the East End, supporting no less than five churches. The pastor of one of them offered spiritual comfort to the German community in the West End; he was chaplain to Queen Victoria's German mother.

The multiplicity of ancestral lines is something we regard as normal. The original European aborigines, the Celts, Romans, Angles, Jutes, Saxons, Vikings, Danes, Normans, Plantagenets, anyone and everyone who fell off the end of Europe and ended up here. Come one, come all, if there is a family in Britain who can trace their ancestry back to 1866, when T. J. arrived in London, and cannot find an immigrant among them, that would be remarkable. In 1866 the Empress of the vast British Empire was a stout little dab of a woman, dressed interminably in black, as German as her black lace mittens, the widow of a minor German prince. German that is, if you left out her distant Breton, Norman, Danish, French, Spanish and Scots forebears, to name only a few of them.

The year 1868 was the year of three Prime Ministers. It started with the 14th Earl of Derby, who unfortunately suffered from ill health and had to resign, and died the following year. The previous year the Tory government had passed the Second Reform Act, which greatly enlarged the electorate, but did little to shift the hands on the reins of power. With Derby gone we fleetingly had Prime Minister Disraeli, but when a general election was called he found he didn't quite have enough to win, which let in the Liberal William Ewart Gladstone.

Disraeli had an ancestral affinity with T. J., being also the son of a Jewish father, in this case a highly respected academic. Just as John Michaelis changed his religion, so did Disraeli. He did it to further his political ambitions and proved very successful. He was a man of culture, author of three novels which sold well at the time, a smooth-talker who knew how to get Queen Victoria out of her grumpier moods. The opposite of Gladstone, who was best described as a garrulous Liverpudlian, someone who never used five words if fifty would do. Victoria complained that he spoke to her like a public meeting.

It was into this huge sprawl of deprivation at one end and wealth at the other that our energetic young Irishman arrived. He started out in hope, in his case of going to the Far East. In our next chapter we will find him in the so aptly named Hope Place in the Far East End. It had only taken his father a couple of years to get started in

Dublin in the 1820s, and it only took T. J. a couple of years to get started in London. Papa Barnardo may not have supplied much by way of encouragement or funding, but he definitely supplied something just as valuable. He supplied the genes.

*

As so much of T. J.'s inspiration was Christianity, it's worth having a look at the state it was in at the time. There was a weekly newspaper called *The Revival*, which in 1870 changed its name to *The Christian*, edited by a man called Richard Morgan. This had a large circulation, quite how large is difficult to verify with confidence, but several tens of thousands. That on its own makes a point. Not a freebie, it had to be bought. Could we imagine a weekly Christian paid-for newspaper with that sort of circulation these days? There was at the time a huge revival in Christianity, but it must be pointed out that it wasn't being led by the Church of England, the driving force was the Evangelical movement.

Leaders of the movement were the Open Brethren and many other Nonconformist groups, as well as the Methodists and missionary preachers like Baptist minister C. H. Spurgeon. The 7th Earl of Shaftesbury was a leading supporter as was his cousin Lord Kinnaird, who later became one of T. J.'s great supporters. Other leading evangelicals included members of the Hoare, Deacon and Barclay banking families, who were just the sort of people any reform movement loves to have on their subscriber list. William Booth and his wife Catherine were part of it through their East End Christian Mission, which was soon to metamorphose into the Salvation Army.

It would be unfair to say that the evangelical movement only belonged to the toffs, because it certainly didn't. The front line was as ever manned by the working class, with much middle-class support and a few aristocrats acting as the cherries on the top. Their motivation was to rescue souls from perdition, but there was also some highly complicated theology floating around involving what was then the impending millennium, which we won't go into here. We've had the millennium, so draw your own conclusions. Fortunately, alongside all the holy writs, there was some sleeves-rolled-up practicality. Something had to be done about the grinding poverty and the filth and disease, not only in the London East End but in the slums of other towns and cities throughout the country.

The economics of Victorian poverty and how it evolved would fill a library. There is a great deal of literature out there for those whom may be interested. Very briefly the Agricultural and Industrial Revolutions, to which add the grandest larceny since William the Conqueror, the eighteenth-century Enclosure Acts, totally changed British society. Britain went into the eighteenth century basically as a pastoral society with a population of about 15 million. It came out of the nineteenth century a fully industrialised society with a population which had doubled. Impoverished and dispossessed by the enclosures, villagers were forced off the land and came into the towns looking for work. Initially there were no such things as labour laws, and they were ground down by all but a very few of the mill owners and other businessmen, who exploited them at every turn.

The mindset developed by those who could hide themselves behind a wall of servants in their country houses was that poverty was the fault of the poor. It was also being said that if there was too much charity, the poor would make poverty their profession and wouldn't go out and look for work. In the conditions of the day that was insane, but the rich held the reins of power, so what they said was what was done. It wouldn't be until the later Victorian years that the mood and the thinking changed, and it was the Evangelical movement that was at the forefront of those changes. By its acceptance and lack of protest of the appalling conditions visible in hundreds of their parishes, the plump, complacent and rosy-cheeked Church of England was regarded by many as more of a hindrance than a help.

From all of this it will be appreciated that while growing up over in Dublin T. J. had ticked all the boxes and joined all the right clubs. He was Open Brethren and YMCA, he had taught in a ragged school, he had prayed for the sick and the dying, he was evangelical to his fingertips. When he arrived in London he had the right credentials, and had letters of recommendation from all the right people over there. A five-minute walk from London Hospital is Sydney Street, where he found a warm welcome from the local Brethren community. This tells us why T. J., who in 1866 was just another young Irish immigrant, did so remarkably well so remarkably quickly. We can sum him up in the phrase, he had what it took.

*

Let us go back a few years and find Doctor John Snow. Born in York but practising in London, he had investigated two outbreaks of cholera. He had the idea that this dreadful killer disease was caused by foul water, which was totally against ideas prevalent in the medical profession at the time, which was that it was caused by foul air. Bad air is the translation from Latin of that other killer disease, malaria. In an outbreak of cholera in Westminster in 1854, Snow was able to show, by analysis of which families used which wells to draw their water, that a particular well was the source of the outbreak. This was proved incontrovertibly to be true, despite the entrenched objections of the local medical authorities. Snow was able to go further and prove that sewage had seeped into the ground around it and therefore into the water in it. Dr Snow had risen to some sort of eminence by then, being part of the medical team attending Queen Victoria, so that at last he was being listened to. It is unfortunate that he died at the young age of forty-five in 1858, which meant that further research into the problem had to be taken up by others.

When we build houses these days, the first thing that the developer has to make sure he has organised is the services. There has to be a road for access, and under that road will be pipes for water in and sewage out, gas pipes and electricity cables. To us this in normal, but in those days it was far from normal. The construction engineer John Bazelgette was soon to be engaged on developing his ideas on a new great sewerage system for the capital, but that would only be the beginning. The realisation that people living in a huge city can't just pour their filth into the nearest river, and that people need a continuous supply of clean drinkable water, still had some way to go before it finally surfaced in the political mind. Ideas like that cost an awful amount of money, which means taxes, and introduce me to someone who likes paying taxes. Most of London obtained its water from wells. The famous Aldgate Pump, which at one time marked the boundary between the City and the East End, was a hand-cranked pump over a well.

Through London ran the Thames, and on the north bank of the river stands the Palace of Westminster containing Parliament. The Thames at that time was a stinking sewer. So much did it stink that at times Parliament was adjourned if the weather was hot. It was this inconvenience to the high and the mighty that finally generated enough concern to get something done. The sewerage disposal scheme headed by James Bazelgette was the result, though his successful solution to the problem of effluent disposal did nothing to deal with the other side of the problem, the lack of clean water to every house.

As a Second World War evacuee to a small town in Bedfordshire I lived in a house which shared an outside tap with eight neighbours. In the middle of the twentieth century, within 50 miles of London, we still had no indoor plumbing and all the houses had outside toilets. In the Victorian period we are discussing all this was barely out of the hopes and dreams stage, and it isn't totally complete now, for there are still some houses in country villages that use cesspits and don't have direct piped sewage disposal, though virtually all do now have clean piped water. It has to be said that the Thames going through London is now clean enough to support fish, though foul water can get into it at times of very heavy rain, when the drains are overloaded.

*

Cholera is a bacterial intestinal disease which leads to vomiting and severe dehydration. Modern treatments stop most cases from being fatal, but these didn't exist way back then. It remains a main danger in areas prone to monsoon flooding such as Pakistan. Where regular safe supplies are not available, the minimum precaution is obviously to boil all water before use, but that assumes the availability of fuel to do it with. It was one of the things which were beginning to be recognised as good practice by an increasing number of doctors at the time we are discussing.

Medicine was moving that way, more and more people were trying to clean up their act, which up to then had been thoroughly unhygienic, especially in hospitals. Joseph Lister, an Englishman practising as a professor of surgery in Scotland, insisted that his operating theatres were kept scrupulously clean, a policy giving him noticeably improved success. Add to that the Nightingale effect; this reclusive but redoubtable heroine of the Crimean War had been bombarding government ministers and her many influential friends. Her mantra can be summed up as mop, bucket, and elbow grease cleanliness, standards of hygiene that in many places the twenty-first century could usefully learn from the nineteenth.

By this time medicine was becoming a lot more scientific, and a lot less mumbo-jumbo. That still left vast gaps in essential knowledge. The Frenchman Louis Pasteur famously experimented with cattle and sheep, vaccinating them against anthrax. The heat treatment of milk to prevent tuberculosis is named after him. Farm animals represented wealth, poor people represented liabilities. If you think that is a crude and awful statement, so do I, but it was logical and relevant in the thinking of the time. Pasteur and others like him were making people take more notice of medical science. Curing animals was a profitable idea, curing people suffering from the Biblical truism that 'the poor are always with us' was tending to come in a distant second.

The main problem at this stage was that while doctors knew what diseases did and could give them names – cholera derives from a Greek word for diarrhoea – they hadn't worked out what caused them. Find and cure the cause is a good line of enquiry, find and isolate the bacteria and find a way of killing it is another. This sort of thing was gathering a head of steam in the hospitals and universities of the period, and steady improvements were being made.

Let's have a look at the words of a recognised Mr Nice Guy of the period, the 7th Earl of Shaftesbury. Here was a man at the very top of society, but not one of the selfish and greedy sort. He is quoted in *Memoirs*, which I paraphrase because of its sheer length. It is from an article he wrote which discusses the state of the gutter children of the London slums. Note that at the time there were slums in Westminster, not just in the East End and the South Bank dockland areas such as Lambeth.

Everyone who walks the streets of the metropolis must daily observe several members of the tribe, bold, pert, and dirty as London sparrows, but pale, feeble and sadly inferior to them in plumpness of outline. Many are spanning the gutters with their legs and dabbling with earnestness in the latest accumulation of nastiness. Others, in squalid and half-naked groups, squat around at the entrances to fetid courts and alleys that lie concealed behind the deceptive frontages of our larger thoroughfares. Whitechapel and Spitalfields teem with them like an ants' nest, but it is in Lambeth and Westminster that we find the most flagrant traces of their swarming activity. There the foul and dismal passages are thronged with children of both sexes, from the ages of three to thirteen. Though thin and haggard, they are singularly vivacious and engaged in every sort of occupation, except the art which would be beneficial to themselves and creditable to the neighbourhood. The matted hair and the disgusting filth that renders necessary a closer inspection before the flesh can be discerned between the rags that hang around them, and the barbarian freedom from all superintendence and restraint, fill the mind of a novice in these things with perplexity and dismay. In this guise they run around the streets and line the banks of the river at low water, seeking coals, sticks, corks, for nothing comes amiss as treasure trove.

One is reminded of what Mother Theresa found in the Calcutta slums 100 years later, and the children scavenging in the city trash heaps, picking over and sorting other people's filthy rubbish on the edge of some distant metropolis, looking for copper wire, rags, bones, anything that will buy a day's food. Those scenes come to us through the television set in the corner of our comfortable, warm sitting-rooms. We can watch as we drink tea, eat a piece of cake, we can nod and we can tut, and we think it's really shocking. Relatively few of us ever do anything about it, we have an amorphous 'them' to do that, though we grumble at the size of the foreign aid budget in the next breath. Do we remember from our history lessons at school that when T. J. was just getting started in London, we and other European nations ruled these places? Shaftesbury was describing conditions in the middle of the nineteenth century, not the early twenty-first. But for hundreds of millions of people nothing has changed, except that maybe in some places it's even worse.

*

All of which is intended to set the scene for the long, hot summer of 1866. We have wondered what T. J. found to do between arriving in London in April that year and finally passing his entrance exam in the autumn of 1867. The answer is that he found plenty to occupy him, and it wasn't always having his head in books studying.

It was things like this that he saw as he went round the area, and it steered him away from the idea of going to China and kept him in the East End from then on. Within a few months of his arrival there was another cholera outbreak in London. We have a medically untrained but very enthusiastic young man, aged twenty-one that July, who was thrown in at the deep end. What could he do? The most likely thing is that he visited the poor in their alleyways and terraces, he sympathised, he prayed long and hard, grieving with those who had lost someone. But he and his medical student friends had very little more to offer. He was able to help the sick but still living get to hospital, praying they wouldn't die on the way. He did whatever he was asked to do with enthusiasm and a great deal of hope. And he learned lessons which in later life he would try to apply, in particular that prevention was better than cure.

What comes through is much more notice being taken of Lister and his methods. We mustn't forget that Florence Nightingale's seminal book on nursing had only been published six years before, and these things take time to gain acceptance. But she was pushing at an open door in many places, and the London Hospital seems to have been one of them. It is quite clear that Dr Snow's work prompted the authorities to make similar surveys to track down the contaminated wells, where they removed the pump handles to prevent further use, and later filled them in. It is clear that the doctors at the London Hospital were now accepting that cholera was a water-borne disease, and were at least boiling water thoroughly before use. After all, the doctors were in the middle of the situation in daily contact with the sufferers, so unless they got on top of it quickly they were right at the head of the queue for catching it next.

The death-toll was appalling, but by luck and hard work the recovery rate was good, quite a large percentage survived. Environment and the lack of a nutritious diet must have taken many who might otherwise have made it through, and those deficiencies were to take off many more in succeeding months who had initially survived. The real killer was social attitude, which over the previous two centuries had allowed this situation to develop and grow.

Recorded deaths finally totalled 5,548, of which 3,909, or 70 per cent happened in the East End. In a three-week period the hospital took in 365 patients and treated 6,251 outpatients. Eye-witness reports say that on one day there were thirty bodies in the mortuary and everyone was far too busy, or their relatives far too sick, to arrange for them to be buried. Of the dead the estimate is that at least 1,500 were children. Yet as appalling as these figures sound, the fact that not all of these desperately poor and underfed people who caught the disease died of it speaks volumes for the heroic efforts and dedicated care of the medical staff, and of the all-too-few volunteers, T. J. being one of them. Something basic and important was learned, when everyone had time to draw breath. The lessons learned mean that London has never had a cholera epidemic since.

The British may grumble about their Health Service, but at least since 1948 they have had one funded out of national revenues. Up to then many hospitals were run as charities, which had accumulated investments over the decades bought from legacies and gifts. Certainly a visit to the family doctor up to 1948 was still chargeable. The London Hospital was in the middle of an extremely poor area where many simply couldn't afford to pay anything. It was kept running by such money as its committee could raise by any method that was legal, and it's fair to say that on the whole it was quite successful.

*

We are still looking for things our hero found to do, apart from having his head stuck in a book doing medical studies. Inevitably T. J. had attracted the attention of those also bitten with the evangelical Christian bug, and these included a man named John McCall. He and his son were in due course to play important roles in the development of the Barnardo organisation. Would T. J. like to spend Easter in Paris? Which does need some explanation.

France had been in a state of political uncertainty, it would be unfair to say instability, for some time. By 1867 it had reverted to a monarchy led by Emperor Napoleon III, in what was called the Second Empire. A monarch with some executive power, in the fashion of the era, it would seem that he was someone who was actually quite good with his domestic policies, but his international adventures usually ended up in a mess. The German Iron Chancellor Bismarck had him for political and military breakfast in the brief and brutal Franco–Prussian War in 1870, and he ended his days in exile in a quiet provincial town in Surrey.

One of his better ideas was to hold a Grand Exposition in Paris in 1867, following the fashion which Britain had set with its Crystal Palace Exhibition sixteen years earlier. McCall's invitation was that T. J. should be part of a team of about a dozen like-minded evangelists, who would go over to Paris and help man what was to be a large Bible stand, alongside French Christians and those from other countries. They would be giving away Bibles and Testaments. On his rapid acceptance McCall gave him a cheque to cover his expenses, and it is understood that the others in the party were similarly funded.

Writing to friends from Paris, T. J. comes up with some impressive claims. He writes that 170,000 copies were given away in a month, with 28,000 given away on Easter Monday. This not only tells us the number, but tells us that he was over there for that long. Giving away freebies is a very easy thing to do, but we will never know what results were achieved from all this enormous effort and expense. In a letter to another friend we read that there were fourteen languages on offer, with Western and other scripts. In a Catholic country, which France then substantially was, he reports that he had sometimes seen people accept the gifts, then throw them away when they found out they were Protestant versions. He writes that this didn't happen all that often.

The visit to Paris was to have one enormously important effect on his future. He met Lord Shaftesbury, who one suspects, though it is never written anywhere, may have been one of the backers of the British contingent. This suggests that his Lordship's appearance at the stand may not have been an accident. Shaftesbury was staying at a hotel in Paris with members of his family, and these included his sister Lady Harriet Cooper. A couple of days later Lady Harriet visited the stand and issued an invitation for T. J. to come to tea at their hotel. Our information is that this invitation was personal, not general to the British team. In an era when lords and their sisters were regarded with awe by the ordinary citizen, such an invitation was enormously impressive. What was it that the great man saw in this young Irishman, such that he sent his sister to personally deliver the invitation? You may call it luck, but as any golfer will tell you, the more you practice the luckier you get. Golf rules apply here. The 7th Early of Shaftesbury and our hero shared very evangelical Christian views, and T. J. had established quite a track record in his not yet twenty two years of age.

The original Anthony Ashley Cooper had a chequered career in Parliament during and after the English Civil War. He was briefly a member of Cromwell's Council of State, but fell out with him and left. On the Restoration of the Monarchy and the reign of Charles II he served for nine years as Chancellor of the Exchequer, becoming progressively a baron, then an earl, taking the title of Shaftesbury. In and out of favour, seemingly a man of competence but also of some strong views, he opposed the succession of Charles's very Catholic brother James. He was tried for treason but got off, went to live in Holland, returning to England with William of Orange in 1688 when James fled the country in what came to be known as the Glorious Revolution.

It was from this colourful character that the nineteenth-century seventh earl was descended. Born 1801, so much the same age as Papa Barnardo, he finally succeeded to the title in 1851. He had meanwhile been elected to the Commons in 1825. In a century when selfishness and greed were normal among the aristocracy, this latest Anthony Ashley Cooper quickly took up the interests of the underdog. While in the Commons he was the driving force behind the 1842 Coal Mines Act and the 1849 Factories Act. As a peer in 1859 he was behind a further Factories Act, and was also promoting an Act aimed at supplying lodgings for the poor. Anyone who has been asked by his employer to work for more than ten hours a day might like to look up legislation Shaftesbury promoted in 1847 on this subject.

We do not therefore find it surprising that such a man should be on the evangelical wing of the Christian Church in England. When T. J. joined the list of people he knew and liked, our hero's prospects took a great leap forward. Mind you, he still had to get his head sorted out, and stop having quite so many ideas and things going on at the same time. It would be towards the end of 1867 that they met again.

*

In the field of social conscience, the giant figure in the mid-nineteenth century was undoubtedly Shaftesbury. He was often the focus of attempts to get the poor – and to use the Marx word there were masses of them – a better deal. During the reigns of four Hanoverian Georges all ideas of social conscience went to the dogs. There was the overwhelming temptation of wealth for the fortunate few by the coincidental emergence of the Agricultural Revolution and the Industrial Revolution. Added to this in the late eighteenth century were the Enclosure Acts, the greatest period of grand larceny against the British working class since the arrival of William the Conqueror. All this, to which add the huge families everyone had in those days, drove people off the land and into the growing cities to look for work. There they were driven into ever more degrading poverty by more corruption and more exploitation.

At the end of the Napoleonic Wars in 1815, that arrogant younger son of a Protestant Irish earl, Arthur Wellesley, Duke of Wellington, decided to go into politics. He even served as Prime Minister for two years. Not for the Iron Duke the notion of *noblesse oblige*. He had famously on one occasion let the cloak slip and revealed his real attitude, when he called his infantry the scum of the earth. He was like so many of his class, all for coming down hard on the poor.

The position in 1830 of the new King William IV was interesting. Sailor Bill as a third son never expected to succeed to the throne. He had served several years in the Navy, so while he never had the common touch, he had met far more common people close up than the rest of his family. The king in those days could still wield a lot of influence. When the Reform Bill of 1832 came before Parliament, those with what we'll call a Wellingtonian attitude were against it, but the Prime Minister was now Lord Grey. The suggestion he made was that the king create enough new peers to force the Bill through the Lords and the king said no! What he did agree to do was to write personal letters to those who opposed the measure, suggesting that they abstain. The opponents knew that if they didn't the Grey alternative would be applied. In the event the opponents largely did as suggested and the Bill became law.

The idea was to advance democracy by getting rid of what were known as Rotten Boroughs; one famously only had a voting strength of nine. It was also aimed at Pocket Boroughs, those said to be in the pocket of the local lord, who was the man who decided who would be Member of Parliament, because he probably employed most of the voters. Shaftesbury, still twenty-one years before he succeeded his father, was of course in the Pocket Borough situation himself. It all looked good on paper, though in practice seats in the Commons were in the pockets of powerful lords for the next seventy years.

An example of what Shaftesbury was up against was the appalling trade of using boy chimney-sweeps. Large houses with large inglenook fireplaces had large, straight chimneys going up to the roof. Up these chimneys every summer were sent boys as young as five, with a brush in hand to sweep away the soot. They were usually dead by the time they were ten. Modern houses either no longer have chimneys in our centrally heated age, or the flue is narrow and has a sharp bend half way up. Shaftesbury tried to get the trade banned as early as 1840, but success only came in response to the social polemic masquerading as a children's book, *The Water Babies*, written by crusading vicar Charles Kingsley. In 1868 employing a boy under the age of eight became illegal, which finally killed off the trade.

There were many other cases where Shaftesbury succeeded, usually in the teeth of the most dreadful attitudes of his opponents. It was obvious that to them Christian churches were places to be seen in on Sundays, not for practising their lessons. He was a prime mover in establishing training ships to train boys for the Merchant Navy. These became famous as the *Chichester* and the

Arethusa. Britain having the world's largest maritime fleet, most of it still under sail, there was a continual need for new men, and these ships gave training for a ready labour market. When trained, what the conditions and the pay were like is another matter.

Shaftesbury was the driving force behind a number of Acts in the field of employment, legislation to regulate child labour under the age of thirteen, work in the mines and work in factories. So it will be seen that when T. J. appeared on the scene in 1866, Shaftesbury was already in the thick of things. Those like T. J. who wanted social change had Shaftesbury as their inspiration. He was a peer, he could get things moving when they couldn't. Having a lord on your side still counted for a great deal in those days. Indeed, would the agoraphobic recluse Florence Nightingale have got so much done if she hadn't had one in the family, together with a great many other upper-class connections?

THREE

The Far East End: 1866–1876

One of the many things going on in Thomas John Barnardo's life takes us along the Mile End Road in search of Ernest Street. To find this unpretentious thoroughfare, which still survives today, look for Stepney Green Underground station, cross over the main road, and it runs parallel, one side turning back. Back in 1867 we find the superintendent of Ernest Street Ragged School was none other than our hero, Thomas John Barnardo. He hasn't yet passed the entrance exam for the Medical School, too busy running the ragged school half a mile up the road. That's apart from his street preaching, his adventures in various gaffs, his trip to Paris, tea with a lord and lady and all the other things we've been looking at. And probably a great many others we haven't.

We have from him the story that one evening the local policeman on his beat strolled in. Having had a good look round the single room containing seventy or eighty lads, he asked T. J. how much he knew about them. We will dramatise the little exchange.

'Not a great deal, constable, except that they're all poor and they want to learn.'

'There's a lot they know already that they shouldn't, my friend,' says the constable. 'I can see twenty I know that have been up before the magistrate at least once, eight who've been inside a prison at least once. If you should get anything into these 'ere, wot might civilise 'em a bit, that would be remarkable. Others 'as tried, and others 'as give up! You 'as bin warned!' And with that the constable gives a glare around the room and departs.

It certainly seems that the demand exceeded the supply in these schools, there was a genuine desire in the area by many of these poor kids to get a bit of education. It's equally clear that what was on offer wasn't blessed with any formal qualifications. There were no teaching certificates, clearance by the local authorities, insurance, or for that matter clean windows, clean desks or a well-ventilated environment. Well perhaps there was that, the door wouldn't have fitted and there was bound to be at least one broken window. The place was as clean as T. J. and his helpers could make it, otherwise it would have stayed dirty. One gets the feeling that, with T. J. as superintendent, Ernest Street School was one of the best in the area. He gives as eighty-six the maximum number his single-room school could take before he had to close the door to others.

His problem was that in an era when there was no lower age limit for the consumption of alcohol or of smoking, those who came to the door too late could always go down to the nearest pub or gaff, and probably did. There they would stay out of the wind and the weather, for as long as they could avoid the eye of the landlord, who would then throw them out. Much of the reason why ragged schools such as Ernest Street were popular was that they were free. Until they locked up, usually about eight at night, you were out of the weather, you could meet your mates, and with a bit of luck you might even learn something, at least how to read. Whether the spiritual message T. J. was so keen about ever actually registered with them is doubtful.

There was a committee of trustees drawn from the local worthies, who raised money by way of charitable donations for its upkeep. What was paid for and what was donated is difficult to ascertain. Equally it is by no means clear if T. J. was being paid, but if he was it wouldn't have been much. His personality and enthusiasm struck up a rapport with his boys – there are no reports at this stage of any girls – and he was determined to do better for them. He brought in an innovation, based on the maxim that the way to a man's heart is through his stomach. That's been a proverb since proverbs were invented. Sympathy for these kids was all very well, but a bowl of hot soup and a slice of bread was sympathy with its sleeves rolled up. He may not have been the person who coined the phrase, but soup as well as sympathy emerged as a key policy underpinning much of his success.

*

The British have traditionally had a lot to say for themselves, but up to the first years of Queen Victoria it cost a lot of money if you wanted to send a letter. As a result the supply of ancient correspondence archives tends to be rather thin, other than those which involved royals, nobles, or some rich merchant. Under the old system carriage of the item was payable by the recipient, which was damned awkward if you didn't really want it. A letter in the eighteenth century might cost as much as 3 shillings to receive. This in 2000 values equates to about £10. In the late 1830s the idea of a universal postal system had been suggested to the government by, among others, Rowland Hill. He it was in 1840 who became the first Postmaster General on the setting up of the General Post Office. Being the Royal Mail, it was established very unusually as a business owned by the state. The original charge for a standard letter was one pre-decimal penny, which equates to about thirty decimal pennies in 2000 values, and some 180 years later, that was what a standard letter cost. It had held its relative price, though that was then and we've had more inflation since.

The result is that the available correspondence archive shoots up; people were writing more letters and doing it more often. The class of correspondence widened, we get the family gossip as well as the strictly business material. It also made possible the 'letter to the editor', such as T. J. was so fond of writing to *The Revival* and other journals. The existence of the GPO generated the creation of the standardised patterns and sizes for envelopes, as well as birthday and other greetings cards. The invention of the telegraph created telegrams, including those famously sent from the Crimean War correspondent to *The Times* in London. Surprisingly late in the day, not until the 1890s, the postcard arrived.

We have been concentrating on the very poor, that has been our storyline, but education and the lack thereof were at the very centre of poverty. Education was gradually seeping down through the class system, if for no other reason than as business grew, traders needed clerks and clerks had to be literate. The dame-schools, the ragged schools and the Sunday School Union were all having a beneficial effect. We have now reached a point in our discussion when there were far more people who could read than there had been in 1801 when Lord Shaftesbury had been born.

T. J. was an inveterate letter writer, sometimes his missives could run to dozens of pages. He corresponded with newspapers, journals and magazines, he unashamedly dropped names when he claimed to know famous people, he worked all his contacts to drum up funds for the Homes after he had set them up. His personal journal was always a bit haphazard, but we have his very meticulously kept business journal. This is one of the things that allow us to track what was happening as his organisation increased in size. He also published articles, and in later years these included tales of how it began. According to *Memoirs*, the Crunch Period for T. J. came in four instalments between late 1866 and late 1868. Crunch Period is my own name for it, and what we also have to bear in mind is that there was a degree of overlap with the various things happening in the East End.

Based on the *Memoirs* version, Crunch Incident Number One brings us the tale of Jim Jarvis, his very first homeless waif. This was one of T. J.'s favourite stories and is true in its essentials. He was then running the ragged school in Ernest Street, the cholera epidemic was over, it was winter and from the surrounding facts probably 1866 going into 1867. The weather was cold, wet and miserable, with London's air full of smoke from half a million coal fires, it would have been more if more could have afforded the coal. The little school was being closed up and T. J. was about to douse the last embers in the hearth. At that point in came a thin scruff, shoeless and hatless, and what clothes he had on were little more than rags, which gave no protection to the biting cold outside. To clarify the convolutions of T. J.'s delivery this is a dramatisation, but it sticks to the essential facts.

'What do you want lad? I'm just closing up, it's gone eight.'

'Tommy said he fort yer might let me stay by the fire fer the night, Guv.'

'Stay by the fire?'

'Bleedin' cold ahrt there Guv! Won't make no trouble Guv, 'onest Guv!'

'Now you run off home lad, I'm just dousing the embers and I'm locking up. Past eight you know. We close at eight. Off home with you.'

'Aint got no 'ome.'

'What? No home? What sort of a tale is that? Be off and go home to your mother!'

'Aint go no muvver.'

'What about your father then? Go home to your father.'

'Aint got no farver.'

'Got no father?' T. J. was beginning to realise just how bad things were for this bedraggled waif. Hesitantly he had one last try at rejection. 'Well go and find your friends then. Where do you live?'

'Don't live nowhere. Sometimes I find a doss in a cart dahn Whitechapel, that's if there ain't a score ov uvvers wots fahnd it first an' there ain't no more room. Got no friends, Guv. There's blokes wot I know, but they ain't wot yer call friends, like.'

T. J. takes a long pause to get his head round all this. He has no doubt that it's genuine. The wafer-thin lad in rags doesn't seem to have the strength to make up any lies.

'Right ... er ... now then! Is it just you, or are there other lads outside who want to come in?'

'There's 'eaps an' 'eaps ov us Guv. 'eaps ov us all over, Guv, 'eaps wots like me, there is.' The lad comes out of his despondency a little and manages a little spirit. 'More 'n' I can cahnt, Guv.'

T. J. checks the street, which is in fact empty, using the time to think things through, then returns to the lad. His Number One Crunch Decision is now made.

'Right lad! ... Right lad, I believe you, but you can't stay here all night. I have to douse the fire, put out the oil lamps and lock up. You'll have to come home with me, and we can get a fire going in the closed stove and boil up some hot coffee. How does a cup of hot coffee and a couple of slices of bread and butter sound?'

In twenty-first-century London the place would suddenly be swarming with police and social workers, and the tabloids would be writing the story before he had stopped talking. Unmarried school teacher takes small boy to his flat! Shock! Horror! This is now, that was then, when we didn't have social workers and tabloids. The shock and the horror was that in the capital of the nation with pretensions of wealth and imperial supremacy, this little boy had been allowed to get into this appalling state, and those who ruled didn't think it was unusual. Even more terrible, they didn't think they needed to do anything about it. The difference was that people like T. J. did think they had to do something about it, at least for this little boy.

He continues his story. We are back in T. J.'s lodgings, the hot coffee has been drunk, the bread and butter demolished down to the last crumb. We discover that the lad's name is Jim Jarvis. Somewhat restored by food and warmth, he tells his tale.

'Never knew me farver, Guv! Me muvver was allus sick, like, an' when I was a kid, like, she 'ad ter go in the infirm'ry! They put me in the workhouse school, like. I was all right fer a bit, but then they told me Ma 'ad gone an' popped orf, an' arter they told me like, I runned orf ahrt ov it.'

'How long ago was that, Jim?'

'Doan know zakly, Guv. Must be four, five year like.'

T. J. does an estimate of how old Jim might be, and thinks he may be about ten or eleven. A small, underfed boy wouldn't have been very good at estimating the passage of years, so his mother may have died two, three as likely as four years before. Even then, Jim went on the streets at maybe eight or nine, but possibly as young as seven.

'What happened then, Jim?'

'I got in wiv a load ov boys, Guv, dahn Wapping way. There was an old lady wot once upon a time said she know'd me muvver, so she said I could sleep in 'er shed, like. Weren't too bad fer a start. Then arter that I done fings fer a lighterman, 'im wot worked a barge on the river. 'e weren't no good Guv. Sometimes 'e give me a big bashing, all fer nuffin' like. Then sometimes 'e went orf fer days and got drunk. Leave me on the barge on me own, 'e did. 'e didn't care wot I 'ad nuffin ter eat like.'

'So why didn't you run away from him like you ran away from the workhouse school?' T. J. is understandably a bit puzzled.

'I would Guv, an' I wanted to, but one day that there Dick, that was 'is name, Swearin' Dick they called 'im, well 'e give me a right bashing, 'e did and swore if I runned orf 'e'd kill me, Guv. That Dick, 'e 'ad a big dog wot knew me smell, Guv, wot 'e said would find me if I runned orf. That were a big fierce dog, Guv. That Swearin' Dick put it on me just fer fun, Guv.' Jim showed him a line of tooth marks down one leg. 'Dun that ter me, that dog dun, Guv.'

T. J. is shocked at the sight of the scars and passes over another slice of bread and butter. There was a pause while this fresh bounty was rapidly demolished, then the story continued.

'That Swearin' Dick, 'e went orf agin, then a couple ov days later a bloke comes on the barge wot I knew a bit. Yer won't see no more ov that Swearin' Dick, 'e says. Got took orf ter be a sodjyer when he was drunk, 'e says. Took the queen's shillin' 'e 'as. Well, yer can just fink abaht it Guv! I runned orf that barge like there was lightnin' arter me, an' I never stopped running until I got ter the meat market! It were like 'eaven Guv, not bein' bashed fer nuffin an' no bleedin' dog an' all! I even got a job wiv an old woman wot sold tripe an' pig's trotters orf a stall, 'elped 'er wiv 'er barrah like. Then there was anuvver lad wot was bigger'n me, wot pushed me orf, like, took the job orf me, like.'

'What about the police? Did you see them about the streets?'

'All the time, Guv. Sometimes they'd just give me a clarht an' move me on. Uvver times they 'ad me up afore the beak, an' I got sent ter the Workhouse one time. That there beak said if 'e saw me agin 'e'd send me ter prison. Arter that I just kept movin' abaht. Earned a penny 'ere, ape'ny there. I even 'ad enuff one time fer a frup'ny doss, but it weren't no good. Their fleas was fighting my fleas and I didn't get much sleep, so I'd sooner sleep ahrt, like, an' save me money. Jus' lately the wevvers bin real bad, Guv, an' I aint 'ad much luck. Afore this lot yer gived me Guv, aint 'ad nuffin sin yistdy!'

Now more used to the sometimes almost incomprehensible East End accent, T. J. was fascinated by Jim's story, in particular his final comment that he hadn't had anything to eat since the previous day, with the implication that starvation of this order was normal. Being an evangelist, the talk inevitably got round to religion. Jim admitted that he'd heard of it, though he didn't know what it meant. It had certainly never reached his life up to then. They then spent some time in prayer. Lots of soap and water were applied to clean the boy up, but couldn't clean up what passed for his clothes. He resolved that the following day he would take the lad to the barbers so that his hair could be shaved off to get rid of the livestock inhabiting it, then to a market stall he knew, where some second-hand but clean clothes might be bought for a shilling.

By this time it was about midnight and Jim offered to take him on a tour of what he called the 'lays', where all the street kids would be spending the night. They set off towards Houndsditch, on the edge of the City, and worked their way through various streets and alleys, until T. J. had to admit he was lost, but Jim Jarvis knew exactly where he was. Eventually they came to a 'lay', which was along the top of a wall high above a market. With a great deal of effort, in the dark of night, Jim was able to guide and help T. J. up a drainpipe. He explained that the boys liked this place because the police didn't want to go to the trouble of climbing up there. Up on the roof there were eleven more street kids.

It had been a stiff climb up and was just as difficult coming down, and he was both saddened and incensed that such a state of affairs could exist, and that this was the only sort of life open to these destitute kids.

'Are there any more like this, Jim?'

'Shall we go to anuvver, Guv? There's loads more yer can see, wot ain't arf as good as this one. Loads, Guv! 'Undreds ov 'em!'

'No more tonight, Jim. Let's go home.'

At that stage T. J. was only running Ernest Street Ragged School. His pupils, as far as he aware, came from homes and went to them afterwards. He had no facilities to take in waifs and strays who had no home at all. He did however, from that time on, provide a home for Jim Jarvis, who was under his care for several years and became the very first of his long line of rescued children.

*

Backed by promises of help from three other student friends, the Barnardo name now made its first appearance in the columns of *The Revival*. In July 1867 he wrote a long letter, which included an appeal for funds. He wrote that he was aiming to find for rent a large building or shed which might hold up to 600 people. Stage two would be to ask for help from the local churches so as to make it weatherproof, and to fit it out at least to a decent level. Stage three would then be to hold a tea meeting service, not just a cuppa, but some eats with it, open not only to the young but their parents as well. Learning from his experience with the boys and their soup, having a tea meeting was a shrewd idea; it was the tea that would fill the benches. They could sing their hallelujahs in thanks for their full stomachs. Whether they believed in the God that this bloke Barney Do was always talking about was another matter entirely.

We should give a little thought to how people moved around in those days. The standard mode of transport, other than your own two feet, was the horse-and-cart, or maybe a little donkey cart. For those who could afford them there were horse-drawn omnibuses and the ubiquitous hansom cab. While today we can park the car outside our door, local council permitting, you can't really do that with a horse, which means that in the nineteenth century there was a need for stabling. Most tradesmen liked to have a yard next to, or close to, their place of business or their home. While much East End housing was poor, crowded and dilapidated as we have been discussing, there were spaces where there were sheds and yards, if you went looking for them. The idea that T. J. was looking for a place the size of a unit on a modern commercial trading estate might strike us as a spectacular ambition, but in those days and in that environment it was quite achievable.

One sentence springs off the page in his newspaper appeal. 'I have therefore resolved not to enter upon the work until I have two hundred pounds in hand. Friends have already promised me twenty-five pounds towards this amount.' In the values of 2000 he was looking for about £14,000. This was a sizeable sum, bearing in mind he was a totally unknown quantity in the journal's readership. Making his plans public, taking them into his confidence, and making it clear how much money he was looking for became his trademarks. He wrote on another occasion, 'I desire that you should pray, my friends, that the funds we need shall be forthcoming. It is, as you will readily understand, useful to know how much we are praying for.'

He was also a great believer in donor anonymity, which accords with the Biblical dictum, 'let your alms be given in secret'. He said in another letter that he would personally acknowledge all donations, but would not publish any donor's name, though in some cases he would go as far as their initials. He further made it clear that anyone sending money was sending it to a private individual, who was not supported by any organisation or committee. Thus he was very open about it all.

A couple of issues later he was able to report that he had found what he hoped were suitable premises. They were bigger than he was looking for and he was this time appealing for forty or fifty suitably inspired Christian people prepared to help him run the proposed event, and it now becomes clear he intends it to develop into a school. No mention of curriculum or qualifications, such things were far in the future. What he had found was the King's Arms pub, landlord Benjamin Catchpole, who was prepared to rent out his assembly rooms upstairs.

This great hostelry stood in King's Arms Place at the corner of Ratcliffe Square, in the area locally called Limehouse. It was on the recently developed route to the London Docks already mentioned, the Commercial Road. We are about half a mile from Ernest Street and just along from Stepney Causeway, an address which would become the centre of the organisation's affairs a few years into the future. So it's all still very local. For a teetotal temperance man like T. J. to hire rooms in a pub must have been very frustrating, but it was the best he could do for the moment. It wouldn't be for long, he was determined on that. Useful to the publican, and also for anyone mounting a tea meeting, the other traders in the little cul-de-sac were a butcher, a baker, a fruiterer and a cheese seller.

When they heard about it, the committee of Ernest Street Ragged School didn't take kindly to such goings on. In his enthusiasm he had completely forgotten to tell them what he was up to, resulting in a very embarrassing misunderstanding. This obliged him, in the 8 August edition of *The Revival*, to publicly apologise. He wrote to explain that he hadn't intended that anyone should think that the Ernest Street committee were connected with his appeal. He didn't regard himself as being in competition with them, his aim was to create extra facilities as there was obviously such a need. In view of the embarrassment he wrote that he had resigned from his position at Ernest Street, though he still had the warmest regard for all the people there and what they were doing. The letter is rounded off by advising that the appeal had raised £90. Anyone who wanted their money back merely had to contact him, and it would be refunded immediately. Likewise if they wanted it passed on to the Ernest Street committee that would be done.

It was obvious that the use of the King's Arms pub wasn't very practical as a place to set up a school, but he was able to make use of it for several weeks. His initial free tea and meeting attracted, he meticulously noted, '2,347 rough lads, young men, girls, women and children'. The following Sunday he staged a street parade and brought about 600 people into the pub, and this was repeated on several subsequent Sundays. Then mine host Benjamin Catchpole put a stop to it. T. J. was spreading the fame of his hostelry far and wide, which was good. However, he had 600 people upstairs in his assembly rooms, none of them buying any beer! Not only that, their leader was preaching a temperance sermon against the demon drink. If that went on it would ruin his business!

*

With his original student supporters he was eventually able to find a donkey shed, which after doing it up they used for a short time as a school. When we arrive at Crunch Incident Number Two, which will be coming along very shortly, this is an example of how events have a habit of overlapping.

Things hit trouble that winter when T. J. collapsed under the strain, and the little school collapsed as well. Whether or not he was sincere about his own studies was his business, but his friends were sincere about theirs, and they couldn't study and run the school as well. He was off sick for about two months, and again we wonder what he did for funds. When he was again up and about he was still determined to start his school. It was in that July that he was able to tell *The Revival* readers of his new plans. He was now calling his venture the East End Juvenile Mission, and up to the day he died all uniform buttons used by the Barnardo Organisation had E.E.J.M. stamped on them.

In the New Year he had acquired on rental two small houses of the type traditionally referred to as 'two up, two down'. These were in a little court called Hope Place, off Rhodswell Road, where Stepney bordered Limehouse. So again we are still in the same tight little area. The Blitz in the 1940s flattened most of these streets and it has all been redeveloped, so many of these roads don't exist any more. Many of them are under the site of what is now the East London Stadium. And news from the medical studies front: our hero has found the time to sit and has passed his entrance exam!

The problem as he saw it was that many ragged schools run by churches were only open on a Sunday. It seemed obvious to T. J. that they needed to be open during the week as well, if not during the day because the kids needed to scrimp and scrape a living, then at least during the evenings. To us that seems obvious, but back then this was pretty radical thinking. He wanted among other things to build up a supply of books, reading primers, writing slates and chalks, and some trustworthy volunteers to stand in as teachers. His own experience was considerable, after all he had taught in a Dublin ragged school from the age of sixteen.

Volunteering at this stage was a very important word; there wasn't any money to pay anyone. His original appeal in *The Revival* had raised only £90, all of which was spent. Illness and other problems had hindered his earlier attempts, but nothing had stopped him trying. Even Hope Place, when it began, teetered on the edge of insolvency. He could, if things got really desperate, call on the kindness of his friends and his family. Papa Barnardo would always have sent him his fare money back to Dublin. However, it's a reasonable thing to say that the Hope Place project wasn't the normal thing for a medical student to do in his spare time. Did we just say spare time? Starting up and finding the funding for something the size of Hope Place and keeping it going was something else entirely. To succeed long-term he would need a lot of donations from the public, and he needed them on a regular basis.

In Hope Place he was renting a couple of tiny run-down terrace houses. He established his Sunday school, and he established the lifelong habit of keeping meticulous and very detailed records of everything he did. Checking these, there is an entry that between 2 March and 15 July 1868 the average attendance was 300 each Sunday. That couldn't have been at one sitting, there wasn't the room, but averaged over the day that is still a big number. He also ran a boys' class four evenings a week, with a good fire going in the hearth, a huge draw to bring in the gutter kids, and oil lamps to give extra light on dull evenings. He claims an average evening attendance of sixty to seventy. This would have been something similar to the attendance he had been achieving at Ernest Street. He tells us that he and a helper used to read to them. As we might imagine from the nature of the man, he and his helpers were using what we might call improving literature, such as *Uncle Tom's Cabin* and *Pilgrim's Progress*. Just being read to was an adventure, even a wonderful luxury for these street kids. It had never happened to them before in all their lives, and it went down a treat. As time passed and success grew he rented more of the little houses in Hope Place, which when you think about it had such an appropriate name.

There was already in Limehouse an organised Shoeblacks Brigade, which T. J. contacted and they agreed to take lads he recommended. Shoeblacks, in a world of filthy streets and piles of horse manure, could make something of a living. They were poor, but they had a vested interest in being honest, or they would lose their pitch. They tended not to go thieving off fruit barrows, or helping things to fall off the backs of carts. His great innovation was to do something for the girls, and he found lady volunteers who taught sewing and how to repair clothes, a desperately necessary skill in those conditions. They were also encouraged to learn how to read, alongside the boys, which was big-time competition. No boy wanted to be beaten at something by a girl! Treating the girls equally was something of an adventure in that society, but it succeeded very well. He established a little savings bank, teaching the benefits of thrift. Fairly soon there was an employment agency, looking for jobs for the boys. It took a lot longer to acquire the resources, and especially the assistance of suitably trustworthy ladies with the knowledge and the skills, to take the risk of trying to find places for the girls.

Inevitably it all had a strong Christian element running through it, not only because of his own character, but because most of his volunteers were coming to him from local churches, or from such people as his friends in the Open Brethren. It isn't surprising that he quickly had what we can think of as a Tract Department. Whether these were acquired from outside sources or he wrote them himself isn't known. Tracts are all very well in a literate society, but in 1868 we have to wonder how many of the people he gave them to could read, or was it a nice bit of paper for lighting the fire. The claim is made that there were about 1,200 being delivered every week.

Knowing the charismatic leadership qualities of the man, which were becoming more and more appreciated, we can imagine his group of helpers going into the lanes, alleys and courts, handing them out, and just doing that was making new contacts, maintaining old ones. It put a face to a name, it discovered needs and produced sympathetic responses, and where possible it found some help. Those contacts were far more important than whether they could read or not. One thing began to emerge, that the people round there liked him and were beginning to trust him. That good opinion was the basis on which his later success was built.

What the local ordained clergy thought of all this he doesn't include in his records, but one feels they didn't mind and didn't feel threatened. A few of the roughs and scruffs were being tamed, and maybe when they got the fleas out of their hair and washed their necks more often, they might be made welcome in proper churches. Meanwhile these ordained clergy were getting feedback from the venture, after all most of the volunteers came from their congregations, and that let them feel they had their fingers on the pulse.

*

The best estimate for the timing of Crunch Incident Number Three is late in 1867. As already mentioned, this overlaps with the attempted donkey shed ragged school. He had at last passed his exam and was now an accepted student at the Medical School. Where he found the hours in the day, and also in the night, with all he was doing is a serious question. Not only that, he was still clinging on to the hope that maybe he would end up in China. As a result T. J. was still on the books of the China Inland Mission.

The *Memoirs* describe a big missionary meeting at the then fairly newly built Islington Agricultural Hall, up the hill from the smoke and grime of the railway termini at Kings Cross, St Pancras and Euston. They sent him a ticket so he went, fully expecting to have to find room at the back, and strain his eyes and ears to see and hear the speakers. In the event not so, for the ticket gave him a seat on the platform, up there with the great and the good. With T. J. things seem to have had a habit of falling out in his favour. The *Memoirs* quote from his recollections of what happened:

> There was a crowded and most enthusiastic audience. Several gentlemen from various parts of the world addressed it, but two or three well-known speakers who expected to be present were prevented from appearing, and they sent word only at the last minute. Thus late in the evening, the chairman found himself in some difficulty, owing to this dearth of speakers. Suddenly he turned to me, as I sat near him on the platform. 'Barnardo! You must say a few words! Tell us about your ragged school in the East End of London!

Are we at all surprised? An unknown medical student with missionary ambitions, but no medical qualifications, is sitting on the platform. He just happens to be T. J., who is now plucked from the chorus line when the star doesn't turn up. How long had he known the chairman, who was a Doctor of Divinity by the name of Thain Davidson? For all we know he'd only just met the man an hour or so before and maybe they'd had a very brief chat. Davidson somehow knew that T. J. taught at an East End ragged school, which seems to be the donkey shed venture – we aren't quite at Hope Place yet.

He records that he was dumbfounded for the moment. Up to then he had only ever spoken to fairly small groups, up to say

100 or so children and adults in his school work. In his talk he specifically mentions his shed under conversion, which with other clues narrows this down to October 1867. We therefore pick up on Davidson again, giving Barnardo no chance to refuse.

Gentlemen! Our expected speaker can't be with us, but by good fortune we have a young medical student who lives in the East End of London, who is by the by intending to go to China. He is going to tell us something about his work in a ragged school.

In an age which hadn't invented architectural acoustics or the microphone, that left our hero with nowhere to go, except stand up and try and do his best in front of maybe 1,000 strangers who had never heard of him. With some paraphrasing and much shortened because of its sheer length, here are the main points in his recollections.

I stood for a moment feeling dazed in front of that great audience, then closing my eyes in an effort to forget where I was, and to concentrate my mind upon the subject, I began to say something, at first I hardly knew what, about my Ragged Night School. Gradually I warmed to the subject…

I remember I could not help revealing what I had seen the previous night in a very miserable quarter of the East End. I found myself there in the early morning, surrounded by a group of the most pitiable children one can imagine, homeless, friendless, foodless and dressed in rags. I dwelt on the pity of it, and the sorrow of the fact that no one seemed to care for either the bodies or the souls of these outcasts…

Then I dwelt upon the heathen darkness in which they lived, and I asked my hearers to pray for the little waif children of the Great City in which we were gathered. I think I can say that my story seemed to impress my audience a great deal. When I sat down I was much impressed by their show of feeling. I was leaving the platform at the end of the meeting when a young woman came up to me.

'I came here to help the missionaries,' she said, 'I'm only a servant and I don't have much to give, but I have saved my farthings for them. But when I heard you, I wondered if you would let me give this for your poor children.' With that she gave me a little packet of coins. This was the very first public money I had ever received.

I know I felt very embarrassed, up to then my fund-raising had been through friends and fellow students. But this was different, it was from a member of the public. When I went home I found it contained sixpence three farthings.

He writes that he kept the money in a drawer for some time. Even in his day it wasn't a large sum, something a little under £2 in 2000 values. Islington was still then almost a village, though rapidly being swallowed up by the muck and grime of the metropolis. Parts of it were still quite genteel, and there were many houses which had servants. Therefore we must add into this gift the complexities of the Victorian social class system. To someone like this young woman, on maybe £10 a year and her keep, it was a tidy sum to have saved up. The value is in the giving, which was far more than the size of the gift.

*

The Agricultural Hall incident had been a completely off-the-cuff talk. The only record of what he said was in an article he wrote many years later. For instance he seems to have forgotten his appeal in *The Revival*, which had raised £90, and which predates the Agricultural Hall talk by several months. He omits any reference to Jim Jarvis, who with his encyclopaedic knowledge of the alleys, courts and pathways of the East End and even into the City, was now T. J.'s guide. Jim Jarvis now had a bed to sleep in, and he was getting regular food and an education. Not only that, but the word was spreading among the street kids that Jim Jarvis and this Barney Do bloke were all right to talk to, and weren't going to make any trouble.

It seems that out in the big wide world his talk had resonated with a great many in the more philanthropic sections of society. We can refer to *Memoirs* again, with the inevitable paraphrasing.

Out of this incident at the Agricultural Hall something unexpected grew. It appears that my statement about the number of children who I had found sleeping out at night had impressed some of my audience very much, and it was repeated by them in their private circles. I am not sure, but I have reason to think that the meeting, and my remarks, were noticed by some of the Press. At that time I did not take a newspaper or need one, I had no time for such reading. I was absorbed on the one hand by my studies and on the other by the claims of my new work at the ragged school. But I heard some time later that a correspondence had appeared in the Press on the subject. Some thought that my remarks described a very sad state of things, which needed redress. Others doubted if such a state of things really existed, and simply questioned my accuracy. I happily knew nothing of this at the time, but about a week later I received a letter, addressed to me at The London Hospital, containing an invitation to dinner. The letter was from the late Earl of Shaftesbury. He said in his invitation that he wanted me to meet some people who were very interested in the condition of waif children. When the appointed evening came I found myself at Lord Shaftesbury's address, one of some fourteen or fifteen guests.

Only casual conversation took place during dinner. Sitting next to me at the table was Doctor M. [we only have his initial], one of the most charming men I ever met. After dinner, as we stood in groups, Lord Shaftesbury came up and spoke to me.

Which introduces us to Crunch Incident Number Three. Versions vary, but for consistency we will follow *Memoirs*. We will again set this out as a dramatised dialogue, as this seems to be the simplest way to deliver the essential facts with clarity. We have to bear in mind that we are working from what was itself a write-up, done at least seventeen years after the event. The reference to the 'late' Lord Shaftesbury means the great man was dead, so the article must date from 1885 or later. That allows T. J. to be a bit hazy on some details. He records the earl's enquiries.

'I've heard of your interest in children of the streets and I was very anxious to meet you, Mr Barnardo. I want to be sure from your own lips that some of the things that have been said are accurate. I've heard it said for instance, that you often find large groups of children asleep at night, in various hiding places in different quarters of London, without proper shelter or care. Is that really true?'

'I'm afraid, my lord, that it's very true.'

'Have you any problem getting these waifs to talk about themselves?'

'No, my lord. As a rule they are quite willing to talk, when I've assured them that I'm genuinely interested in their conditions.'

'Well, do you ever get them to leave their miserable surroundings?'

'Yes my lord. Occasionally I've been able to get them some help to get off the streets, but my resources to help such poor children have necessarily been very limited.'

'I suppose then that you wouldn't find it difficult to find a group of such boys tonight.'

'Certainly not, my lord. Any time after half-past eleven or thereabouts, at one or two places I know I could find quite a number of homeless children sleeping out all night.'

Shaftesbury and T. J. are centre stage in this conversation, all the others listening intently. He says that at this point, by the look on Shaftesbury's face, it was quite clear that the earl had his doubts. For an aristocrat of his eminence and standing, Anthony Ashley Cooper had a surprisingly wide knowledge of the slums and who inhabited them. He was one of the exceptions to the usual rule, he really cared and wanted to do something about it. He'd been proposing and cajoling legislation through an unwilling

Parliament, trying to improve the conditions of the poor, since before T. J. was born. However, even he for the moment couldn't bring himself to believe that the situation was as black as was being painted. The earl made a definite decision.

'Right then, Mr Barnardo! Could you take us to such a place tonight?'

'Certainly, my lord. I'll take you to one of these places with pleasure, but we'll have to wait until it's late enough.'

At about midnight the party all put on their hats and topcoats. This class of person wouldn't dream of being seen on the streets without them, even allowing for the chill of an October evening.

Hansom cabs were ordered, and under T. J.'s instructions they headed for Billingsgate Fish Market in the City, off Lower Thames Street. They set down at a cul-de-sac called Queens Shades, where they were accosted by a police constable, suddenly surprised by a large party of well-dressed gentlemen in the wee small hours of the morning. We imagine his instinctive, "'ello, 'ello, what's all this then?' As things turned out the constable proved very useful, and could give backup to T. J.'s experience with quite as much of his own. One wonders how many beers he was bought in the next day or two on the strength of his telling the tale.

Queens Shades was used to stack crates, barrels and boxes. Over many of these piles were tightly roped tarpaulins, intended to keep out the damp and hinder pilfering, a somewhat pious hope. They also marked out each lot from the others. The tarpaulins were also useful in an entirely unofficial way. All too often T. J. knew that he had found large groups of street kids dossing down under one of these coverings, which they had managed to work loose. There was a tell-tale gap at the bottom edge of one covered pile, which clearly hadn't got there by accident. Remembering that T. J. was small and wiry, he was able to use this gap and work his way carefully underneath, under the watchful eye of the constable, the earl and the other gentlemen. He soon found a bare leg. Grabbing it and pulling, but trying not to hurt the lad it belonged to, he soon hauled out a dirty, ragged and half-asleep street kid. As we can imagine, the air was immediately rent with protests of his innocence, before he'd ever been accused of anything. It was the earl who put a stop to it.

'We're not here to take you to task, my lad, what we want to do is get you a bit of help. There's more of you under there, I dare say. No harm in telling us lad, seeing we're all here. How many more are there under there?'

'Lots Guv. The 'ole pile's covered wiv 'em!'

The earl fished a coin out of his purse. 'You get them to come out and talk to us my lad, and I'll give you this sixpence.'

'Cor!' This was as much money as a lad like him saw in days.

'Well?'

'Cor!' The ragged and grimy lad gave the matter a few more seconds thought. 'I'll root 'em arht fer yer!'

With that he clambered up to the top of the tarpaulin and proceeded to jump up and down at spots where he knew there were other waifs dossing. Very quickly the whole pile was heaving and the occupants were tumbling out through the gap, to be grabbed as they appeared by the constable and the earl's party. That didn't get all of them out, until one of the older ones suggested that the earl should promise to make it worth their while. Shaftesbury said he would give each one who came out a penny, and he would stand the cost of some food. The lad went back through the gap, and in a minute the tarpaulin was heaving again as more of them emerged. There were so many under it that when the last one emerged the covering collapsed in folds around what it was supposed to be protecting. Others emerged from under nearby piles, attracted by the noise, and the numbers grew. It took another minute or so to take a count, which came to the amazing number of seventy-three, all equally thin, dirty and all in torn and grubby clothes.

'Well Mr Barnardo,' Shaftesbury had to admit, 'Whatever doubts any of us might have had have certainly been blown away. This is a terrible proof, if ever one was required, of the need for action such as you are attempting. And obviously not just in the

East End, here we are in the City itself. Something must be done everywhere that this is happening!'

There were nods and serious faces all round. These prosperous middle- and upper-class gentlemen had never seen anything like this face to face, and they were all badly shocked.

'I promised them some food, Mr Barnardo. What can we do about that at this unearthly hour of the night?'

'Dick Fisher, my lord. There's a tea and coffee stall just along the way that serves all the porters who work at night in the fish market. We could take them along there. Fisher probably knows quite a few of them already.'

'Fisher's stall it shall be,' said the earl, turning to the youngsters. 'Hot coffee and as much bread and butter as you can eat. What about that, my lads?'

This raised a cheer and they set off along the street. Dick Fisher had never done so much trade an hour after midnight, as the boys took the place by storm. For a lot of them it was the biggest meal they'd had in a week.

'Mr Fisher, I shall need some change, if you please.'

'Why bless yer, me lord, anything fer yer lordship I can do, 'course, me lord!' Fisher had heard a member of the party address Shaftesbury by his title, and realised the quality of the people who had invaded his place of business. Never having met a real lord before, he was quite overcome by the honour.

'I promised all these lads a penny each. Can I ask you to change this half sovereign for me, please?'

A proper gent and even said please, a word the stallholder hadn't heard used in earnest for more years than he cared to count. It took some delving in a large wooden box out of sight round the back, and he asked T. J. to check the number for him. The earl then made them all line up, and gave each of them their penny as promised, and gave Fisher a sovereign to cover the cost of the bread and butter and coffee they'd consumed in their feast. That raised another cheer and brought a broad smile to the stallholder's face, as he hoped that a lot of those pennies would find their way back into his large wooden box over the next day or two.

Members of the party were now talking to the boys, one or two of whom promised to meet up with T. J. a couple of nights later.

Shaftesbury was clearly stunned. When they parted later outside the earl's house, T. J. reports the earl as saying in most earnest tones, 'I tell you, Barnardo, all London shall know of this.'

As his organisation grew, T. J. openly worked all his contacts and was only too happy to drop names. However, when it came to donations he never revealed who had given how much, that was always kept confidential between him and the donor. The guest referred to as 'Doctor M' proved to be one of many who became enduring friends and supporters of the Homes. The original biographer James Marchant came up with 1867 as the year of the Islington speech, and he did after all have access to all of T. J.'s papers, and also had the help of his widow. The Billingsgate sojourn would have been not long after that. Clearly T. J. didn't take Jim Jarvis with him, the lad would have been out of his depth in that company.

*

Which now brings us to Crunch Incident Number Four. This is the one that at last put some financial flesh on the bones of his hopes and dreams. At last someone came up with some money, and in a sizeable amount. Again we have T. J.'s own words to introduce it.

> I received an amazing letter, the contents of which were so surprising, so unexpected, and as I judged, of so manifestly a providential character, that I was brought to a solemn and sudden decision concerning my life's work almost there and then. For although many days passed before I spoke of this letter or of its contents to anyone, or even admitted to myself that I had arrived at a crisis in my life, I felt as if guidance, the answer I had been seeking, had been vouchsafed to me in a wonderful manner. The contents of that remarkable letter were to this effect, that the writer would provide 1,000 pounds for the furtherance of my child rescue scheme if I felt able, for the present at all events,

to give up the thoughts that I had entertained about China, and would be content to remain in England, and to establish in East London a Home for Waifs and Stray Children. No other condition was attached. The letter came from a well-known Member of Parliament, who I had at that time never met, but who afterwards became and continued to be up to his death, a warm and close and generous friend of the work. It will be understood with what amazement I received such an unexpected letter from a person to whom I supposed I was absolutely unknown. For at least ten days I told no one of it, lest I should be persuaded one way or the other. It raised anew, in a fresh and practical fashion, the whole question of what I was to do with my life.

Like the other three Crunch Incidents we are looking at, these are recollections written in an article many years later. He very often wrote about such things, on the one hand to explain himself and his work to the magazine's readership, and also as vehicles to keep in the public eye because there was such a lot of fund-raising to do. One will realise that magazines tended to be bought and read by people who might have a few spare pennies to donate to a worthy cause. We cannot be absolutely accurate over the details, though we can be happy about the main facts. We have to admit that T. J. was a man with an active imagination, and little touches may at times have been added. The important thing is what he achieved – the odd detail in what was, after all, the very early days won't change anything. The available clues suggest that the letter referred to was probably written around August 1868.

The writer of this life-changing missive was a Member of the Commons called Samuel Smith. It would be forty years yet before any provision would be made to pay such Members a salary. That meant that if you wanted to be there you either had to be wealthy in your own right, or have the patronage of wealthy backers, or of course both. Smith was a wealthy Liverpool businessman in his own right and had access to serious money. We again refer to the Office of National Statistics for an idea of how much he was offering, and between 1868 and 2000 the multiple is sixty-seven.

So in 2000 values we are discussing £67,000, as further increased by inflation since. That is a very large sum to offer a relatively unknown and basically unproven young man of about twenty-three years old. Smith was a prominent evangelical Christian who may well have read the appeals in *The Revival*, where T. J.'s attempts to get things moving first appeared back in July 1867. To that we can add the notice he was given by the press after the Agricultural Hall meeting. He had by then also issued his report on the first five months of his work at Hope Place. That report did mention China, which Smith refers to in his offer.

Smith wouldn't have just taken the report in *The Revival* as enough to persuade him to spend this sizeable sum. T. J. wasn't even an established charity, indeed in *The Revival* letters and reports he made it clear that he was a private individual, who didn't even have the backing of a committee. However, wealthy men have wealthy friends, and an evangelist like Smith would almost certainly have known Shaftesbury, for instance. Before making the offer our friend would have made a great many enquiries, quietly taken up references. But it is true that a man like Sam Smith often made his own best deals by going by his instinct.

Let us all agree that if we happened to have £67,000 available, and felt like making a dramatic, philanthropic gesture, we would also do a lot of checking first. This young Irishman, in days when just to be Irish could bring its own problems, was basically unproven in running a charity, and was on record as having made a bit of a mull of his relationship with the Ernest Street Ragged School Committee. With these tiny drops of information as all he had to work on, Sam Smith took the plunge. Well, actually, it was a bit more than that. Ever since the Billingsgate sojourn, quite a few people in surprisingly high places had begun to hear his name mentioned. Not so much him dropping Shaftesbury's name, but the earl every now and then dropping his as an authority on the destitution in the East End. To sum all that up, at long last someone was going to put his hand in his pocket.

But things are never all that simple. What appears to have happened is that Smith, a much older and more experienced man, had offered to provide the funds. In all this 'offered' and 'provide' become important words. He wasn't fool enough just to hand over a cheque for the full sum and then stand back. There would have been serious discussions, the donor was a businessman, he had contacts. People would now do things for T. J. with Smith behind him that they wouldn't have done for him on his own. However, a great deal of caution is necessary as we work our way through the story. From what we can discover, quite how much financial support Smith supplied over the course of the next year is far from clear. As time passed we realise that money was often in short supply, and that plans were delayed from the lack of it.

FOUR

Young Man on a Mission: 1866–1876

William Notman and his wife lived near Hope Place, and Mrs Notman had heard that Thomas John Barnardo had started something up which, to use the phrase Notman recalled, was some sort of religious work. Urged on by his dear lady, he tells us that he went along the street to see what was going on. He not only looked, but he was one of the very first to join the enterprise. He was to become an enthusiast for the work. We can pick up from Notman's recollections of T. J. several years later.

> He had a power in him that seemed to be in no other man, which compelled us to work and could not be resisted. From that time he drew the poor people together in an evening service, and preached to them in an upper room of this small house, till the room could hold no more, and they had to divide the front and the back room. He stood there midway at the parting wall, discoursing at one moment to those in one room, then turning around, discoursed to those in the other. He introduced the method of going into the poor streets round about with large boards, on which were advertisements of the Sunday school, evening school for the boys, and adult meetings. It was a terribly

rough neighbourhood where they went, Barnardo leading the way. They were pelted with all manner of garbage at first.

Notman began working at Hope Place in 1868, totally untrained like all the other volunteers, and was still with the organisation thirty-seven years later in 1905 when T. J. died. He goes on to tell the story of when an ordained vicar, the Reverend Brown, came to preach at Hope Place. Seating capacity was completely overwhelmed, so T. J. first tried the neighbours.

Will you go to the homes and ask them to lend us their chairs? They went and got some chairs from the people, but even then there weren't enough. Then Barnardo said, let's ask the World's End pub. Do you think the landlord would lend us his benches? Let's go and see. It was about two in the afternoon of Sunday and Barnardo went to ask the landlord, who said yes, provided they were brought back promptly. They collected the benches, and set them up in the body of Hope Place, and made an aisle and the meeting took place. The work among the children grew very much. The principal work was done among the young people. They divided the rooms and had classes for the older boys and girls, with infants classes as well. The girls came from factories such as Bryant and May, Bell and Blacks and Burgesses. From that time they began to add to the church from the schools.

This gives us a vivid picture of the area, as well as reinforcing our understanding of our hero's dynamic character. 'He had the power in him that seemed to be in no other man.' The docklands of Shadwell, Wapping and Limehouse were tough areas. We can well imagine the boys round there letting fly at anyone who looked a bit better off than they were. In particular, we mustn't lose sight of the fact that he was essentially an evangelist, this was still a Christian venture first and foremost. The Church of England especially, but one or two of the others in varying degrees, weren't popular with large sections of the poor, who viewed them as canting middle-class hypocrites.

The first thing the school he set up needed to teach most of its pupils was just how to read, before they could go on to other things. In the days of the British Empire, one of the leading textbooks from which to learn to read was the Bible. The story of borrowing the benches from the pub is typical T. J. and we've met it before. He was preaching against the boozers, yet the landlord did him the favour. Bryant and May was a leading local employer, though at that time not a good one. They manufactured matches and used phosphorous in the process, which actually rotted the jawbones of the operatives. Employing mainly women, it was the subject of a famous strike over their appalling and particularly unhealthy conditions a few years later. The confidence instilled in some of the women by the Hope Place school had a lot to do with how they handled themselves, and how they came to win a notable victory. The firm still had a presence in the area until the 1950s.

1870 was a year when many things happened. It saw the first Married Women's Property Act, which is a mind-boggling concept; what on earth was the legal position of the ladies up to then? George Eliot published the famous book *Middlemarch*, an archetypal middle-class Victorian novel better written than most. It is mentioned because Mary Anne Evans thought it necessary to use a male pseudonym to get her books published and more widely read. Still with books, also in that year the reform-minded author Charles Dickens died.

Of more interest to T. J. and those of a like mind was the first Education Act, creating the first of the School Boards, giving limited publicly funded education to children between the ages of five and ten. The children were initially taught what were called the 'three Rs': reading, writing and arithmetic. It would be a century and several Education Acts later before the upper age limit at which they were legally required to remain in school reached sixteen. Also of interest to T. J., Britain had about 350 orphanages and homes for waifs and strays, serving a population which at the time included all of Ireland, of about 30 million.

From the general to the particular, in that little slum street in the East End, Hope Place was still a ragged school. It was a much better ragged school than a lot of them, because it was open weekdays as well as Sundays, but it was still a ragged school, and one not financially backed by any of the established organisations. By 1870 Barnardo was determined to move the venture on. Samuel Smith had offered to provide support if he would open a home for waifs and strays. Still a single man, and completely at a loss when it came to setting up a home for girls, he went in search of a place big enough to convert into a home for boys. This he found half a mile from Hope Place, in a street which at the time boasted among other things a sugar factory, Stepney Causeway. We have a record of him writing to a friend, all the clues suggest in August 1870. He had acquired the property and is reporting progress.

> In reply to yours about our Boys Home I write you a few hasty lines. The house, 18 Stepney Causeway, has been taken on lease. Various workmen, carpenter, painter, plumber, gasfitter are now busily engaged in fitting it up. When completed, it will contain five dormitories capable of accommodating sixty lads in all. There are also four rooms fitted up as lavatories, with basins, baths etcetera, and a private room for the mother and the father of the family. Space for healthful recreation is provided at the back of the premises, which consists of a good yard and coach house with stable and loft. The rent for all is £45 per annum, taxes are about £12 more. I need not tell you that we are fitting it up as plainly and as economically as is consistent with its permanent usefulness. Those friends who have already visited it agree with the various plans we have. I long to see it completed and ready for the reception of the lads. If the supplies are to hand, this could easily be accomplished in three weeks. [He now interposes the problem we have already mentioned] For want of funds I fear I shall be compelled to call off the workmen and suspend operations, as I am quite determined not to go into debt.

It is this matter in particular which raises the question of his relationship with Samuel Smith. There is another letter of 29

September, again mentioning the lack of funds. However he was able to advise the public through the columns of *The Christian*, which was the new name for *The Revival*, that 18 Stepney Causeway was open for his first intake. If we are looking for it now, the nearest reliable landmark is Limehouse railway station.

Now things could really begin to get moving. If we look at the rent, the 2000 conversion is about £75 a week. There is no way you could rent a property of the size he describes, not just the buildings but the land they were occupying, for that sort of money in the modern world. Whatever the conversions are for household goods and chattels, property is another financial world entirely. Not only are there the many rooms mentioned, there must have been a sizeable kitchen, scullery, dining-room and probably one or two others. Outside there were outbuildings, as becomes obvious as the story unfolds. It seems to have been a huge step up from Hope Place, which at this time he was still also running. Most importantly this wasn't a ragged school, it was a residential home.

We must make a last mention of the lack of funds which caused delays in the conversion work. It is perfectly possible that Samuel Smith was there in the background. It is also emerging that there were several other people, though we don't know the scale of their generosity at this stage. Meticulous records of cash flow were always kept; T. J. records figures starting 15 July 1866, only three months after his arrival from Dublin. Ignoring the odd pennies he tells us he had an income of £214 for the two years to July 1868. For the eighteen months to December 1869 he received £818, and there is a figure for the fifteen months of January 1870 to March 1871 of £2,429. One suspects that Smith may have put in quite a proportion of this last amount.

With some more help from the Office of National Statistics index we can update those to 2000 values. The multiple is about seventy, so the first figure converts to a modern £14,500, the second converts to about £58,000, and the fifteen months to March 1871 to £170,000. We have to admit we are not comparing like with like. Today we have all sorts of things we regard as necessities that in those days hadn't been invented yet. The social differences were very marked, for instance there was a huge deference to the aristocracy, and in the absence of modern trade unions and employment laws, there was unbridled exploitation in the workplace by unscrupulous employers.

As a fund-raiser T. J. was clearly someone special. Working in such a poor area as the East End, you would expect that he could get things done cheaper than had he been in the West End. Yet as good a fund-raiser as he was, he was obviously desperately short of money during the Stepney Causeway conversion. The property was very much bigger, it needed far more spent on it, and he made it clear that while he had to accept plain fittings he wasn't going to accept low standards.

The letter shows that his standards were higher than others were allowing for in their own projects. The description of the variety of tradesmen is revealing. We would expect a carpenter and a plumber, but note that he had not only the several inside toilets, but also as many washbasins all plumbed in. The gas fitter indicates a gas oven in the kitchen and possibly a water-heating system. Might they even have piped hot water to those hand basins? Almost none of the great country houses of the land in 1870 had such things, yet the gutter kids of the East End would have them as standard. Most East End houses still had an outside toilet, often shared between several families, and if you were lucky a tin bath to wash in front of the kitchen fire. Goodness gracious! Regular soap and water, clean hands, clean faces for destitute boys. Whatever next?

And he lays out very clearly what he wanted next. This was not to be an orphanage. Though some of the lads were inevitably orphans, about three-quarters of the children he was to deal with over the next thirty-five years had family, who for a wide variety of reasons needed help. Initially 18 Stepney Causeway was to be only for boys, and he divided them up into three categories. The first of these were older lads who already had a steady job, but needed a home. They were willing and able to pay something towards their keep. For these lads we would call it a sort of hostel. The second category were lads willing and able to work, but at the moment without a job, and needing a home. These would be given training in the Home, so they could acquire the skills needed to find work. When they found employment they also would be expected to contribute out of their wages towards their keep.

Category three, as we would expect, was the biggest problem. These were the destitute and homeless, and a lot of them really were orphans with no known family. They were the Jim Jarvis sort of street kid, even though some of them still had tenuous contact with a family member; some even had a parent, for all that the parent had abandoned them to the streets. The same rules applied as before, but dealing with this category took longer and was far harder. They needed to be shorn and deloused, hot water and a lot of soap applied vigorously, inspected for various livestock both internal as well as external, fed the medicines of the day to rid them of their parasites and sores, clothed, fed, and in some cases tamed of their tempers, as not all of them were instantly grateful for the sometimes rough attention all this entailed. Having got them that far, the usual rules applied. Educate, train with some skills and get them a job, at which point they were expected to pay something towards their keep. Category three, as you can well imagine, eventually overwhelmed categories one and two, though it cannot be said that they ever totally disappeared. Lives can only be lived one at a time, and each had their own needs. Over the years T. J. learned and he developed better ways of helping them.

Taking Limehouse railway station on the main Commercial Road as our landmark, Salmons Lane is around 200 yards north. That keeps us in our tight little area. In 1872 he set up a branch of his ragged school. He was for the time being still running Hope Place. At 18 Stepney Causeway and its outbuildings there were now workshops and a laundry. He had established a brush-making department and was in the early stages of making footwear. In the days of coal he claims that income from selling the chopped wood used to start them was £766, which converts to £54,000 in 2000 values. The time taken to earn this huge amount isn't clear, but it must have been a valuable addition to his funds. Because many of the lads knew the City like the backs of their hands, which were now clean enough to be seen in public, he was able to set up a City Messengers Brigade, which in time grew in reputation for its honesty and reliability.

Stepney Causeway didn't open until December 1870. At that time his accounting, which was meticulous, was April to April. Adjusting the figures a little to account for the slightly awkward fall of events, it would be fair to say that his income from January 1871 for the fifteen months to the end of March 1872 was about £7,500, which is £500,000 in 2000 values. That means this was no longer a little organisation scraping along the ground. The record of receipts includes some self-generated money, the chopped wood being an example. By the middle of 1872 the residential numbers had expanded to 130, from the thirty boys he had opened with eighteen months earlier. Add to those the twenty-four paid employees and the seventy-six volunteers. Now add all the supplies such an enterprise needed on a daily basis. All of that needed funding and finding the money was not easy. But just so that he didn't feel underemployed, add Hope Place and Salmons Lane.

He was twenty-seven years old, an inspiring, dynamic ball of energy, always on the go. About this time he laid down some rules. 'We do not beg, we do not get into debt, we do not publish the names of our donors.' He had to admit that seeking donations was an honest form of prayerful begging, and he liked to suggest the amount he had in mind to be prayed for. While the rules sounded wonderful at the time they weren't always stuck to, and a couple of decades into the future they did get horribly into the red. But we will come to that in due course.

We can never allow ourselves to think that with all this going on he ever lost sight of his original aim. At heart he was always a Christian evangelical missionary. At the heart of what he did was the central idea that he was working for the good of the children's souls by sorting out their lives. In his mind Hope Place was a missionary church before it was anything else. There he was regarded as its pastor, general factotum and centre of all works. To T. J. that little church was as important as anything else he did. Did we say he might be underemployed? Just to dispel that thought, in August 1872 he started up a Tent Mission, acquiring some sort of very large marquee, and we will paraphrase more of his quotes.

> We were obliged to take to the open air, and we had not been very long at work when we were chased through the streets by people of the neighbourhood. Finally we took up our stand in a very busy part, opposite the World's End public house. I had to quit that speedily because someone, who I suppose did not mean to do a friendly thing, opened a window above me and poured out a vessel of not very pleasant water on my head, which speedily extinguished my fervour.

As a method of extinguishing fervour it has its supporters. From Ancient Greece there is a story that Socrates suffered the same indignity from the action of his wife. Later in T. J.'s report we discover that the tent could hold 3,000 people, apparently all seated, night after night. One wonders if they can get that many into St Paul's Cathedral, but that is the claim. How reliable the figure is I would hesitate to say, but give or take an enthusiasm and an exaggeration or two, it does seem that he was attracting large numbers.

Among his assistants as things developed were Joshua and Mary Poole, both well-known evangelical preachers, and they became long-term supporters of his work. They are an interesting couple. Joshua had been a violent drunk, and he had served time in prison for GBH on his wife Mary. Now sober and completely reformed, he had given up the drink entirely. Whatever we may think of T. J.'s claims, one thing has to be a fact. Whatever the size of the tent and however many the chairs, there is an indication that there was a sizeable amount of money coming in. Even in 1872, investments of this size were not going to be cheap.

Another large pub in the area was the Edinburgh Castle, which will shortly feature prominently in our story. We get from our hero descriptions of the pubs, gin palaces, gaffs and music halls, and this is one of his examples. He complains at the length of the songs, that they were full of double entendres, that there was a roaring trade in drink, and also that there were nude statues set in niches around the walls. He was of course preaching the temperance message, and there had been a strong temperance movement in Britain since the end of the Napoleonic Wars. The law at that time had no control over drinking, either by age, hours of opening, or strength of alcoholic content. Booze being what it is, this was guaranteed to lead to trouble and inevitably to exacerbate the already endemic poverty. Boozing still causes trouble in our own day, though not quite as much, because we have some controls and laws, as far as they are enforced at any rate.

In the First World War, there were large munitions factories with explosions abounding, with a far from well-trained workforce. The government brought in the Defence of the Realm Act. Recognising the effects of alcohol on workers in the industry, they included in it, among many other things, restricted opening hours for pubs, and forbade the sale of alcohol to persons under the age of eighteen. This produced the famous cry of 'Time Gentlemen Please' at closing time, which persisted in pubs for decades afterwards. It was originally aimed at stopping munitions workers having too much time to get drunk, and blowing the place up by their carelessness. In no way does that suggest that the temperance message T. J. was expounding fifty years earlier had won the day. None of the pubs shut, but they were at last subject to some serious regulations. As prohibition in America in the twenties proved, you can't stop people drinking alcohol, you can only try and reduce the amount of damage some people inflict on themselves and on others.

*

The Tent Mission soon began to make a noticeable impression. The favourite pitch became a piece of ground 100 yards along Rhodswell Road from Hope Place, just across the road from the Edinburgh Castle pub. There exists a wonderful photograph of the building, which seems to have been taken around 1873. Again we are still in the same tight little area, all these places are a ten-minute walk from each other.

Such was the Mission's success that eventually the owners no longer thought it worth staying open. What happened to mine host James Mullett is not recorded. What is recorded is that the leasehold, still with thirty-eight years to run, came up for auction. With some friends, T. J. did a tour of inspection. These friends were of the well-connected and prosperous sort; he no longer just had to rely on Samuel Smith. It had eighteen rooms, one claimed to hold 2,000, with a capacity of 1,100 for another. The reserve price was £4,000, they only had £2,800. They put in a 'stopping' bid of £4,200 to get it taken out of the auction for a period of days, which was accepted in return for a 20 per cent deposit. Our hero did what he usually did in such circumstances, he told all his friends how much to pray for. Somehow, on the morning the 'stop' ran out, the last of the extra £1,400 they needed came in. It appears to have been a damned close-run thing.

So what's all this then, T. J. and his mates owning a boozer? Well first things first, which was to vest the property in a trust. From this evolved the overall trust which eventually covered the whole enterprise. The *Memoirs* quote T. J. as describing it as an enlargement of the East End Juvenile Mission, but it must be said that it became a lot more than merely juvenile work. We have the names of the original seven trustees, and one suspects that in varying degrees they were the people who found most, if not all of the £1,400 needed to complete the deal. It was always his habit never to divulge who had given and how much; this he held to be confidential with the donor. All of them were people who had no need to count their pennies; two were younger sons of wealthy earls. Apart from Shaftesbury, T. J. now knew a large number of such people, and by the time he died he probably knew half the

House of Lords, and had got money from most of them for his charity.

The property market today in no way compares with the general figure for inflation over the period. Let us merely say that in 1872 the Hope Place houses, mean little two-up-and-two-downs, might have been had for £30 or £40, or rented for maybe 3 or 4 shillings a week. That's 15p or 20p rent. The Edinburgh Castle was not only enormously bigger than Hope Place, it was quite a bit bigger than the house in Stepney Causeway. The use of this new purchase was not going to be to increase the space for residential child rescue. What it allowed was to greatly increase the range of activities provided for the poor of the area.

Temperance had become a national movement, and it was the first real cause of a political nature that women could get involved with. Very rightly, the wives were getting fed up with being knocked about by drunken husbands, and equally having to 'pop the weasel down at uncle's', so often. With birth control unheard of, that means pawn the press iron, usually in order to buy food for a legion of children, the husband having drunk what money they had down the pub. While many women also drank, most had the yearly baby, families of twelve were normal, some even had twenty. In those situations, with so many mouths to feed, poverty was hardly a surprise. Women were beginning to speak up for themselves a little more, and the temperance movement gained momentum.

Two things had helped. The Sunday School Union founded in 1804, and the Ragged School Union founded in 1844, were formalisations of things that had been around for several previous decades. First and foremost they taught reading, so that at last the poor were in some small way literate. In view of the fact that businesses needed clerks, the more literate working class were getting some of those jobs. With literacy came awareness of their social condition, which led to demands for betterment. By the time T. J. came on the scene this movement was well underway. Indeed the whirling wheels of industry increasingly needed their skills in order to turn. Shaftesbury had been pushing for change for several decades, now along came numerous people such as T. J. to take up the baton and carry it forward.

With that pause for reflection in mind, let us now stroll down to the Edinburgh Castle. But what's all this? It's a tea and coffee bar! Yet the place still looks very much like the pub it used to be. Let us have a few words from a Northern gentleman, Walter Hinde Smith, who hailed from Leeds in Yorkshire.

> I think it was about 1867 or 68 that Doctor B came to Leeds to see my wife's work. She then had the oversight of sixteen 'British Workmen's Public Houses without Drink'. Each one had a Mission Hall attached. He was charmed with the idea, and declared that he would eclipse our work by going in for something on a much bigger scale, but keeping to the main idea, which is what he did.

The date seems wrong, it was much more likely after 1870, and he wasn't yet Doctor B., only Mr B., so this is clearly a much later recollection. The Hon. Arthur Kinnaird was a trustee of the Edinburgh Castle, and his family already had a temperance venture in Dundee, aimed at competing with the pubs. Apart from Dundee and Leeds there were temperance taverns in Liverpool and Manchester, and several other towns. We also notice that it wasn't Walter Hinde Smith, it was his highly organised wife who was running what must have been a considerable business; he claims sixteen such taverns. No small enterprise at any time, and being run by a woman who didn't have a vote, and barely had legal control over her possessions. Not to criticise any of this, but do we also get a sense of absolute earnestness, and a ghostly slogan, 'We are your local do-gooders', written in large capitals over the door?

Not only was temperance something people weren't used to – after all, St Paul preached 'take a little wine for thine stomach's sake' – but T. J. recalled that what he saw in Leeds did seem dull and dingy, these places were putting people off even going inside to look round. They were also called working men's public houses, but a large proportion of the mill workers in Yorkshire and Lancashire were women. That registered very much with T. J. and the Edinburgh Castle from the start was designed to cater for the factory women, who were in just as large numbers in the East End as they were up North. He explains his reasons for taking a different course of action from the lady in Leeds.

> Why play at public houses? The answer is that the establishment of coffee houses isn't play at all, it's hard work. The publican understands human nature, he adopts common sense methods of attracting custom. In a general business way there's no harm in adopting the same lines. The working man is caught by the guile of the publican, why shouldn't he be diverted to better ways by the same means. The Coffee Palace is fitted up in the style of a first-class tavern, because the light, warmth and general cheerful aspect gives satisfaction to the poor customers, whose homes are at best only too bare, and whose life is undoubtedly monotonous. The well-conducted Coffee Palace has an abundance of attractions, and there is nothing that customers of a higher class can object to. Customers accustomed to good food at home can appreciate the tea and coffee, and relish the bread and butter.

In other words, let's not frighten them off before they even get through the door, give them something they're used to, bright, warm and cheerful. He kept the old name and he kept the old pub sign on its high wooden mast set in the pavement outside. Don't just make it welcoming, make it acceptable to the local traders and shopkeepers. It could never close down the nearby pubs, but a much better class of establishment had come among them, raising the tone of the road, something that was good for their trade. In fact quite soon he had such people coming in and having a meal themselves.

He understood people and the Edinburgh Castle was a great example of his instinctive people skills. The people around there felt that he was a good bloke and they liked him. If we go to a later recollection dated 1886, we have an idea of the realistic way he thought and acted. As usual it is paraphrased. 'I always thought that to teach total abstinence was worse than useless, if I couldn't offer a substitute for the social advantages of a pub. There was a missing link in our temperance organisation, unless they had somewhere to go to be social.'

Once it was up and running, the Edinburgh Castle offered good cooked meals at affordable prices, all drinks were non-alcoholic, so mainly tea or coffee. It also offered newspapers and allowed for darts, dominoes, chess and other pastimes. Above all it was a place to go for a gossip with your friends. You could be free with your opinions and pretend to listen to what others thought, as is only natural. It was essentially run as a pub with no beer, and particularly in the winter an evening spent in the warm there didn't burn coal in your own grate, which was something else that the poor appreciated. With its several large rooms this was the future, as T. J. saw it, for his mission to the poor and needy. It soon had offices staffed with people who could be turned to in times of trouble.

There is a splendid photograph taken in 1873, which is remarkably clear. The sharpness of the image gives enormous credit to the photographer, in an age when he only had a primitive camera and photographic glass plates, and all exposures for outdoor photographs had to be judged according to the sun, or lack thereof. We see the Edinburgh Castle, a large establishment in any era, standing on a locally important thoroughfare. To the left we have a two-horse, low-sided cart bearing the name W. J. Cook. We can read the address as 20 Commercial Road E, and professional enlargement indicates that the cart was carrying sacks of coal. To the right is a one-horse covered cart of lighter construction, which belonged to A. W. Matthews, fruiterer and greengrocer of 125 Well Street NE. In passing, Well Street is where the 'Tesco' family had their original market stall.

The pub was a three-storey building, and taking into account all the available clues, it seems to have had a frontage of some 60 feet. Over one of the entrances is emblazoned Working Men's

Club. So no concessions to the ladies yet! Beside the main entrance is a large board. An enlargement allows us to read this.

GOSPEL SERVICE
Tonight at 8 o'clock
Last appearance of
FRANK L SMITH
Where do we go when we die.

*

Just below the eaves there is the pub sign, 'EDINBURGH CASTLE', in big bold gilded capital letters. 'The Peoples Mission Church' is written in an elegant sweeping arc over the main entrance and is repeated over a second doorway further along. Solidly set into the pavement is the original 20-foot-high sign mast, which is a good bit of public relations with the locals. No change of name, no big changes other than a fresh coat of paint. Oh! And no beer!

However, there is an important addition, for nailed to the big solid mast, just under the actual sign in its Victorian wrought iron frame, there is a big oblong board. This takes a lot more magnification, but in the end it is readable.

NO
DRUNKARD
SHALL INHERIT
THE KINGDOM OF
GOD

Before you buy a building always get a survey! It transpired that the Edinburgh Castle was in a pretty dreadful condition, so bad that in 1882 they had to pull it down before it fell down. It was rebuilt and reopened in 1884, bigger and more splendid than before. The grand opening was attended by no less a dignitary than the Lord Mayor of London. It was from the beginning always run as a commercial proposition, and it always gave a fair return on the money invested.

In all this talk of grinding poverty, we must not miss the point that the majority of East Enders were respectable working people. Apart from dockworkers and the lightermen on the barges, seamen of all nations, there were warehouses for the cargoes of the world, outgoing as well as arriving, rope making, sugar refining, there was a rice mill, a pottery drainpipe factory, and a corrugated iron works, all within a few hundred yards of the Edinburgh Castle. Add to those several hundred other trades and professions; London in those days was a hive of manufacturing and trading. Though the working class were not well paid, they tended to be decently sober most of the time. Without much in the way of labour laws, and the trade unions only recently legalised, any man annoying the foreman could be fired at a minute's notice. Workers tended to be less abrasive, for fear of the consequences. It was mainly these people who were attracted to the new Mission church at the Edinburgh Castle. Shall we paraphrase another recollection?

> At the Edinburgh Castle on Sunday we have a crowded morning congregation of decent, respectable working people, at an hour when all such are popularly supposed to either be in bed, or at the pub on the corner. Others besides Miss Ellis Hopkins have wondered what secret nexus connects Christianity with broadcloth, and I have been asked why our hearers, all East End workers, are so respectably clad. On a Sunday afternoon we have usually 2,500 in attendance. In the evening the full capacity of the hall is tested, and I know of no more hopeful and inspiring sight than between 7 o'clock and 8.30 in the evening, all our 3,200 seats are occupied.

Picking up on an old-style word, broadcloth was a type of wool serge, popularly used for men's 'Sunday best' suits. Quite who Miss Ellis Hopkins was is not explained, but she may have expressed some public doubts about the enterprise. The number of 3,200 in the congregation is staggering, set against church attendances in our own century. The recollection is not dated, but is thought to be from the 1880s.

There is an adage from the world of the media: if the truth becomes a legend, publish the legend. As with what may have been the doubts of Miss Hopkins, the claims which Barnardo makes are worthy of a little caution, or we'll only be left with the legend. Most of these recollections were written years later, and we don't know if he was using contemporary notes or trying to remember. Let us admit that there may have been lapses of accuracy. There is no question that he made a huge contribution to the social improvement of the poor, but can we for instance believe 3,200 people attending his church? Well, if you know you have 3,200 chairs and they are all occupied, then yes! Another of his claims was that there were often as many as 200 people at a time to be converted to the faith. Billy Graham was getting those numbers at his evangelical mission at Wembley Stadium a century later, at a time when people were far less religious, so we know the claim is at least credible.

Let us agree that times have changed. That was then, this is now. In the nineteenth century Christianity was the normal thing, atheism was thought of as very oddball, you were not considered a safe sort of person if you discussed it. In the twenty-first century there has been a role reversal. In much of society Christians are now thought of as the oddballs. We will have to agree that while we wouldn't go along with the last dot and comma of every claim, it is abundantly clear that the Edinburgh Castle Mission church was a tremendous success, the congregations were consistently big, and many people did come forward for conversion and blessing. It's where the staff and the volunteers came from, as the crusade against poverty and social deprivation in the area gathered momentum. It was T. J. who generated the enthusiasm, it was the congregation who became the seedbed of a rapidly growing self-help organisation. In fact, in later generations the authorities had them as a blueprint to work from when social welfare properly arrived. The support systems were set up, and the intense effort that went into them can be understood from the next paraphrased quote.

> Of the host of allied agencies which have sprung up out of, or have grouped themselves the Edinburgh Castle centre, one of the foremost of these is the Deaconess House in Bow Road, filled with educated Christian ladies who devote their whole time to visiting the poor, the sick and the ignorant. The neighbourhood of the Castle is divided into districts, and every house and room within the radius receives regular visits. All our relief agency is founded upon intimate knowledge, and this knowledge the ladies supply. We know who friend 'A' is, what he works at, whether he is out of work or not, what his earnings are, whether his wife is a good manager or not, what rent they pay, how many children there are, whether and where they go to school, whether they attend any place of worship, etc. This systematised intelligence guides our actions in case of relief being wanted. Then too, the largest ragged schools in London have been carried on for years within a stone's throw of the Edinburgh Castle, these being a direct outgrowth of the Mission Hall work. The whole staff of teachers is selected from the converts made at the hall. One of our most valuable rules is to set our adherents at work suited to their capacities and aptitudes. In this way we have filled not a few of our agencies with the very men wanted for such posts. In connection with these schools, situated in Copperfield Road, we have for years supplied the hungrier scholars with free breakfasts and dinners.

The Deaconess House opened in 1875 and remained in existence until 1897, and as one can see, Scotland Yard would have been proud of its information-gathering abilities. Where the money came from is always an interesting point. Were these ladies of independent means, or was the trust paying all the expenses? One feels a bit of both, because such an agency would not have been cheap to run. What those apparently genteel ladies didn't know about their patch would probably have been easier to write down than what they did, because it's clear that they were the Social Services of their day. If anyone was in trouble, get on to the Castle people.

Thinking about it in our own times, it sounds like a load of interfering busybodies, a lot of it might even be illegal. Back then there was nothing else, and the situations were often a lot more desperate, so help was welcomed with open arms. Previous attempts at philanthropy had been very hit and miss. What T. J. did was stick to a patch he knew well and could handle, then get the locals organised to do what was needed. And there is the key point, they were locals helping locals. Quite where the deaconesses were recruited from is another matter, but the movers and shakers were all locals, they lived round there, it was their manor.

Copperfield Road Ragged School is where the Hope Place school eventually went, and as the recollection says, it became the biggest of its type in the whole of London, as well as probably the best. So many of these quotes are not dated, one has to pick up the clues to give an idea of the time to which they refer. Copperfield Road was another turning off Rhodswell Road, and is these days the site of the Ragged School Museum. While publicly funded schools under the charge of the local authorities and the School Boards came into existence in 1870, ragged schools were still open for about another thirty years. For some but by no means all of that time, until it closed in 1908, the Barnardo Trust received a local authority subsidy to help with its expenses.

FIVE

Marriage and a Village of Girls: 1876–1886

It would be as a result of his evangelism that the greatest change in his personal life came about. In the suburb of Richmond, Surrey, William Elmslie was what is described in the archives as a Lloyd's subscriber, a status somewhat different from a full member of this great insurer of ships and more or less anything else you can think of. Thomas John Barnardo was now earning a reputation because of his work in the East End. He was also known as a charismatic preacher, for which he charged a fee, which he needed to give him a personal income. The daughter of the Elmslie household who we met briefly in our earlier mention was Sarah Louise, always called Syrie. She is said to have been the prime mover in urging the invitation for him to speak at the church the family used in Richmond. It was therefore natural that they should meet, but it seems it would be eighteen months before they met again. However, things then moved swiftly, he proposed and she accepted.

Having himself a few years earlier been in severe financial straits, Papa Elmslie was not too happy about Syrie marrying a man whose sources of income seemed insubstantial. He was persuaded by his determined daughter to agree, and in June 1873 she became Mrs Barnardo. There were to be seven children, three of whom died young. General life expectancy was under sixty in those days, but barely forty in the poorer areas of the big cities. T. J. himself died in 1905 aged sixty, but Syrie lived until 1944, when she died in quiet retirement in Sussex aged ninety-six.

They married at the Metropolitan Tabernacle, Newington Causeway, the pulpit of C. H. Spurgeon, a well-known Baptist minister of his day. On the main road from London Bridge to the famous Elephant and Castle junction, it was said to seat 6,000, so twice the size of T. J.'s own mission hall. Spurgeon was yet another of his legion of friends and was happy to let him use the church, but was himself unable to officiate, having been booked to elsewhere that day. We might wonder why they didn't use the Edinburgh Castle? It wasn't because of the upper-class company expected, after all Newington Causeway isn't Mayfair either. It was simply that the Edinburgh Castle wasn't licensed for the conduct of marriages. The *Memoirs* tell us that the stag night of this ex-wine merchant's clerk and champion of temperance was really more like a prayer meeting.

The wedding guests included anyone who was anyone in the evangelical and Nonconformist wings of Christianity in and around London. Sons of peers being entitled to call themselves lord or honourable, there were several of those, various other wealthy backers, his old friend the Revd Grattan Guinness, and, in a nice touch, the Church of England Rector of Limehouse Parish. He had been most helpful to T. J. in many ways, and much of the growing enterprise at this stage was in his parish.

The six-week honeymoon was the first holiday T. J. had managed to organise in nine years. Who paid for the trip is an open question. What is on record is that they came back to a slap-up reception at the Edinburgh Castle, where the congregation had subscribed to a silver tea set as their wedding present. Not least in all this, once he got back to work, was that as a married man he felt that he could now start on something he'd up to now been avoiding: rescuing destitute girls.

A strong supporter of her husband and his work, Syrie actually took relatively little responsibility in the day to day running of the

Trust itself, concentrating on being a wife and mother, which is really what he wanted and needed. Now being married gave him the status of respectability he felt he needed to tackle the problem of the girls. That sounds terribly prim and Victorian, but then he was a Victorian, and an awful lot of his supporters were very, very prim.

It's worth repeating that Barnardo Homes, as they developed, were never orphanages as such. About a quarter of the children being cared for were orphans, but three-quarters were not. That meant of course that he was not only responsible to the child, he had the family in the background, something which could be awkward and led to a great deal of trouble at times. It makes it easier to appreciate that where a home situation, in a desperately poor family, made it sensible to get one or two of the sons out of there to ease the pressure, equally it made sense to do the same for the daughters, so long as a safe home could be found.

Up to this point T. J., as an unmarried man of the strictest religious principles of morality, had run shy of tackling the issue. He employed by this time a great many ladies, both paid and as volunteers, in his rapidly growing organisation. Now he was married, and with Syrie as an enthusiast for the same Christian morality and philanthropy, his circumstances changed. Now he could rescue girls.

*

One of the more practical projects in the care of destitute children had been set up in Addlestone, Surrey, by a group of worthy wives who had rich husbands. One of their supporters, after whom the place was named, was Princess Mary Adelaide, Duchess of Teck. Though a German title, the family mainly lived in England. They had an interesting daughter, also called Mary, who married King George V, and was thus grandmother of Queen Elizabeth II.

The Princess Mary Village Homes were based on the cottage system, a rather experimental idea. The girls lived in small groups in a cottage, though the definition of cottage was fluid; we are talking of maybe twelve girls in a very roomy house. There they lived under the watchful eyes of a resident housemother, which was totally opposite to the publicly funded workhouse system. It was also far better than the large dormitory system used by many charities, and was being used by the boys in Stepney Causeway. In the days of empire it could be made to work with boys, military discipline and systems, eh! It certainly couldn't be made to work with girls. As he developed it in later years for his girls, he aimed to create a family atmosphere in his cottages. We have to bear in mind that we are among Victorians, when twelve was a quite ordinary number of children in a family. Queen Victoria only stopped at nine because Prince Albert died.

John Sands, a wealthy lawyer and one of the trustees of the Edinburgh Castle, gave the newly-weds a fifteen-year lease on Mossford Lodge, a large house in 24 acres, in what was then rural Barkingside in Essex. This later became a freehold, and is the reason why so much of the organisation developed in later years in the immediate area. Such properties in that era had servant's quarters, a coach house and stabling for horses. It also suggests that T. J., either out of his own pocket or with the help of his father-in-law, felt sufficiently financially secure to take it on. He was wrong in this, it proved to be ruinously expensive, and after a fairly short stay they moved back to the East End, to one of the better-class roads in Bow. This took him back to what was in those early days his main area of operations.

They did however keep possession of the property, with the idea of developing it for the girls. The coach house was remodelled, furnished and generally kitted out, and twelve girls were brought in from the slums. With clothing and bedding it seems about £1,000 was spent. That would multiply up to about £70,000 in 2000 values, so no stinting on the expenditure. There is no record of where this money came from, but John Sands is a leading candidate.

It hit trouble from the start, which takes us back to the remarks about the Village Homes at Addlestone. The girls were being housed in the open-dormitory system, we might think of it as a barrack-room system. By early 1875 the number of girls had risen to fifty-four, and things were rapidly going horribly pear-shaped! These were rough, tough girls from the slum streets and alleyways. Let us say that the bigger girls knew only too much about things which weren't at all respectable, and the smaller girls were getting a complete education in them. In no way had it registered with T. J. that such a state of affairs could be possible. When he realised what was happening it blew his Christian socks off! We will go to his recollections, paraphrasing as usual from articles he wrote in later years.

I was rescuing little English nomads, some of whom might be rightly described as girl savages. The life stories of some of my first inmates were shocking in the extreme. The period of which I write was the heyday of beggars. There was nothing but the Vagrant Law to touch them, and that wasn't used often. They could sleep where they liked, drag about boy and girl savages with ignorant minds and stunted bodies who never went to school. They were capable of fighting viciously, and becoming drunk at an early age. Debauchery followed as soon as possible. Among my first group of girls I had as many depraved children gathered in our little Home as I suppose have ever been under one roof since then. These were mostly criminals in embryo. If they continued in their environment, together with the simple neglect by Society and State, that was all that was needed for them to become abandoned women. It was with such as these that I had to deal. Knowing nothing better, I supposed a home in the country under Christian influences, with simple education and some degree of training, would at any rate be the first steps towards a better life. I saw what I had to do.

That certainly tells the tale. Debauchery and abandoned women, so prostitution and all the crime that goes with it, and these girls were only eight or nine, maybe up to fifteen. What he was saying was that society was ignoring them, that the state was failing in its duty to protect them. It was about time someone got their act together.

It was people like T. J. who persistently hammered away at it, and slowly attitudes began to change. Here was a well brought-up, well-intentioned man who had been in the thick of it trying to help the poor in Dublin for five years, and now doing the same in London for another five. Yet even he, with all his experience, had been a bit of an innocent when it came to the girls. Rescuing them was the easy part, now he had to civilise them out of the sordid nature of their early childhood. That was going to take a damned sight more than just soup and sympathy! His first attempts were clearly way off the beam, his approach would have to radically change. Let's pick up our quotes where we left off.

> I saw what I had to do. There should no longer be a great house in which sixty of these motherless girls would be herded together, clad in some dull uniform, generally divested of all prettiness. Instead there would be cottages, each one presided over by its own 'mother', in which all the members of the family could be dressed as ordinary working people's children were under ordinary circumstances. The girls would be of all ages, from the baby of a few months or weeks to the growing girls, some of whom would be nearly out of their teens. There, family life and family love might be reproduced. Such was the rough outline of my new plan.

Now he was thinking along the lines of the Princess Mary Cottage Homes. There are some people in the world who not only think of good ideas like this, or borrow them as in this case, but they go out and bang on the world's door to get things done. What he was doing was banging loudly on the Victorian world's door and the smarter the house, the louder and longer he banged. He already had 24 acres of land, and immediately adjoining there was more available. In the end he accumulated 60 acres, on which the Girls Village was progressively built. Today the site is a short walk from Barkingside railway station along Tanners Lane.

Three weeks before he was thirty, on 9 June 1875, not just one or two but eleven foundation stones were ceremoniously laid by the Earl of Aberdeen, grandson of the Prime Minister who had taken us into the Crimean War. After 400 days not just those eleven buildings were completed, but another two as well, and add to those the laundry. This time the celebrations called for not one lord but two. Back came Aberdeen, accompanied by Lord Cairns and his lady. There was a grand opening, followed, as we would expect, by a slap-up tea. Cairns was the Lord Chancellor, and having such a tremendous supporter who was also a leading lawyer proved to be very useful in years to come.

One of the extra cottages had been paid for by a wealthy supporter in memory of a daughter who had recently died. As was the Barnardo custom, we do not have his name, or the many other donors who made similar in-memoriam donations. The *Memoirs* tell us that by the end of 1906, so a year after our hero died, there were sixty-five cottages and eleven other ancillary buildings, and at that time there were plans for more. A panoramic photograph of the village exists, which includes a distant view of the church. As the church wasn't completed and dedicated until Easter 1894 the photograph must date from then or later. The cottages are seen as substantial brick-built, two-storey, tile-roofed houses around a green. There are roads and paths, a large number of trees and shrubs and what was clearly then still countryside in the distance. The church and all the other buildings seen on a visit in 2006 appear to have been built to very high standards, and the church at that time was well cared-for and in use.

The Barnardo Trust no longer has any children in residence. The organisation still exists in a form suitable for today's needs in today's century. There stands along Tanners Way near the church, on the site of the old apple orchard, the current head office, relocated from Stepney Causeway in 1969. Several cottages have been sold to a housing association, and when last checked on were in use as sheltered housing for the elderly. A total of fifteen cottages around the green have been 'listed', which means they are regarded as having historic significance. Some of the properties are still used by the trust, but about 30 acres were sold to the local authority. The local magistrates court is one of a number of developments thereon. Both in respect of this and of the head office built at around the same time, some of us might regret the sixties style in which they were designed, and wish that they were more in keeping with the original Barnardo village.

*

T. J. was a great one for reports full of details and all sorts of statistics. Up to the time he died in 1905, the village had seen 8,700 girls pass through, which gives us an average of 300 a year. Obviously the numbers would have been less to begin with and progressively grew. We have some details of Miss Southgate, one of those kindly but also redoubtable Victorian maiden ladies of sterling worth. She was the 'mother' of Forget-me-not Cottage from 1876, so one of the first, until 1887. She then ran Peace Cottage up to about the time T. J. died, and she herself passed away the following year. We can see from the figures the age mix she dealt with. In twenty-nine years she cared for two babies under a year old, sixteen aged one to six, sixty-four aged five to ten, seventy aged ten to fifteen, and five above that. That adds up to a remarkable 157 in twenty-nine years. That means she had a turnover of about five or six in and five or six out every year. Where it could be made to work, this was the deliberate strategy for the cottage families in the village. We will shortly come to the special circumstances where it couldn't be operated, and the problems involved.

In an era when the wealthy lived in large houses and employed servants, the girls were among other things trained for that line of work. There are two stories which illustrate this, case studies of how such destitution, or at least severe poverty, could sometimes overwhelm even hard-working and respectable families.

In the first case the girl lost her mother when she was only six years old. She had three brothers and her father, who was a poorly paid farm labourer. To assist the family the girl was taken in by a kind neighbour. However, this kind lady died when the girl was ten. Back with her family, we have the five of them trying to live on the father's meagre income. Things are going from bad to worse. Someone who knew the family organised an application to Barnardo's and she was accepted. She was at the village for six years and at the age of sixteen was found a position as a maid, in which she is said to have prospered.

The second case is that of a girl arriving at the village on the application of her mother. The father was dead, and the mother was only making 3 shillings a week, that is 15p, as a machinist in a shoe factory. Even with the most generous application of the Office of National Statistics multiple, they were on the breadline with no butter. The girl who was accepted was one of several children in the family. She was also trained for service and found a position with a good family. She later married and is reported to have visited some time later to show her housemother her baby son.

Neither of these girls were orphans. The organisation could have filled both Stepney Causeway and Barkingside Village with orphans quite easily, but that wasn't the intention. The working motto was 'No destitute child will ever be turned away'. Not all the destitute were orphans. To the limit of the money he was able to raise, T. J. stuck to that principle. Exactly what 'never turned away' meant was subject to some fine-tuning out of sheer necessity on some occasions. What he refused to allow was the donor election system in use by some other charities. In those cases a donor could nominate a specific child to be accepted, in return for a large donation. Barnardo always insisted that the only criteria were the needs of the children, and that no donor was ever allowed to have control over how the money was spent.

One outstanding and beneficial effect of the Village was the health of the children. There were no such drugs as antibiotics. What the system relied on was hot water, soap and a lot of elbow grease. Keep the place clean, keep the children clean, don't let dirt settle. The Village was receiving girls with all sorts of illnesses caused by dirt and damp, particularly what was then called consumption, now known as tuberculosis. This terrible killer disease was endemic throughout society, the rich could get it as well as the poor. But TB was especially rooted in the slums, where people lived in continually damp conditions in which the disease thrived.

Add to TB such things as scabies, intestinal worms, fleas, lice, polio, scarlet fever, all sorts of things to put you off your tea, you name it, they probably had it. Because of malnutrition many had the bone malformation called rickets. On initial intake many might show an apparently low intelligence, though that was usually sorted out when the diet improved. The constant insistence on personal cleanliness, plus high standards of sanitation, proved to be big winners. In fact the Village had sanitation fitted as standard which was way ahead of that in place in most London homes of the time.

Inevitably there were some deaths. In the big cities as the century turned, official figures for the child death rate were about 16 per 1,000. In the year 1902 there was a residential population of 6,399 in the Barnardo Homes, boys and girls added together. There were in that year thirty-four deaths, or 5.3 per 1,000. Tragic as each individual case was, the Barnardo Homes came in at a third of the national average, and a quantum leap better than the rate in the slums the children emerged from. Many of course were ill when they arrived and failed to make it through their first few weeks. While there is no medical analysis of causes of death available, one feels that if one took out the TB cases, there would be almost no other deaths to count. A special note of the excellence of the Barnardo systems was shown when there was an outbreak of scarlet fever, in those days a serious childhood illness, in the Village in 1879, only three years after opening. While a few deaths might have been expected, none of the 150 children affected were lost.

If we are talking about the health of the children, there exists a remarkable picture of twelve disabled lads from the boys' home, all of whom are on crutches having lost a leg. The reason is easy to explain. Living in filth and dirt, an injury that we in our clean world wouldn't think twice about could get infected, or, as they said in those days, turn septic. In the days before antibiotics that was very serious. The victim could get not only blood-poisoning, but also gangrene. The only cure for gangrene was to chop off the affected limb. It sounds drastic, but the state of medical science then allowed no other option, in fact it is still being done in today's world in severe situations. Modern hygiene and modern drugs usually prevent such situations happening. The picture reminds us of the enormous range of children the Barnardo Homes dealt with. Among the many things the picture demonstrates is T. J.'s determination to prove to the world, and to the children themselves, that only having one leg still left them with two hands and a brain in full working order. It wasn't a disability which could stop a determined person from doing a worthwhile job and earning a wage.

The biggest problem almost from the start was self-inflicted. This was the declaration that no destitute child would ever be turned away. What if the child was not only destitute and starving, but also permanently mentally handicapped? Soap and hot water can clean the child up, it can be fed and clothed, but what if there is no possibility of letting the child back into the community because it simply couldn't cope? This was to become a major problem, and it had a special significance in the Barnardo household.

In all, T. J. and Syrie had seven children. Herbert and Ken both died as youngsters of one of the childhood scourges of the time, diphtheria. Tom died as a baby. That left William, Gwendolyn, always called Queenie, Cyril, and the youngest was Marjorie. Family records confirm that she was born with Down's Syndrome. So the family had been repeatedly shaken by the personal tragedy of losing the children. They also had to tackle something which, with their middle-class status and the attitudes of their generation, was usually shunned with horror. How were they to raise Marjorie?

It brought the problem home to them at the most personal level. It made them more than usually sympathetic to the plight of the mentally handicapped. However, it wasn't something that the growing Barnardo Homes organisation had been created to take on board. Very importantly, it wasn't something that their donors thought they were giving their money towards. There seems to be no other way of saying it: T. J. went into the situation with his eyes shut to the difficulties, but his heart wide open and his compassion in full working order. From the earliest days the expense of accepting mentally handicapped children made inroads into the Trust's income disproportionate to their numbers. Let's paraphrase another quote, where he discusses such girls.

> Those classed as feeble-minded present very special difficulties. Quite a large proportion of our deaf and dumb inmates are feeble-minded. The term covers however a wide range of disabilities, although the line of demarcation is not easy to draw. Some never rise above the unclassified class, or the second standard at school, but they can develop intelligence for good hard work. Some of these can be placed out with careful mistresses. Some can be taught needlework, but are incapable of further education. Among girls such as these, the result of careful teaching in our Embroidery School at our Girls Village Homes has been little short of marvellous. They are not as a general rule, however, capable of being placed away from institutional care. Older girls, for whom we frequently have applications, are almost helpless.

One hopes no one will object to the terminology he uses, that was the language of the day. One also has to realise that he had no training as a mental healthcare professional, nor did any of his staff. His genius was kicking the society he was a part of in the backside, getting it to start thinking about this problem. The quote makes it clear that just as he could so easily have ended up with an orphanage, so he could have ended up with a vast mental institution. In either scenario, if he took all the cases offered he would have been totally swamped.

A further quote about the dangers of this situation is from the pen of T. J.'s successor William Baker. We will again paraphrase from something much longer, and he is also writing about the Girls Village.

> Our main difficulty arises from the fact that the number of cases that cannot be allowed out of the Institution is continually increasing. We therefore have to devote money subscribed for the benefit of children to supporting those who have really become women. Many of these inmates are, however, partially able to support themselves by their work. There seems a real necessity in dealing with this question for wider statutory powers and for the establishment of special institutions to deal with such unfortunately afflicted individuals. We find that our method of family life at Barkingside, with two or three more or less feeble-minded girls in each cottage, is a most valuable method of education, so long as progressive education is possible. If however the intelligence ceases to grow, the presence of such a girl in the family is disturbing, and the peace of the home is upset. For such cases undoubtedly proper establishments should be supplied. Already two cottages at our Village are devoted to such cases, and a third is to be added.

That is how William Baker found it after 1905, and it was a situation which had been building up over the previous twenty years or so. What we get from the comments is that the Barnardo Homes were, in the first decade of the twentieth century, committed to housing and caring for maybe sixty of these ladies for the rest of their lives. That wasn't what the Homes had been set up to do. Then we must realise that the actual situation was even worse. Baker discusses the horrors of sending them to the asylums and workhouses, dreadful and grim establishments which still then existed. If sent there then all the progress, all those little triumphs they had achieved, all that they had made of their lives despite their severe limitations would have been completely destroyed. What Baker was calling for was a properly thought-out and publicly funded policy of humane social care for these unfortunate people. There are many who would contend that

Britain still hasn't managed to get it completely right, even these days.

You and I are adults, probably middle-class if that phrase still has a meaning, well fed and fairly well educated. The girls being rescued from the slums were… girls being rescued from the slums! Let's fix that idea in our heads. They were rough and tough, had lived desperately rotten lives up to then, they thought and often fought like that, because that's what they were, slum kids. It must have taken a long time and a great deal of skill to calm some of them down. They certainly didn't become little angels and little princesses overnight. With that sort of background, they were being put in with young women who had mental and other physical problems.

Let's start with you. Could you do it? Could you take it on, you with your childhood, as against them with theirs? I have never had to, and I have to say I don't know. I did work for a charity for several years, so I know a little bit about some of it, but that was when I had grown up, not when I was seven or eight! These rescued slum kids had their own problems, their own history. You can therefore understand William Baker's comments about having a mentally handicapped girl in a family cottage with other girls. It must have been disturbing, it could have been very frightening for some of the very young ones, it needed to be very well handled. It says a huge something for the housemothers that it worked as well as it did. However, it couldn't be allowed to go on forever.

The Barnardo people did what they could, and it would appear that in some cases these girls and young women could be encouraged into needlework. By patience and the expenditure of a lot of hard work by the staff, some of them became proficient in hand embroidery. At that time embroidery was still popular and therefore saleable, so much so that in 1903 a School of Embroidery was established in the Village. Apart from embroidery the school also taught lacemaking and knitting, from which the Homes were able to gain a small contribution towards their ever-rising costs. At the time that T. J. died the capacity of the Village had reached 1,000. Including the fifty who could, by their own efforts, generate a small income, there were about 200 who would always need some sort of institutional care, and could never go out into the general community. That is 20 per cent, a huge proportion! The drain on resources for other work is immediately apparent. We can see the mountainous task William Baker found himself trying to tackle.

How many of us have been asked to sponsor someone for a parachute jump, a cycle ride, a swimathon, or a runner in the London marathon? We applaud their courage and their humanity, we put our name down for a fiver or a tenner, pay up when they give us a nudge the following week, and we feel good about it, we've done our bit for a good cause. That's how we deal with it today, when Britain has a full array of social services, the National Health Service and the hospice network. This is now, but way back then none of those existed, and organisations like Barnardo Homes relied entirely on donations. It is obvious that some fundamental decisions were having to be made every day, and the bold and virtuous Christian determination never to turn away a destitute child was often under the severest pressure. It is amazing how it managed to stand up so well to the tests it had to weather, and it must be accepted that every now and then it buckled under the strain.

Let's turn our attention to education, something of a favourite subject with T. J., our ex-ragged school teacher. We have some figures which indicate the rate at which the population of the Village was growing. With education from 1870 increasingly but not yet entirely publicly funded (as the headmaster of Eton will confirm), there developed the school exam. Where would schools be without exams? The exams were in what were then called the 'three Rs' of reading, writing and arithmetic. Remember that this was a girls' school, in an age when teaching girls to be clever was still frowned on by the grumpier of the upper and middle classes. In 1877 we have 112 passes in all three, plus an extra one in writing. By 1879 there were 303 triples, to which add 27 in reading and 19 in writing. That suggests that about 10 per cent of the girls found sums difficult, but it does mean 90 per cent found them easy. In 1906, that is the year after our hero died, there were 843 on the school register, which indicates the considerable rise in numbers over the period.

To that number we must add those below school age, and those not on the register, being completely unable to benefit for reasons already discussed. In other words there were over 1,000 girls in the Village at the time. The school inspector's report is full of praise for the results achieved by the pupils, and for the dedicated hard work of the staff. The school as a separate building made its appearance in 1893, so quite what accommodation was like for the education of the children before that is a little unclear. Like many of the cottages, it was built from a gift *in memoriam* by the parents of a child who had died, like the Barnardos' two sons, from diphtheria.

The church belonged to the Anglican Communion, with a Church of England vicar, which may at first be surprising given the very nonconformist stance T. J. took most of his life. The point is that most of the wealthiest of his supporters were Church of England, and it made a great deal of sense not to risk offending them. He was always a shrewd operator when it came to raising money. The church is, because it's still there, a sound and solidly 'chapel-built' structure, and when he was alive they had three services a week. The vicar would have been guaranteed some of the consistently largest congregations, but with the financial status of most of them being what it was, the collection plate might have been a bit light.

*

Life doesn't happen in two dimensions, so shall we take another look around the country and the world, to give our story a bit of historical perspective. In medicine and public health Florence Nightingale wasn't the only one beating the drum for cleanliness. Joseph Lister was expounding its benefits from his hospital surgery in Edinburgh, and pointing to his improved results as proof. Barnardo Homes took it on board with enthusiasm, and their mortality rate being so superior to the national average among children was testament to its benefits.

Around the world let's make a note of the births and deaths. Among the deaths we find a classic example of when the truth becomes a legend, publish the legend. This was the Battle of Little Bighorn, also known as Custer's Last Stand. One-time general (now rather oddly a colonel) George Custer was in command of a company of the usually successful Seventh Cavalry, when they tangled with Crazy Horse and Sitting Bull, heading up a big war party in the western state of Montana. Very few of the Seventh Cavalry came out of it alive. The legend that they all perished is not quite true. The reason for mentioning it is because this would be about the last big battle, one of the few won by American tribes, and they would lose all the rest from here on. The white man was taking over, and this was a part of the world that since 1776 the British no longer ruled.

News came from Dublin that Papa Barnardo had died aged seventy-four. In those days, that was called having a good innings. The youngest of the Barnardo boys, Henry Lionel, took over the business in partnership with his mother, and shortly afterwards they moved from the Dame Street address to Grafton Street. Papa Barnardo left about £1,500, worth £100,000 in 2000 values. That suggests that the Dublin branch of the family were comfortable, but not what could be called wealthy.

Looking westward to America again, Jennie Jerome was a New York socialite claiming descent from the First Nation tribes, through her great-grandfather having married into one. Her marriage to Lord Randolph Churchill, third son of the then incumbent Duke of Marlborough, produced in 1874 a son, Winston Leonard Spencer Churchill. While Jennie brought a nice dowry with her, Randolph's eldest brother and heir to the dukedom topped him by marrying Consuela Vanderbilt, daughter of a fabulously wealthy American railway tycoon. Two solid chunks of American money to prop up the spendthrift habits of the English aristocracy. In due course Winston was to marry another American, Clementine Hozier, from a wealthy banking dynasty. Americans were happy to spend their money marrying their daughters to the British aristocracy, and the British aristocracy were exceedingly happy to let them. Winston is known to have said on several occasions that he was always happy to visit America; it was where most of his relations came from.

On the other side of the world in 1869, so only twelve years after the Indian Mutiny, a prosperous Hindu called Karamchand Gandhi was presented by his fourth wife with a son, who they named Mohandas Karamchand. He grew up to be known to the world as Mahatma, meaning Great Soul. Both Churchill and Mahatma Gandhi came from political families. The Mahatma's father was First Minister in his state government. Lord Randolph was for a time Chancellor of the Exchequer. Winston is known at times to have made disparaging remarks about Gandhi, when discussing Britain's imperial role in India. In return, the Mahatma is not on record as having ever said anything entirely complimentary about Winston when discussing the British Empire, its role in India, and the determination Gandhi had to persuade them to leave.

Another interesting pair, both born in 1879, were the Caucasian Georgian Ioseb Dzhugashvili and the German-born Albert Einstein. Ioseb rose to power in Russia and was known as Stalin, Albert became a Swiss citizen and a mathematical theoretical physicist. Both in their own way moved the world society they lived in, and helped shape the twentieth century.

Of more interest to our East End story is the career of William Booth. Born in Nottingham, he became a Methodist minister on Tyneside, in North East England. He transferred to London in 1865 and founded a Christian Mission. This was very similar to T. J., but Booth was the older man by some years. The Booth Mission developed by stages into the Salvation Army. This was an actively evangelical organisation which was also proactive in helping the poor, but it concentrated on adults rather than small children. The 'Sally' was famous for its 'doss houses', places where down-and-outs could get a bed for a penny a night. In later years they developed a highly confidential missing persons bureau, where worried families might with luck trace lost relatives. Reunions then always depended on whether the lost person agreed they wanted to be found. So the Booths and the Barnardos proved to be complementary to each other in a lot of the services they offered. If one asks if they ever personally met, there are no records but it is perfectly possible.

Also in 1879, a reform-minded lawyer, Richard Pankhurst, married a Lancashire lass, Emmeline Goulden. The social legacy of that marriage was the militant Suffragette movement. The much older Richard may have been able to restrain his more enthusiastic wife initially, but after he died in 1899 the rest, as they say, is history. Men have traditionally blamed women when things go wrong. With the eventual victory of Mrs Pankhurst and the arrival of women's suffrage, 50 per cent of the blame became legal.

*

The Victorians were great ones for telling people how things should be done, even though they had been doing it without such instructions for centuries. As they ruled so much of the great big wide world out there they took it upon themselves in particular to tell everyone how to play games. They even invented a couple. It was their forte that they made up such splendid sets of rules and organised them so well. After that, at least when we lost we would understand why, which is something we have proved damned good at, and terribly decent about it when it happens.

Picking up on that thought, in 1867 the Marquess of Queensbury, a sporting gentleman of some note, formulated the rules for boxing, taking it out of the bare-knuckle age. Many years later he was to famously clash in court with Oscar Wilde over what was in those days the highly illegal practice of homosexuality. Oscar Wilde lost both the case and his career as a playwright, and was locked up in Reading Gaol for a couple of years.

Over in India in the 1870s some army officers, bored with the long-established game of billiards, invented snooker. In 1863 in Britain the Football Association was formed and they used the round ball, and in 1871 the 'pick it up and run with it' oval-ball faction formed their own Rugby Union. 'Soccer' derives from Association, for the round-ball faction. The FA Cup as a knock-out competition dates from 1872, but the Football League for soccer had to wait until 1888.

In the arts Gilbert and Sullivan were entertaining the upper classes with their satirical comic operas. Oscar Wilde, already mentioned, was Irish, as were both T. J. and the very socialist-minded playwright and theatre critic George Bernard Shaw. In France the Impressionists were beginning to be noticed. Their leader, Claude Monet, always acknowledged that his own inspiration had come from seeing the works of John Constable and J. M. W. Turner.

The engineer Charles Parsons invented the turbine in the 1880s, greatly improving the generation of that new thing called electricity, and also leading the way eventually to the gas turbine engine for jet aircraft. Henry Royce was in the electricity industry before he linked up with the Hon. C. R. Rolls and began to make rather superior motor cars. Over in America, Thomas Alva Edison set up in business, much of which was also involved with electricity, picking other people's brains quite frequently on his way to inventing things for either its generation or its use. Sam Morse died. He had invented the electric telegraph and then proceeded to invent his eponymous dot-dash code which made it usable. Alexander Graham Bell also picked other people's brains a bit and added his own ideas, which led to inventing the telephone. In Italy the Marconi family were delighted to have a new son who they called Guglielmo. He grew up and like so many picked other people's brains, added his own ideas and produced the first working radios, which also of course led to television and a great deal more. Quite why the first practical typewriter was invented in the workshops of a gun maker isn't quite clear, but in America the Remington Arms Company claim to be the first to do it.

*

What thought does all that lead us to? It says that T. J. didn't live in isolation; this is just a tiny flavour of his world. The second half of the nineteenth century was when the modern world was invented, and it wasn't all invented in Britain. There were all sorts of changes afoot, the horizon was bustling with new ideas, new inventions, new social attitudes in among the old and stubborn ones. Beavering away in the basement were people like T. J., Booth and others. They were living in that era, they were affected by all those things in one way or another. It gives us a feeling of their lives, what they would read about in their newspapers and magazines in the last decades of Victoria's reign.

The old attitudes of those who called themselves society would have to change, but they hadn't changed yet. The world had a bright tomorrow, pouring out from the minds of bright young people with bright young minds. In Britain at that time 2 per cent of the population owned over 90 per cent of the wealth. More and more people, made literate by advances in education, were saying that such an imbalance was wrong, that things had to change. Over the coming decades, as the nineteenth century changed into the twentieth, huge changes were made, but history tells us of the huge cost in blood and slaughter it took to achieve them.

Where it failed, both in Britain and in mainland Europe, was that left over from the past there were still a few aristocrats wedded to the old order, the old ways, the old attitudes who simply didn't understand that those changes were inevitable. Democracy hadn't caught up with them. In Russia there were still serfs until the 1870s! There were still European empires. Apart from Russia there was the Ottoman Empire based on Turkey, the Germans newly unified under the Kaiser, the Austrians with a multilingual empire based on the Danube Valley, the Christian French with largely Muslim African colonies, and the British, an empire covering a fifth of the world's land surface and maybe a sixth of its population.

If the aristocrats who had managed to hold onto their executive power didn't make an absolute hash of everything, everyone could breathe a sigh of relief. Instead, nine years after T. J. died, they made a hash on a monumental scale. They called it the First World War.

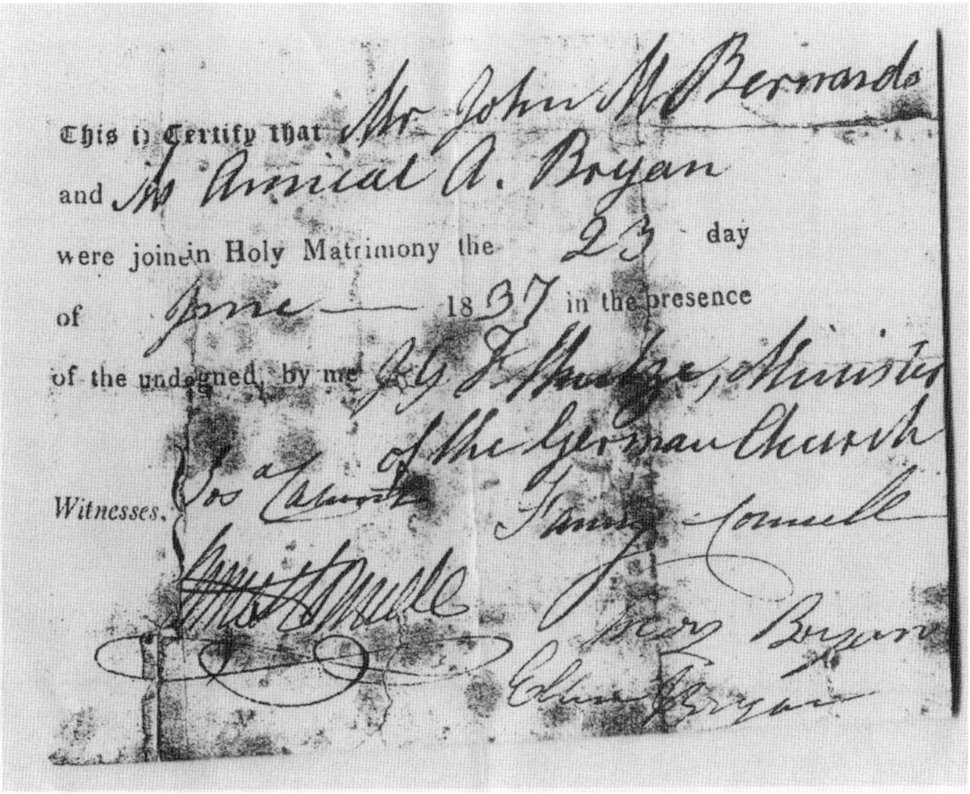

This is to Certify that Mr John M Bernardo
and Ms Anniciat A. Bryan
were join in Holy Matrimony the 23 day
of June 1837 in the presence
of the undersigned, by me J. G. F. ... Minister
of the German Church

Witnesses.

Mary Bryan

Above: 1. The marriage certificate of Thomas John Barnardo's parents. (Family Archive)

Right: 2. Hope Place. (© Barnardo's Image Archive)

3. The Edinburgh Castle. (© Barnardo's Image Archive)

4. Outside the Sunday school in 1909 (the building stopped being a day school in 1908). The children are waving invitations to the Christmas Treat at the Edinburgh Castle (once over the road from Copperfield Road, now the site of Mile End Leisure Centre). (© Ragged School Museum Trust)

5. Artist's impression, Copperfield Road Sunday and Free Day Schools, 1879.
(© Ragged School Museum Trust)

6. 'The Elder Lads at Dinner in our Free Schools' from *Night and Day*, April 1879. First-floor classroom in the Boys School, Copperfield Road – now the Ragged School Museum. (© Ragged School Museum Trust)

7. Doctor Barnardo. (© Barnardo's Image Archive)

8. Martha Ward. (© Barnardo's Image Archive)

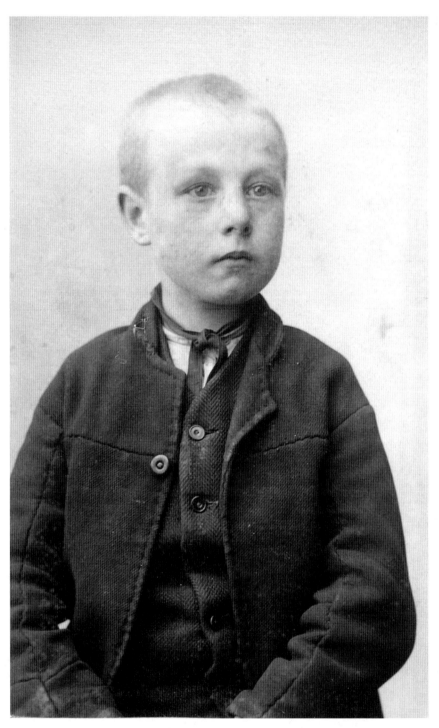

9. Harry Gossage. (© Barnardo's Image Archive)

10. Doctor Barnardo. (© Barnardo's Image Archive)

11. The classroom at the Ragged School today. (© Ragged School Museum Trust)

12. The exterior of the Ragged School Museum today.
(© Ragged School Museum Trust)

13. Doctor Barnardo.
(© Barnardo's Image Archive)

SIX

How to (and not to) Run a Charity: 1876–1886

After that extensive excursion into the great big world outside, with its happenings and its looming dangers, we will return to our hero and his doings in aid of the poor.

You don't need a committee to run a cake shop, but you do need a committee to run a corporation. The Barnardo Homes was becoming a large and complicated organisation, and Thomas John Barnardo was still trying to run it as if it was a cake shop. As early as 1875 questions were being asked, and before we should be surprised that they came so soon, we should realise that by then Hope Place had been open seven years, Stepney Causeway for four. Those two parts of the rapidly growing enterprise were well established. Then we have the Edinburgh Castle and a quantum leap again to the Girls Village. Surely he wasn't still trying to run all that as a one-man band? Indeed he was, without proper formal organisational backup. Is it surprising that he became vulnerable to attack? He had a growing band of wealthy backers, and there were beginning to be one or two people who were shaking their heads and carrying worried frowns.

There were enough complications to fill a book, but we will deal with the essentials. Here was a brilliant man in many ways, a good organiser and a wonderful motivator, but at times we are reminded of the remark famously made a century later by the head of the Civil Service, Sir Robert Armstrong. In a court case involving the Official Secrets Act he said that 'there are times when it is necessary to be economical with the truth'. With regret, T. J. was to be caught out doing something rather like that.

An example of this was when he started to build another pub with no beer, intending to call it the Dublin Castle, and to run it along the lines of the now well-established Edinburgh Castle. In 1875 he purchased a site at Mile End Gate, at the junction where Mile End Road joins with Whitechapel Road. On this site he started to build, only to hit opposition from a surprising quarter. The objection came from a local missionary, F. N. Charrington, who was a member of the wealthy family who owned the nearby Anchor brewery. It was never a fight with the family, just between the two men.

A committed Christian who had given up booze for good works was just the sort of person T. J. ought to be able to get along with, indeed they knew each other. However you can only get on with someone if they want to get on with you. Charrington had been doing his missionary work in the area for some time, and objected to T. J. butting in on what in the local terminology was 'his manor'. Just how much it was Charrington's manor when T. J. had taught at the Ernest Street Ragged School a quarter of mile along the road is very debatable. At first T. J. tried to be reasonable and co-operative, but Charrington wouldn't leave it alone. Considerable money having been spent on the project, T. J. wasn't in a position to just drop everything and walk away.

Enter now the Revd George Reynolds, minister of a small local Baptist church. His bitter complaint was that the hugely successful Edinburgh Castle Mission church, less than a mile away, was robbing him of his congregation. If this new extension of their work was allowed it would close his church down. There were several other local churches who never actually got involved, but felt Reynolds wasn't the only one who might close.

All of which ignored what the Edinburgh Castle Mission church was already doing in the area, all the social work and all the community work now being delivered. Reynolds had been in the area for far longer and all he managed to do was run his little church, and that was all he ever would do, he was that sort. The fire was well and truly lit when Mrs Johnson was dragged into the affair. She had been T. J.'s landlady for a time when he was a student. It was being wildly alleged by Reynolds that she and T. J. had enjoyed an improper relationship while Mr Johnson, a merchant seaman, had been plying his trade in places far away. It was never wondered in all this what Mr Johnson might have been doing in those faraway climes to relieve the monotony on his occasional shore leaves. Now divorced and with a new man in her life, Reynolds was to all intents and purposes calling Mrs Johnson a prostitute, while leaving her with no right of reply in the matter.

We now get another entry into the fray. Formed in 1869, the Charities Organisation Society boasted Shaftesbury as one of its vice-presidents. These people appear to have supported the laissez-faire style of economics, which is basically dog eat dog and damn the poor. Whether our friend the earl realised what he was getting himself into is a good question. What is clear is that the Charities Organisation Society was a self-appointed pressure group, and just as much a charity as Barnardo Homes. On the mention of the earl, by now it might be said that while T. J. was boasting about knowing him, the earl never greatly boasted in the other direction. It was an emerging truth that while T. J. was a wonderful man in many ways, he could at times be very difficult to get along with.

The declared aim of the Charities Organisation Society was to get charities properly organised under a sound and recognised legal system, which on the face of it was a good idea. Where it wasn't a good idea was that they were advocating some pretty lunatic principles, in particular that old chestnut we've met before, that poverty was the fault of the poor. They were regrettably off their heads on the economics of poverty and its causes. As we are dealing with charity for the poor in the East End in all this, let's have a look at the government-run system then in use, called the Poor Law.

Alms for the poor go back to ancient times. In Biblical times 10 per cent of the income of the temple in Jerusalem was supposed to be devoted to the relief of the poor. Poor Law of one sort or another has been around since the dawn of history, these days we call it social benefit. In Tudor England, population maybe 5 or 6 million, the most immediate contact the common people had with their rulers was the local parish. The parishes had the responsibility of raising a 'rate' to cover its cost. In 1576 the law required that all able-bodied poor seeking relief should be given parish-approved work in order to earn it. That meant that the poor could get what was called outdoor relief, it meant they could still live at home. In the eighteenth century the system changed. Now the wages of the poor would be subsidised out of the rate. It doesn't take a genius to work out what happened. Employers paid desperately low wages, and looked to the parish to make up the difference. The results were catastrophic all round.

In the reign of William IV we get the seminal 1834 Poor Law Amendment Act. That was the Act on the books in the period we are looking at. Recipients were divided into the deserving poor and the undeserving poor. The deserving poor could go into the workhouses, the undeserving poor went into what were termed Houses of Correction. Again we are back to this dreadful chestnut of lunacy and ignorance, that poverty was the fault of the poor. It was tyrannical and in the long term unworkable. It was also a lot more expensive to run than the old Tudor system, both in time as well as money. One of many reasons that Victorian Britain had so much poverty was the mindset of the ruling class on this particular question.

The population of Britain was exploding. The census of 1851 gives us a population of Great Britain of 21 million, to which add the whole of Ireland, another 7 million. This was the census just after the great potato famine in Ireland. Fifty years later Queen Victoria died. In the census year of 1901 the relevant figures in were 37 million and 4.5 million. In half a century Great Britain's population had gone up by 75 per cent, while that of Ireland had plummeted by 35 per cent.

There were two things affecting these figures. In Ireland there had been depopulation directly through the deaths in the famine and subsequently the flight of many of the survivors, either to Great Britain or to America. In Ireland this far outweighed the effect of the second reason. In both Ireland and in Great Britain there were vast families. As we have already said when discussing the Village Cottages, twelve wasn't an abnormal number. Improvements in health in Great Britain in particular, and the emergence of philanthropic endeavours such as Barnardo Homes and others, meant more children survived. Given that these vast families of children had more chances of survival, there simply wasn't the work in the countryside for such numbers. That drove down country wages and led to a move to the towns. The same economic forces applied there, only with far worse housing. Plentiful supplies of something always drives down its price, and that includes the price of labour. The employers followed the economically natural path, and were able to exploit the workers and keep wages low.

It has to be said that in the midst of this there were some decent employers, Salt of Saltaire up in Leeds for instance, and the remarkable Cadbury enterprise in Birmingham paid what was, for those days, good wages and gave their people good housing in 'model villages'. That was always, of course, so long as you toed their line, otherwise you were out at a moment's notice. With some rare exceptions things were grim, and through the years they would get grimmer, until the two sides were so far apart it inevitably led to trouble. But it becomes very clear in this discussion that poverty wasn't entirely the fault of the poor, there were pressures causing it which those fortunate enough to be wealthy chose to ignore.

One particular factor in London concerned the development of roads and railways. Most of the national railway network was in place by about 1870, but comparisons between Ordnance Survey maps of 1860 and 1890 show that some development continued. In the countryside wealthy landowners who disliked the smelly noisy things could arrive at arrangements with the railway companies which took them through fields a long way from their elegant abodes and beautiful gardens. In the middle of the East End they came straight through your bedroom wall.

Between 1860 and 1890 several thousand houses were demolished to make way for network extensions out of Liverpool Street and Bishopsgate and various other termini. If you were the landowner you might expect something in compensation. If you were renting a couple of rooms for 3 shillings a week then tough. It's coming down on Monday, clear out or it'll fall down all over you. Compensation!? You must be joking! And it wasn't only the railways. Road developments such as the Commercial Road route to the India Docks complex were also being built. The road network was by this time developing even faster than the railways.

Which means that these factors destroyed the homes of many thousands of London's East Enders and others. With all these families put out of their homes pressure on housing increased; short supply drives up prices, 3 shillings a week rent quickly became 4 shillings a week. Add all that up and you can begin to see how way off the beam the Charities Organisation Society really was. There were hundreds of factors in the equation leading to poverty. Certainly shiftlessness and dishonesty and drunkenness were three of them, but they are far from all of them. Most people were honest and decent, they liked the respectability that went with having a regular job. The Charities Organisation Society not only defended the statute that was on the book, they seem to have deliberately supported the worst interpretations of it.

They thoroughly disliked T. J. for a variety of reasons. They regarded him as a presumptuous little exhibitionist for claiming family, status and rank, which as my own researches have later proved he actually didn't have, so on that score they were right. He ran his charity as an individual, without even the backing of a committee, which was at the very least unwise. He'd been caught out for telling far less than the truth about his medical qualifications. If that claim was false, what else was untrue.

The whole thing simmered, spat, and at times boiled over. A couple of times T. J. issued writs against Reynolds, but was persuaded to withdraw them. If Charrington's involvement had been exclusively his own, no one else involved, it is very possible that things could have been amicably resolved, but Reynolds wouldn't leave it alone. He had a church with a relatively small congregation, and he was steadily losing regulars and their money in the collection plate as the Edinburgh Castle Mission church drained away his attendance figures. An inveterate letter writer, T. J. would have been far better employed holding himself above all the turmoil in a dignified silence. Instead of which he wrote to the local press, who of course lapped it up. Two of the area's leading ministers slagging each other off was wonderful for the sales figures. Neither of them appears to have read the verses in their book of rules, the New Testament, about resolving disputes.

Things came to a head with the appearance of a booklet claiming to make 'startling revelations' about Barnardo Homes. There were claims that the children had diseases, there was poor sanitation, poor food, poor care, a lack of moral training or religious education. This was a 'shock horror' attack on T. J. and all he was doing. It was intended to cause a sensation among those who didn't know much about him but it was very largely dismissed as rubbish by those who did. Accusing T. J. of being backward with religious education was ludicrous.

These are street kids, they arrived with backgrounds which put even Christianity somewhere down the agenda until their other problems were dealt with. They arrived full of diseases and in poor health. The food was better than they had experienced before and was at least regular. Much the same could be said of all the other charges, that they were based on fabrications and distortions and ignorance of the facts.

Instinctively a good publicist, in 1874 T. J. had begun to use photography in what was then a novel way. All children were photographed on arrival and again six months later. This gave a visual identification record of each child, and an idea of their progress. From the administrative point of view it was wonderful, and is the ancestor of all photo ID cards we have today. However he then started to sell 'before and after' pairs of photos to his supporters, showing the improvements achieved. His critics began to accuse him of faking the initial intake pictures to make the children look worse than they really had been. That some of their suspicions were not entirely unfounded came out later.

There is absolute certainty that the Charities Organisation Society were acting as *agents provocateur* in the matter. They were stirring things up with a giant-sized paddle. The problem they saw in him was that while he was very independent, he was shockingly successful. He was well and truly under the skin of several of the leading Charities Organisation Society members. His success was cutting the ground from under the feet of the worst of the bigots, and showing up their whole façade of prejudice for what it was.

If your shopping list of grumbles is long enough, you're almost sure to get lucky with one of them. Though he had never at that point qualified, T. J. had got it into his head that he wanted to be known as Dr Barnardo. Back in 1870 he had given himself the title of doctor when signing the lease of 18 Stepney Causeway. In fact his only medical experience was as a drop-out student at the London Hospital and its medical school. Now a regular contributor to *The Christian*, the new name for *The Revival*, material began to appear over this new-style signature. Picked up by his critics, he went dotty. He appears to have gone through a highly complicated rigmarole of trying to get a mail-order medical degree from the German Geissen University. It was futile and quite stupid and it badly dented his standing with many of his supporters and donors.

This added to the criticisms that had been brewing for a year or so. On the urgent advice of some of his friends he quietly went north to Edinburgh, where he did what he had failed to do at the London Hospital, he got his head down to some serious study for four months. Being a highly intelligent man, his IQ must have been up in the Mensa bracket. On 30 March 1876 he became a Licentiate of the Royal College of Surgeons in Edinburgh, a fact which he also registered in London. However it was not a full degree and wisely he never practised as a medical doctor, but it was just about enough to let him use the title. After he had made his name he did become an Honorary Fellow of the College.

Not only was there this foolishness sometimes in his character, there was the hard-headed matter of money to think about. As has already been said, he was at this point still running the place like a cake shop, no committee, no treasurer. It would have been so easy for him to have slipped a gold sovereign into his pocket and no one would have known. His enemies were telling the tale that they were sure he was. The added fact that he was an Irishman, so in the opinion of many was never to be trusted, was further fuel to the fire. He and Syrie were now living in Bow, but he appeared to those not close to the action to still have Mossford Lodge, which was surely beyond his wealth to afford. All these were fair comments and questions from those viewing things from the sidelines. Where was all the money coming from to afford it all?

He was bringing all these things down upon his own head. He was up to his ears in work to keep the enterprise running, which was good. He was a very prickly customer who wanted to stay independent, which was the difficult bit. It was clearly time for him to get his own legal status and the status of the enterprise sorted and settled. What happened unfortunately was that during all this simmer and fizzle, as the story gradually moved from a little local difficulty to a national story, trust in him began to fray, donations began to tail off and money became increasingly tight. By then his enterprise was caring for about 600 children, and if it wasn't dealt with properly and quickly they were going to suffer.

Several times T. J. and in particular his many friends tried to get the thing settled, but Reynolds was a nobody who had suddenly found fifteen minutes of fame and he wouldn't let go. The leading lights of the Charities Organisation Society locked their teeth firmly onto it and they wouldn't let go either. The accusations of the 'shocking revelations' booklet constituted a clear libel. There is a famous legal adage, the greater the truth the greater the libel. So the question was, should T. J. at last go to the High Court and sue?

The government had changed while all this was happening and Disraeli was back as Prime Minister. That meant Lord Cairns was back as Lord Chancellor. Having on your support team a shrewd and wily lawyer like Cairns, who was not merely brilliant but was being free with his advice, gave T. J. a very strong hand. Having John Sands, who was another leading lawyer and the man who at the time still owned Mossford Lodge, was an extra bonus.

They insisted that T. J. get his act together. There had been a trust created for the Edinburgh Castle. Sands agreed to convert the Mossford Lodge lease into a freehold in favour of the Barnardo Homes, and cover that with a trust as well. T. J. didn't want the East End Juvenile Mission made into a trust, but Cairns and Sands, backed by other major supporters, required that he join the real world and get all these loose ends sorted out and properly tidied up. It was time to close the cake shop and do things properly. The thing was so big and so successful, a glowing credit to his dynamic drive and ability, that there was now no other option.

One odd thing that came as a bit of a shock when the dust settled was that technically T. J. was now an employee. The Trust Deed guaranteed him a job for life, and he acquired the title of Honorary Director. The word honorary implied that he was unpaid, which sort of clashed with the idea that he was an employee, and it was never properly resolved. The Trust Deed did contain the safeguard that he could be asked to resign if two-thirds of the trustees demanded it, or of course he could always leave of his own accord.

By 1877 all efforts at reconciliation had been exhausted. On the one hand T. J. was a damned fool for rising to every bait, on the other hand Reynolds went even further by publishing yet another blast of accusations. It was obvious that the case would have to go to court, but the question was which one? With Lord Cairns pulling the strings in the background, the choice came down to the Court of Arbitration of the Court of the Exchequer. Heard of by only the most astute legal eagles of the day, this worked to very special rules and these rules were likely to fall in favour of T. J. and his supporters. Whether it was within those special rules for

Fitzroy Kelly, President of the Court, to add his signature to an appeal for funds to help T. J. with his legal bills one has to put in the startled raised eyebrows column. Kelly was obviously a friend of Cairns; let's face it, so was every other lawyer in the Inns of Court. There is also the fact that Kelly is a very Irish-sounding name and T. J. was born in Dublin.

Three very respectable gentlemen were convened to hear all the evidence from both sides and draw a conclusion. To use a legal phrase, they would come to a judgement and make an award to one side or the other. John Maude QC was the Recorder of Leeds, so a senior judge from Yorkshire. John Cale Miller was Canon of Rochester Cathedral in Kent, but he had come up the ranks via a pulpit in the London East End. He therefore had local knowledge of the area where the affair was happening. William Graham had been, but was no longer a Member of Parliament for Glasgow, so his connections were north of the border. He would have a view on any major political implications and public morals, should these be raised. It seems to have been a balanced team of eminent men of acknowledged respectability. They should be just the sort of people one would ask to consider this unusual case, which was now exciting considerable public interest. Not all the court records have survived over the years, but a lot of the juicier bits have come to us via various press reports. The press, as you can imagine, were well represented in the public seats.

The hearings were spread over three months in the late summer of 1877, and the entire production had the benefit of well-known lawyers of the day. None of these gentlemen were thought to be arguing their client's case so eloquently for a mere pittance, as they glowed under the public gaze. In the end, had it been a football match the panel's award would have been called a draw.

In respect of T. J.'s honesty in his financial dealings, this section of the report can be quoted without paraphrase.

The statements of accounts are printed yearly, and are sent to those donors who supply their names and addresses and have requested to receive, for any sum they contribute, a printed receipt bearing a number, with which they can compare the list in the yearly statements and reports, and there find their respective donations, and thus be assured that their gifts have been duly accounted for. Mr H Bishop, of the firm of Turquand and Young has in addition personally investigated the system of bookkeeping and accounts, and gave evidence before us of its thorough efficiency. There are no traces of any part of these donations and earnings, or of any other such funds having been, as suggested under this head, expended by Dr Barnardo in his own house and in household expenditure, or improperly appropriated to his own personal benefit.

So far so good. Much as we'd expect, T. J. hadn't had his hand in the till. All the financial misconduct charges were therefore thrown out.

When discussing the unduly harsh discipline allegations, the Barnardo side did agree that their tactics did include, when needed, what we would now call the sin bin. When one of the lads became just plain impossible, he was locked up in a cellar, often for several hours, and told to calm down. The main witness to this was an ex-Barnardo boy, William Fletcher. He told the tale of some pretty awful punishments and brutality. If he was to be fully believed then T. J. was allowing his staff to go too far. The arbitrators chose to believe T. J. and his team, who claimed that while discipline was strict when necessary, what was being alleged simply hadn't happened, and records were produced claiming to prove it. In those days thrashing children heavily was an everyday occurrence, no one thought much about it. One has the quotation already used in Chapter One of T. J. remembering his schoolteacher in his own teenage years in Dublin. The arbitrators were of the same era, they had themselves suffered thrashings when young, and had doubtless dished some out to their own children a time or two.

With the benefit of hindsight one tends to believe much of what young Fletcher told the court, but it was viewed by the habits of their generation, not ours. In Victorian England what was being described only raised an eyebrow, such things were normal, it was how children were brought up. At about this time an eight-year-old Winston Churchill, grandson of a duke, came home from his boarding school and his mother found him severely bruised from a thrashing. Herself the daughter of an American millionaire, she had the status and the money to hit the proverbial roof, which her wealth was after all keeping over the family's heads. Winston was immediately withdrawn from that school and sent elsewhere. That was the Churchill family, T. J. was dealing with street kids.

The director of Stepney Causeway, one might think of him as the headmaster, was Frank Fielder. He was a rough, tough reformed drunk who had taken the Temperance Pledge never to drink again. William Notman we have already met in the early days of Hope Place. He is an example of a tough but decent East Ender who had found a mission in life. None of the staff had ever had a day's professional training in how to teach, or even what to teach. They were teaching themselves how to do it as they went along. There weren't any teacher training colleges, remember that publicly funded education was itself only seven years old. Above all they were products of their time and their environment, just as we are products of ours. The results they were getting were generally excellent given their sort of background, bordering on the remarkable. But they were the sort of men who, if you gave them a back answer, would clout you. If you argued about it you got well and truly thumped. They can't be judged by our standards.

Just as an aside, here is another quote. 'I don't know what the world will be like in the years to come! The way children behave today is terrible, they are insolent to their elders and misbehave all the time!' A senior official in Ancient Egypt gave instructions for that to be inscribed on his tomb wall. Not much changed there then!

Taking a view about the photographic records, the panel classified them as artistic fiction. They didn't criticise them as a method of obtaining and maintaining records, or their use in publicity. They did however make the point that in the before-

and-after situation, where money was being asked for, the truth must be shown without hint of blemish. The hint was taken and the sale of the before-and-after photographs was discontinued soon afterwards. However their use in maintaining records was continued and was still being employed up until the 1960s when the residential part of the organisation ended.

The arbitrators agreed that the children were being well fed, were being educated to a good standard and that they were being taught the Christian religion. As has already been said the majority of the children were not orphans, they had family. The allegations in the notorious booklet had caused a great deal of upset, and there were a lot of very worried mothers and fathers around wondering what they had let their children go into. Not everyone in the East End was a criminal, most of them were respectable.

We now take contraception for granted, but in Victorian times it didn't exist, other than the highly dangerous 'women who could do something about it'. Resorting to this was highly illegal, and the results could very often be fatal. Much of the poverty was caused by having hordes of kids with not enough money coming in to feed them. There was a general ignorance of how to prevent pregnancy, both among the public and among the medical profession, and there was a religious fury against anyone who researched it. Queen Victoria had nine children, but then she could afford them. 'Go forth and multiply and fill the earth' was the Biblical exhortation. What the Bible does not ask is what we do when we've done that? And these families had done that in abundance. None of which is intended to imply that mothers didn't love their children. When the stories began to circulate about the Barnardo organisation being a lot less than perfect, families who had placed children with them were rightly worried, and started to ask a lot of questions of their own.

The arbitrators were forthright about the muddle of legal status governing the organisation, and insistent about the need to put it all on a proper footing. We will do our usual paraphrasing, particularly in this case, as one of the sentences would otherwise run to over 150 words.

We are of the opinion that these Homes for Destitute Boys and Girls, called the Barnardo Institutions, are real and valuable charities worthy of public confidence and support. As regards the conduct and management of these Institutions, whilst there have been matters upon which it has been our duty to disapprove, the general management has on the whole been judicious. With a view to avoiding the recurrence of controversies, to strengthen the claim of these charities to public confidence, and to ensure their continuing efficiency and wellbeing, we recommend that the Trustees as soon as possible seek to engage the services of a working committee. These gentlemen should be associated with the Director in the administration of these Institutions and should take a real and active interest in the oversight of the Homes. They should afford to the Director their advice and assistance upon the many questions which must constantly arise in the experience of such work, such alteration should be made in the Trust Deeds as may be necessary to this end. The necessity of such a committee is enhanced by the fact that the authority and discipline of such Homes appear to be self-constituted, and have no legal sanction where parents and guardians are not parties to the children's admission.

Everything that came out of the arbitration was acted upon with urgency under the particular guidance of Lord Cairns, who offered himself as president with that purpose in mind. By now he knew T. J. quite well and realised what a prickly character he could be at times, so it needed someone with enough personality to deal with him at the helm. It was a great shame that Cairns was to die in 1885, because he was the one man who, in the nicest possible way, could bully T. J. into listening when he didn't want to.

There already existed the trust which covered the Edinburgh Castle. All the various ventures were now brought under a single legal umbrella and in 1899 this was further strengthened by having it 'incorporated'. The 1877 imperative was to establish a properly constituted committee, active in running the institution and being legally responsible for it. The committee would also be responsible for the actions of the director. Therefore from that point in law the committee was the superior legal entity. During the discussion of the discipline, especially the 'sin bin' and the beatings, there was a legal grey area. The depth or otherwise of that greyness is far too complicated to discuss here, and in any case the law and the social attitudes are now totally different. The arbitrators dealt with it by giving a warning rather than directly issuing an order. Cairns was, after all, head of the judiciary as Lord Chancellor, so could there be a better man to know what to do about it?

During the hearings they had at one point come up against the tendency T. J. too often had, which was to be ridiculously economical with the truth. Let's rephrase that, plain haemoglobin awkward, mulish, stupid and obstinate beyond belief. Correspondence in the local newspaper, *The Tower Hamlets Independent*, had become more and more vitriolic over the previous couple of years. One of the correspondents called himself 'Clerical Junius', which was so pompous it was silly, bearing in mind the East End context. This individual had written a couple of long letters which had been published.

One can only be glad that no one writes in that style these days, because to the modern mind they are almost unreadable. They are full of pseudo-academic multi-clause sentences, a veritable sludge of verbiage. Taken together, the two letters came down heavily on T. J.'s side and very much against that of his opponents. When the counsel for George Reynolds asked him who wrote them, T. J. refused to tell him. He then admitted that he had seen the second of the two letters before it was sent and had arranged for it to be delivered to the editor. He said that he was therefore prepared to accept moral responsibility for its contents. Which is an answer we can reasonably have trouble with, because a couple of weeks after that second one appeared in the *Tower Hamlets Independent*, he had sent and they had published his own letter saying it was all wrong, it was terrible, and he disassociated himself from its contents entirely. This, remember is the man who went through the rigmarole of trying to get a mail-order degree from Geissen University. Have we been here before?

The problem was that everyone else in the court was sure that T. J. had written them. The refusal in a Court of Law to come straight out and say so was a shattering blow to his legal team. Here was a court that with great ingenuity Cairns had contrived, and he was among those furious at this turn of events. If his counsel had just walked out it would have been understandable. The letters had T. J.'s writing style running through them like Brighton through a stick of seaside rock! Yet here he was, claiming confidentiality in favour of the alleged author, refusing to give him a name. Had the court charged him with contempt no one would have been surprised. And yet let me put in my own observation, never raised at the time. Had he then challenged counsel to show the relevance of bringing the matter up, questioning whether it had anything to do with the matters before the court, he might well have won the point. He didn't, and equally important neither did his legal team.

This rigmarole contributes to the result being a one-all draw. He had created an institution which was doing great things. The conduct of the employees and the volunteers was usually excellent, but could be less than the best on some occasions. His own conduct was under fire, and his reaction in court to the questions over the newspaper correspondence made him no friends at all. The panel of arbitrators were clearly very angry about it.

The trick Lord Cairns had played had kept the Charities Organisation Society out of things, other than sending their own observer. Even Charrington was kept out other than as a witness, so the affair was played out as a straight tussle between T. J. and Reynolds. On the one hand, Reynolds and his backers had hardly any evidence which in that Victorian society would have been sufficient to get T. J. booted out of his position as director. On the other hand, T. J. was clearly a man with an imaginative view of what constituted the truth on occasions. What more proof was needed that he needed to be called to order, and the whole institution put on a proper legal basis?

Whatever the arbitrators thought of him in private, there were limits to what they wanted to say in public. On balance they thought that it was safe to leave him in office, given that Cairns was there to keep him in order, and also because much of the legal work had been accomplished by the time the hearings began. It came out afterwards that Canon Miller was so angry over the 'Clerical Junius' letters and T. J.'s refusal to come clean about them that he threatened to write a dissenting report, and it took a great deal of effort and tactful persuasion by the other two to talk him out of it. In the end he unwillingly agreed to add his name to their report, which made it unanimous.

There were some complicated exchanges when the letters controversy blew up, and you would need a lot of money to pay an expert in Victorian law, social views, ethics and a good deal else to explain them to you. The lawyer for George Reynolds quietly advised his client that now would be a good time to withdraw. This was a shrewd move! Far from leaving T. J. triumphant in command of the field, he was now enmeshed in such a controversy that he almost dragged total defeat out of the jaws of victory. Along with the Charities Organisation Society observer, Reynolds and his lawyer walked out, which caused quite a stir. That left T. J.'s lawyer, who was the personal choice of Cairns, to talk him out of all the trouble he had made for himself. Counsel managed this brilliantly, but it was obvious that he was as angry as anyone else at what had happened. Miller allowed himself to be talked round, but what emerged in the gossip and rumour afterwards may have had the canon behind it. It was said that he did it for the children. While he joined a select band of people who couldn't stand T. J. one little bit, Miller did acknowledge that he had produced a track record of achievement second to none, so it was perhaps in order to let him get on with it.

The Charities Organisation Society continued an underground war against T. J. until the day he died. Their immediate reaction was to issue a circular, *Mr Barnardo's Homes, Cautions to the Benevolent*, of which 2,000 were circulated. At the time the award had not yet been published, so this appears to have been in contempt of court, though no action was taken. As we can well imagine T. J. was furious, and prepared and printed a riposte, which he advertised would be circulated when the final award had been officially declared. The committee met urgently, expressly put into the minutes their refusal to allow this, and wrote to *The Times* asking that this minute be published, which it was. Did it ever dawn on T. J. at this point that he was an employee, admittedly unpaid, and that the committee could actually give him instructions which he would have to follow? It was as well the committee acted as it did. The final award when published contained an injunction upon both sides not to publish any more leaflets which were defamatory to the other party. That was a wise inclusion.

Press reaction was generally even-handed. Several made the point that T. J. could no longer be allowed to run the Homes as a one-man band. Others wrote that future plans he had been discussing were very attractive, but they asked what he was going to use for money. The Charities Organisation Society had technically won a victory, because the organisation no longer 'belonged' to him, legal control was vested in the trust through the committee. Quite whether that limitation meant very much in practice was to be severely tested at times as the years passed.

For those seeking more about the arbitration, may I refer them to the bibliography, which lists a book by Gillian Wagner. She gives a more academic and objective review of it. For those wondering if Junius was some ancient Roman philosopher, he wasn't, but dates from about 100 years before these events. He wrote some controversial letters to the press on political matters. As in this case his name was never officially discovered, but again there was a leading candidate.

*

During the 1870s there had been a growing swell of Christian evangelical revival. Britain had been visited, one might even say invaded, by Moody and Sankey, an American duo of great fervour and intent. Like T. J., Dwight Moody had caught the evangelical bug big time and had founded his own church in Chicago, and was later to found a Bible college. He was the preacher part of the team after he linked up with Ira Sankey, who was the one who did the music and the singing. They went on the road and in 1873 they arrived in England. After a highly successful tour they left behind a considerable evangelical movement. Moody and T. J. became firm friends and stayed in contact for over twenty years.

Taking all that on board, it wasn't surprising that a number of the fifteen-strong committee should have been from that wing of Christianity, and that five were men of the cloth. The other ten represented a wide cross-section of society. Robert Anderson was a Doctor of Law and worked for the Home Office. He was very briefly involved in the earliest stages of the Jack the Ripper case. Mr J. E. Gordon was an MP and a member of the Stock Exchange. The Hon. Tom Pelham was a younger son of the Earl of Chichester and proved to be a staunch supporter. We have already met Lord Kinnaird and John Sands. Chairman of the Stock Exchange Samuel Gurney Sheppard we have also briefly met. Lord Cairns held the post of president until he died eight years later. By no means least after such a run of distinguished names, there was Colonel Noble, a retired businessman, William Paton, and Dr Heywood Smith, who was a friend of T. J. It was thought useful to have a fully qualified doctor on the committee. Lastly there was a respected East End church worker named H. Nairne Dowson.

The breadth and scope of the membership gave the committee public credibility after all the uproar that had been buzzing about. It could be noted that there was a Home Office connection through Dr Anderson, a judicial connection through Cairns, and people with connections all through the establishment. Whatever might have been going on before, this looked like a blue chip committee if ever there was one. The days of the one-man band cake-shop mentality were relegated to the past.

By 1877 there were eight Homes and Mission branches to supervise and in the Girls Village there were fourteen cottages occupied, with several more coming on stream. Remember, T. J. had only been in England eleven years. Everyone was drawing a deep sigh of relief and getting on with things when a sad note was struck by the early demise of John Sands. It had been Sands who had covered the considerable cost of the arbitration, and had been a tower of strength and support during the hearings.

You may have noticed my penchant for figures, and in the arbitration a lot of money was spent that would have been far better used in support of the children. The legal costs are reckoned to have come to about £4,600, which is about £350,000 in 2000 values. If you are elderly and infirm and a nice policeman offers to see you across the road, you would almost certainly say yes. If a lawyer made the offer you would be wise to say no, because you wouldn't be able to afford his fee, plus VAT. Or in other words, lawyers don't work for nothing. At the end of it all T. J. was left about £2,000 in debt, which these days translates to about £145,000. The special appeal that Kelly endorsed somewhat dubiously proved a flop. This case never had much general support. Bearing in mind he was still at that point a volunteer, he didn't have a salary, the trustees in the end took over the debt. Quite what is the legal position of taking on board the debt of a private individual by a 'charity in trust', you must ask your faithful legal eagles, who would as usual be happy to charge you a fee for their opinions.

He had only arrived in London in 1866, and T. J. had ever since meticulously recorded all the institution's income. The figure we have for the twelve years up to 31 March 1878 is £154,099 13s 6d. That equates to about £10,575,000 in 2000 values. In that period there had passed through, or were still boarding, about 1,500 children. Starting with Jim Jarvis, we must allow a build-up from zero. To those 1,500 we must add all the soup-and-sympathy assistance that had been given to probably thousands of others. And not just soup, but other essentials as well. Operational costs had to include supplies and staff wages; not everyone was a volunteer, not all supplies were donated. For those being boarded there had to be food and clothes, good old hot water and plenty of soap, education included textbooks and exercise books, writing slates, pencils and pens, there were tools and equipment for those who needed them when jobs were found, there were building maintenance costs, even the costs of running the laundry. And that cannot be the whole list by a long way.

Donations were paying for building the Village cottages and for work at other centres. The Barnardo community was raising very large sums from their own resources. Not only did they have to fund the care of the children, they were doing a huge amount of social work in the community at large. In today's values the economy with which he was running the organisation was fantastic. Today he could do the job of Chancellor of the Exchequer on that performance. How on earth did he do so much on so little from a standing start twelve years earlier? It is the economic wonder of the age! And this was the man some of his enemies had been saying had put his hand in the till!

*

Two Frenchmen were having a conversation. One said that of course women were a lot different from men. The other exclaimed, 'Vive la Différence!' It's quite obvious that T. J. fully agreed. He certainly treated the girls in the Village differently from the boys in Stepney Causeway. The girls lived in cottages in what was for those days a large, but not unusually large family. The cottages had pretty names like Woodbine, Myrtle, Forget-me-not, Honeysuckle and so forth. The rules of residence were strict, their behaviour had to be exemplary, but the care delivered was equally high, far better than could be found anywhere else. One might even say that the middle class didn't look after their children any better, and some a lot worse.

The lads lived a much more barrack sort of life. In the days of empire it was much more chin up and do your best. It was necessary to find them jobs; bootblack is hardly a lifetime career, nor was chopping firewood. There were firms who would take a Barnardo boy as a first choice, because they gained a reputation for honesty and reliability. There were a whole range of trades available then which simply don't exist now, where active youngsters were wanted. It has to be agreed that coopering, which was making barrels, wasn't T. J.'s favourite trade because of the connection with beer that could be put into them, but he accepted that. The Stepney Causeway workshops taught fourteen different trades on site. Our good friend William Notman eventually came to be in charge of the boot-making department.

It was essential to get these young people fit for work and gainfully employed, because there was a tide of others not yet rescued who wanted their places. The difference of course extended to what was thought suitable. The girls majored on a life in service as maids and cooks, etc., though some went into nursing and various other jobs thought appropriate for them. And equally with the boys! There were for them a wide variety of trades: leather work, blacksmithing, jobs in the building trade, van boys on the horse-drawn carts, what you might call trades with dirty hands. Nothing which expected intellectual prowess, though in later life many of them surprised people by just how well they did. The time taken and the effort made for these children, an effort they usually responded to, was remarkable in that Victorian age.

In 1875 he made a tour of Scotland and Ireland, deliberately to find out how other people did things. He had no compunction about picking their brains and using their ideas. Many of his so-called 'dreams' happened after he had made such visits. One such dream involved Burdett Road, which is an important road in the Mile End area, were he had begun to use Burdett Hall to cater for some mission work. Plying a one-horse hansom cab and out in all weathers, the driver up on his high seat had no protection if it started to rain, other than such oilskins as he might have to wear. While he could do nothing for them while they were plying their trade, T. J. established on the corner of Burdett Road a cabman's shelter. Practical and didn't cost a fortune, but the credit with the locals it brought him in the area was enormous. Another case of good old Barney Do!

As we go into 1877 the Deaconess House was opened in Bow Road. In Stepney Causeway an infirmary was established to bring medical care to the sick children, and a lot were sick on arrival. Initially it was desperately restricted in what it could do, though this rapidly improved as time went by. Nearby was the London Hospital, then with over 400 beds, where the public at large would go for help. Fortunately the Nightingale effect was being felt throughout the medical profession, and there was a rapidly improving standard of care on offer.

Linked to the Stepney Causeway infirmary was a large house at Crowborough, near Tunbridge Wells, made available by a wealthy lady benefactor as a convalescent home. In 1878 a further medical mission was set up on The Highway, in the Shadwell Basin docks area. A large house in Jersey was donated by a Mr McNeill the following year. This is recorded as being for small boys with delicate health. That most likely meant the dreaded scourge of tuberculosis. There was a philanthropic explosion going on, because by 1880 the number of departments had grown to twenty-four, operating from eighteen addresses. The Mission Statement for all of them was the Ever Open Door.

There is a dramatic but entertaining description of an early morning scene in Stepney Causeway, which includes what that Mission Statement meant and what was claimed for it. There has been our usual paraphrase treatment.

When we open the Home today we see that the waiting hall is full with women, men and boys, but the boys are the most numerous. Little boys, big boys, fat boys, thin boys, tidy boys, merry boys, sad boys, fair boys, dark boys. In short, almost every sort of the genus called boy. When we are seated at our little table in our private room we ring a bell, and in they come one by one. Then for three or four hours we listen and advise, warn and pray, take copious notes of such cases as are likely to call for future action. We have however made a rule that no really destitute lad shall ever apply in vain at our door, and can now thankfully write that we have never turned away one houseless and destitute boy since the Home has been doing its work.

All of which is fine so long as the final claim rang absolutely true. While they honestly tried, it was impossible; the problem was so vast and so widespread. What T. J. claims is really as regards those he heard about, and they at least got soup and sympathy until he could do more for them. The scene in the quote is of children from poor homes coming into Stepney Causeway with their mothers, a few with fathers, seeking help. It all seems very orderly and polite. They will do what they can, in particular help keep the children at home where possible, and accept the most desperate cases if space is available. However, in the brief history of the enterprise it hadn't always been that orderly, and the kids hadn't come with their parents. It had started with the street kids, this scene is in a class way above that! Which leads us to the tragic story which created the Mission Statement. The tale of what happened to Carrots!

John Sommers was a ginger-haired street kid known to all as Carrots. He might have been eleven, no one really knew. He'd never known his father and his mother was a drunk, and probably half a dozen other things as well. The boy appears to have ended up on the streets at about the age of seven. A bit like Jim Jarvis, he had managed to scratch a living, had tried to sell newspapers, been a bootblack, done anything to make a penny. Even among the small and thin he was smaller and thinner, and couldn't stand up for himself. Most of the time he was on the edge of starvation. Sometimes his mother would find him and clout him, and rob him of the penny or two he might have had. The Queens Shades was one of his favourite dosses, in among the sixty or so other lads usually to be found there, and where T. J. first found him.

One night T. J. calculated that he could take five lads, and went with Jim Jarvis to pick out the five most desperate. Despite that description, Carrots came sixth. What T. J. then did was to promise the boy he would definitely come back for him in about a week. The trouble was that Carrots didn't last that long. It was a cold, hard winter that year. The next morning when the market workers came along to roll the kids out, one of them didn't move. Carrots had found an old fish barrel and curled up inside it, and there he had frozen to death from starvation and exposure.

T. J. never forgave himself for what had happened, and that was the origin of the Ever Open Door. Always after that when he didn't have a bed for someone, he made sure that any destitute child at least got a bowl of soup and a slice of bread and butter. If John Sommers had a memorial it was that Mission Statement. In his very precise way T. J. put his thoughts down on paper, in one of his famous reports to his supporters and the public. Some of these ideas we have yet to cover, but this is a good point to introduce them. This was written in perhaps 1870 and for a change the language is straightforward. On this occasion no attempt is being made to paraphrase.

OBJECTIVES

1 To rescue, educate, industrially train and place out in life orphan and destitute children
2 To evangelise among the masses of the East End.
3 To heal the sick and relieve the deserving poor.

MEANS

1 (a) Search agencies to discover waif and stray children
   (b) Free lodging houses
   (c) Large industrial homes
   (d) Small family homes
2 (a) Mission halls
   (b) Deaconess houses
   (c) Temperance aids
   (d) Ragged and Sunday schools

PRINCIPLES

1 Without any limitation as to age, sex, creed, or nationality.
2 Irrespective of any kind of physical infirmity. Crippled children, blind, deaf mutes, incurables and even those given over to death are eligible, if really destitute.
3 At any hour of day or night.
4 Solely on their merits, without election and without the intervention of wealthy patrons.

Having said that the statement laid out above has not been paraphrased, the next quote must be, if only to deal with a sentence which would otherwise run to 180 words. What follows is from an article written in Queen Victoria's Jubilee year of 1887, in which he is thinking back for his readers to the earliest days of the institution and how it began.

I am set primarily on the saving of children. The Homes under my care may be said to effect this upon a wider basis than any other institution in the world having the same end view. But in addition, our East End Mission has from the first undertaken the task of evangelising among the adult poor.

It comprises as well, agencies for visiting the sick, the aged and the fallen.

For relieving and nursing the sick, both in a medical mission and in their own homes. For educating on a scriptural basis the children of the labouring poor.

For supplying free meals or food at nominal prices to the hungry, both adults and children. For distributing clothing of various kinds, boots etc.

For supplying needy mothers with bedding and other articles during childbirth. For sending the convalescent poor to the seaside or country homes.

For paying rents for the aged and infirm.

For redeeming from pawn tools or implements needed to obtain work.

For enabling persons out of work, particularly girls, to obtain situations.

To help poor women with their struggles with starvation, with loans of sewing machines, mangles etc.

In general, by many like methods of systematic and carefully applied relief designed to raise the fallen, to cheer the faint and infuse fresh courage into the discouraged warriors in the grim battle of life.

That is not, we need to remind ourselves, a manifesto from some politician for a future they would like to create with Christian magnanimity, and weren't they being nice about it, so please vote for them. By the time he wrote the article, this was what the Barnardo organisation had built up and was actually delivering in its 'manor', the East End of London. This was well over half a century before Beveridge put pen to paper with his famous report, which historians all say became the basis of the welfare state.

The committee, and Cairns in particular while he was alive, desperately tried to keep T. J. in touch with the real world, and get him to understand that there wasn't a never-ending stream of money coming in. When you realise what was being achieved on the funds they were managing to raise, it is staggering. It irked T. J. desperately, because he was always full of new schemes, and the committee had to painfully explain why they had to say no. The reason was the money wasn't there, no matter how worthy the thought. It further irked him that he wasn't the master of all he surveyed any more; the committee did have the right to refuse, and in order to stay solvent it had to do it more and more often.

While in the public mind, which probably includes you, Barnardo's was a children's organisation, some sort of orphanage charity, the facts were so very different. It focussed on the care of children most definitely, but it was also, in the Barnardo manner, doing the job we'd expect from Social Services. And being largely unpaid, coming from the heart.

On top of that it had the Christian dimension as an article of faith. The children's work was always the East End Juvenile Mission, the word 'mission' was always central. Whatever your faith or the absence thereof, you have to admire their efforts, even as you totally damn the social conditions which made their efforts necessary. Quite what the legal position in respect of the donations might have been, your faithful legal eagle would be happy to charge you a fee to research. Victorian law wasn't our law of today. Should the social work finances have been separated from the children's work money? It's obvious that his Mission church congregation at the Edinburgh Castle knew full well the collections money was all going into the same pot. Let's not wonder too long, that was then and what they did then was the start of where we are now. Is it a wild exaggeration to claim that the thinking behind the modern welfare state was invented in Stepney Causeway?

Charities are always short of cash. As already noted, the first period we reviewed had a 2000 translation of £10,750,000. Come forward to the Golden Jubilee year of 1887, and the £550,460 reported in the accounts translates to a 2000 figure of £41,376,000. To give us an idea of what money would buy then, part of Stepney Causeway was demolished and in Jubilee year they built Her Majesty's Hospital for Sick Children. Do not confuse this with Great Ormond Street, no connection. Not by modern standards large, it had seventy beds. Built in good, solid Victorian brick, it cost £9,000, so translates to about £700,000. What could you buy these days for that money? Certainly not a seventy-bed specialist paediatric hospital. Annual income in ten years grew by 250 per cent, and allowing for a decade of inflation, which isn't a recent invention, clearly the institution was growing rapidly.

In 1887 we pick up on a report of activities in Stepney Causeway. Remembering that this was still the age of the horse-and-cart, there is a blacksmith's forge, a mat-making shop making harnesses and tack for horses, and a print works. Five properties have been bought to house destitute children. Sturge House in Bow Road had been acquired for work with older girls, and was also used for a time as extra office space. It focussed on finding work for them, especially in service as maids and cooks. An extension was built there to provide more shelter for destitute girls. In nearby Burdett Road they had established a hostel for working lads, which eventually had space for 200 beds. We are, you will note, still in that tight little area we are thinking of as the Barnardo 'manor', all locations within about a mile of each other. And of course the Girls Village in Barkingside. And let's not forget the Edinburgh Castle, the convalescent homes in Kent and the Channel Isles, and a great deal more the report doesn't list.

*

There is something we need to pick up on which has been mentioned obliquely a couple of times. Up to now we have been thinking of T. J. as the Honorary Director, in other words he didn't have a salary, not even, we are led to believe, an expense account. That has to mean that somehow he had become a man of substantial independent means. We cannot closely discuss where those independent means came from, because little definitive information percolates down to us, other than to say he came from a prosperous middle-class background. What he may have inherited from Papa Barnardo couldn't have been much when shared out with his brothers and sisters. Papa Elmslie had died in 1880 leaving only about £2,000, all of which went to his widow.

What gives rise to this is a letter of 20 March 1883 to the trust solicitor. Something devastating had clearly happened to his finances. We will pick up halfway through the letter, which is not paraphrased.

> Painful and distressing therefore that it will be to take even one shilling from the Homes, on which I would, God knows rather spend than be spent, yet no other honourable course seems open to me, if I am to recover the ground unhappily lost through no fault or improvidence of my own, but by the dishonesty or folly of others.

In other words, his financial sky had just fallen in, the details of which we never discover. One is, however, reminded of what happened to Papa Barnardo over in Ireland, who lost heavily on a speculative investment. However, Papa Barnardo had a prosperous business and made a complete recovery, while T. J. was running a charity and giving his time for free.

On 23 March he writes again, clearly replying to the suggestion that his friends pass round the hat to recover whatever little local difficulty this might have been. He turns this down flat, and writes, 'I have always had a strong feeling about the race of philanthropists and evangelists generally, who live by faith and postage stamps.'

Which is an elegant way of saying thanks, but no thanks to the offer, from a past master of the art he describes. Instead he asks for a salary as a proper and permanent way out of the dilemma, if the trustees would kindly agree. It's clear he would feel very embarrassed by charity, indeed he says it would be humiliating, even though they were such good friends. He didn't want the story to get out, which it would if they held a collection for him. In the background there were also all the nasty things that were said in the arbitration case, and the fact that the Charities Organisation Society would make a meal of it if they found out. Such was his position at the centre of the organisation that if any idea that he was personally deeply in the red got out to the general public it would send shudders around the donating public and would almost certainly hammer the cash flow.

The outcome was that the trustees agreed to pay him a salary of £600 a year, which translates approximately to a modern £45,000 a year. When you think what he did to earn it, this is nice but not enormous in our modern way of thinking. This of course could never stop him from being the founder, but it set in concrete that he was now an employee of the trust. When he worked for nothing, claiming expenses was optional; now as an employee he would have been perfectly entitled to claim. His extensive travels, which included five trips to Canada over the years, would have been legitimate claims under this heading.

Looking for clues to his private resources, we find that he privately owned a children's magazine, *Children's Treasury*. This was a vehicle for stories he wrote, and gave the public information about the organisation. From this he gained a steady income for some years. He was also paid for articles in magazines and a London newspaper, *The Echo*. Further, he was in demand as a preacher and charged for that; we recall that's how he met Syrie. He made the mistake of setting up a second magazine, *Night and Day*, as the official house journal, but this had the effect of killing off *Children's Treasury*. People would buy one or the other, they didn't want both, so he lost his income when a catastrophic fall in sales meant he had to close it. All in all he was guilty of some errors of judgement in the publishing field, and this may have had a lot to do with his problems, but the background feeling is that it was not responsible for all of them.

By 1879 the Barnardos were living in Oliver Terrace in Bow. From there they moved to Banbury Road, South Hackney, then a pleasant road close to Victoria Park, so ideal for a family with children. We will recall the photograph of the Edinburgh Castle. Did they buy their fruit and vegetables from A. W. Matthews, who traded from nearby Well Street, whose delivery cart was outside the Mission church? They hadn't moved very far; even now they were still inside the Barnardo manor.

SEVEN

Children as Property: Legal Cases

The position of children was probably not sorted out in what we would call the full legal sense until the Children's Act of 1908. Up to then, in varying degrees, whichever part of society you belonged to, children could be regarded more as the property of their parents or guardians, rather than citizen of the realm. Cynics may note that the National Society for the Protection of Animals had existed since 1824, whereas the National Society for the Protection of Children didn't appear in the scene until 1884. In Victorian England it was probably more of a crime to kick your dog than kick your child.

When children were admitted to the Homes the parent or guardian, if they had one, was required to sign a formal agreement with the organisation. The law as it stood was so dysfunctional about the status of minor that the agreement was very difficult to enforce if disputes arose. It became obvious from the earliest days that a child could be put into the Homes while the family was in trouble, which meant deloused, scrubbed, fed, clothed and other troubles sorted, only for the youngster to be reclaimed a year later. The child was a year older, may have learned to read, was a lot healthier and could be found a job to bolster the family income. The Homes had spent all that time and effort and they barely got a thank you. It was costing a fortune that they didn't have, and they couldn't afford that sort of thing. If the family was honest and respectable they would, if they could, often join the list of donors. Some families proved to be so dreadful that there was a fight to stop the child ever going back to them.

Probably the best way of summing up this problem is to say that we regard children as citizens and the Victorians didn't. Today we say the state has a duty of diligence and care in ensuring that the citizen child has a safe and secure upbringing. The state ordinarily delegates that duty to the parents, in the reasonable expectation that the parents will discharge that duty diligently. However, the state reserves the right to act for the citizen child if the parents fail to be diligent in their care. Our modern phrase for what comes into force when that happens is that the child is deemed to be 'at risk', and there are various systems which can then be energised. In practice, whatever the theory may have been, the mid-Victorian parent or guardian more or less owned the child, with superior rights to the child than even the state, except in exceptional circumstances. Those rights were superior to any institution such as Barnardo's Homes, despite any agreement signed on the child's behalf upon entry. In all this the state very largely stayed out of things.

Just to go through the provision of care in cases of poverty, it was organised in Parish Unions. As the name implies, several parishes combined together to run a workhouse. Publicly funded to the meanest subsistence level, and as different from today as chalk is from cheese, the parent–child relationship wasn't affected, and the parent still essentially owned the child. Workhouses were so awful that often throwing the child out on the streets was regarded as the better option, and many of the Barnardo children arrived in their care because of it. The 1834 Act was an abomination abominably administered. The far better alternative, the philanthropically supported Homes for Waifs and Strays, gradually emerged from the wrack and the ruin.

The Barnardo Homes came under this general heading. Throughout London alone there is a figure for 1884 of twenty such philanthropic institutions supporting destitute children. That's before we consider what was going on all over the rest of the country. Most of these institutions had a Christian basis, some were better run than others, but every one of them was far superior to the public workhouses. Some like Barnardo's were specifically Protestant – there was one in Bonner Road, also in the East End, which was Methodist – others were Catholic, and several were non-specific.

This is where we have to consider some special characteristics in T. J.'s nature. His father was a Prussian Jew who had converted to Anglican Christianity for the love of a lady. Papa Barnardo's first wife, Elizabeth, despite having a Catholic father, was staunchly Protestant, which had an extra frisson in Ireland. Things were not so different then in Ireland than they are now. Irish Protestants don't always like Catholics, and the dislike is equally often reciprocated. T. J. wasn't just running a home for destitute children, it was also the East End Juvenile Mission. As the entry form the parents had to sign made clear, it was a Protestant mission. He wasn't just feeding and clothing them, he was trying to save their souls. In fact, whatever spiritual feeling they may have had when they arrived, which was usually zero, when they left he wanted them to have Protestant souls. There were cases where he would fight the family head on in trying to keep a child, even trying to retrieve it if it had been taken away. He always said it was for the good of the child, saving it from the family influence, for instance they might be violent or indeed be criminals. All of which, in many of the cases that he had to deal with, was true. To T. J. his idea of what was good for the child was his only consideration.

We might agree that in such cases he was justified. However, would we agree that he could be allowed to stretch things to the point of deliberately preventing a child from being a Catholic? Looked at from the balanced perspective of hindsight, there were several cases in which this most sectarian of Irishmen did just that. He sometimes did things which we would think were completely irrational, but because of his sectarian viewpoint, they were rational to him. When we try to think with his brain, we find that all his adult life his first thought was his mission, and by that he meant his Protestant and therefore anti-Catholic mission. Taking a child out of destitution and away from bad influences was all aimed at saving the child's soul from damnation, and to his way of thinking that soul had to become a Protestant soul. That was simply the way he thought. Bear these thoughts in mind, because they will eventually become relevant to things that come up.

Things were moving on. In 1878 he lost John Sands, and in 1885 he lost Lord Cairns. The deaths of these two good men as trustees and committee members were sad blows, and the influence they were able to exert was never fully replaced by others. One of the new faces was a barrister, Charles Baker, who in 1885 wrote a treatise on the law as it applied to children at the time. This was a very appropriate subject of great interest to his fellow trustees. What came out of it was that the law in this respect was deplorably deficient at every point of the legal compass. His conclusions were that were the public to be asked for their opinion, which in those days they almost never were, it would want girls in particular to have far more protection in respect of rape, and generally tougher laws were needed in all areas involving the relationship between children and their parents or guardians. In the *Night and Day* magazine, circulation up to 100,000, T. J. ran a series of articles hammering away at this theme.

Calls on the conscience of various churches and Christian organisations were beginning to bear fruit. The Church of England got its act together somewhat, not always an easy job in those days, and it created the Children's Society. The Methodists in Bonner Road were on friendly terms with T. J., and probably with a lot of encouragement from him their work eventually evolved into the Methodist Children's Homes. There was also the Waifs and Strays Society, which acted as an umbrella group for several Homes.

As already mentioned, the NSPCC came along in 1884, and there was an unfortunate echo in its founding. Our old friend Sam

Smith was much involved and T. J. was an early supporter. In fact, at the inaugural meeting at the Mansion House, his name is down as the seconder of the motion to formally create it. What could go wrong after that? What could go wrong was T. J. picking an argument entirely of his own invention, and a couple of years later resigning in an acrimonious manner. He saw in the management of the society the presence of some Catholics. Whenever and wherever he saw Catholics involved in childcare his eyes glazed, all the gaskets blew, and he just went right off the rails. That was T. J. and it explains why this man with a heart of gold so often lost support with the public. He turned irrationality on this subject into an art form. The situation is made even clearer when one reads the leading relevant clause in the custody agreement the parents or guardians had to sign to get a child admitted to Barnardo Homes.

> The nearest friend shall place the said child in the said *Protestant Homes* to be taken care of, maintained and educated therein, or in one of the Branch Establishments named at the head of the paper, or boarded out in the country for a term of years from the date hereof, or for less time if the managers for the time being of the said Homes think fit, during that time to be brought up in the *Protestant faith*.

So long as they could read, and despite increasing efforts in that direction not everyone could yet, there it was in black and white and specifically in italics. Barnardo Homes would bring the child up in the *Protestant faith*, there was no other option available, take it or leave it.

*

We now arrive at the reason for all this discussion. In the year 1888 there were three admissions which led to a most monumental upset and uproar, which put the arbitration hearings completely in the shade. Arrivals that year included two boys and a girl, and apart from their own variations on the all too common theme of neglect and need for help, initially there seemed nothing unusual about them. The girl was Martha Ann Tye and the two boys were Henry Gossage and John James Roddy. All three had at least one parent living and the parents were all *sent*, note my emphasis on that word, the standard intake agreement. The agreement in law, as has already been mentioned, had the adhesive qualities of Teflon in a great many respects. Within a year of the child being accepted, in all three cases there was an attempt by the parents to reclaim their child. We do not find these cases in the *Memoirs*; the biographers seem to have hoped that by ignoring them they would fade away. That attitude was nonsense, as by then the cases had proved to have been of huge significance to the running of the Homes.

For a much fuller discussion of the devils in the details of these cases I refer you to the bibliography and the book *Barnardo* by Gillian Wagner. My own researches have traced official documents on some of the participants. In particular let us interest ourselves in a comparison between the attitudes then, and our modern attitudes towards children. We do have some surviving judicial comments to work from, which emerge from what are, one must regret, apparently incomplete survivals of the court proceedings.

We can usefully begin with the case of Henry Gossage. From the Family Records Centre I have obtained a birth certificate which seems to soundly fit. This shows him born 8 January 1878 when the family was living in Oldbury, West Bromwich. This is on the north-west edge of Birmingham, bearing in mind the city has grown enormously since then. His father was Edward Gossage, a brickyard labourer, his mother Mary, maiden name Toy, no employment given. We find them in the 1881 census living in Leamington near Coventry, which is 30 miles away. Edward remains a labourer, Mary is still apparently just a housewife, and we learn that three-year-old Henry had two older brothers: Thomas, then aged nine and William, then seven. Other background research suggests that Gossage was a bit of a Midlands surname.

In 1888 young Henry, now aged ten, comes to public notice. He is found in a dreadful state of neglect, wandering around Folkestone in Kent. The story varies as to whether he was found by a clergyman or a policeman, and whether for a few days he was put in the local workhouse. What is known to be a fact is that there was a clergyman involved who knew of the Barnardo Homes. He it was who contacted them and persuaded them to accept poor Henry. So far nothing greatly unusual; they had accepted kids in the same terrible state all too often.

The lad's story was that his father was now dead, and that his mother had handed him over to an itinerant street musician who played a barrel organ, a rare item now only found in antique collections. The organ grinder had mistreated him, starved him and finally abandoned him, though possibly the lad had finally run away. Not all details can be absolutely vouched for. One version even says that his mother had sold him to the man for a drink of gin. Whichever version is the true one, we have a lad of ten years in a dreadful state and in need of help.

The crucial thing, and where it all goes terribly wrong, is that underneath all the grime and the desertion and awful treatment, here was a bright enough lad. He knew where his mother lived and could give an accurate address for her. It would have saved a vast amount of trouble of all sorts if he had shut up and said nothing, but after all he was only ten.

Barnardo Homes followed all the rules and wrote to the mother. A reply was received which confirmed that the father had died. Mary Gossage added an interesting fact, which was that the two older boys had been sent to Canada. There were by then several organisations promoting emigration to Canada, and the previous year T. J. had started one of his own. Mrs Gossage confirmed that she wasn't able to maintain her son and asked that Barnardo Homes take Henry in. Having made contact and confirmed that she was where young Henry said she ought to be, a standard agreement form was sent, and that is where it all started to go wrong. That she asked Barnardo Homes to look after Henry was always agreed by all sides, but it was also agreed that she never signed the form.

It now descends from the unfortunate to the positively 'believe it if you like'! With T. J. as the teller of the tale, here we go. It was sometime in November 1888 that he had a visitor at Stepney Causeway. According to the teller of the tale this smartly dressed gentleman introduced himself as Mr William Norton. He had with him several letters of introduction, all of which seemed to be from people of respectable standing in Canada. Now there's a coincidence, Canada again! The teller of the tale related that Norton asked to adopt one of the poor Barnardo boys, say, a lad of about ten, and take him back to a prosperous life in Canada. It sounded a wonderful offer, and an assistant was told to find several who fitted the bill, so that this very nice gentleman could make his selection. Of those called in, so said the teller of the tale, William Norton chose Henry Gossage, the lad who had remembered where his mother lived.

Yes! Quite! In our own generation all the whistles would have blown, all the sirens would have gone off and the place would have been swarming with policemen and social workers, pouring through every door and window! Shock! Horror! Attempted abduction of small boy! This is now. But even then, surely to goodness T. J. ought to have smelled a rat! He is the teller of the tale and he says no, he didn't! From his viewpoint this was a wonderful chance for young Henry, he was being offered adoption, not merely a servant's job. William Norton seemed to be prosperously well off, and the letters he carried appeared to be authentic. Looked at with our benefit of hindsight, here was a man whom T. J. didn't know, a Canadian he couldn't check on for maybe three or four months if correspondence went by sea, unless he used the transatlantic telegraph system recently installed. Even using that, verifying any response might have taken up to a month.

To us it seems to be a total non-starter! Without question there was a gay community in London and there were also perverts here and there. Oscar Wilde was a leading homosexual and he and his friends had a known meeting place in the West End. Then called rent boys, youngsters inveigled into the business were not a new invention, they existed in Ancient Greece and Rome. If not gay, Norton could have been a pervert, and they were around in ancient days as well. The elusive William Norton, and there has only ever been T. J. who said he existed, could have been anyone and the alleged letters could have been forgeries. Bearing in mind all the terrible things he had seen in the East End, we have to ask ourselves if he could have been so blindly innocent of the potential for disaster awaiting Henry Gossage in all this. When the case came before the courts he insisted that this was the truth. Are we in any way surprised that the alleged letters of introduction do not seem to have survived?

Not a man of robust health, T. J. was off sick for a few days at this crucial time. You will understand that in the days when letters were all handwritten, his correspondence got behindhand. Norton came to collect Henry during this period of absence. What we next discover is a letter on file from a Mr Newdigate. This enclosed a 10-shilling donation, 2000 value something just under £40. That was a nice friendly gesture and the office clerk had sent a receipt and filed the letter. However the letter, when brought out into the light of day, had been written on behalf of Mary Gossage, advising that it had been arranged to take Henry out of Barnardo's, and transfer him into the care of St Vincent's Home in Harrow Road. It doesn't take a genius to work out that St Vincent's was a Catholic institution. It is alleged that at the time T. J. never himself saw the letter, which is why he never answered it. It is the story we get from the teller of the tale, and it is the one we are therefore stuck with. We cannot prove the existence of Norton, we have none of his introductory letters, and we cannot prove the chronology of the correspondence in the Stepney Causeway office and how it relates to the Norton visitations. All we can prove is that the 10-shilling donation arrived and the receipt was sent to Mr Newdigate. And that young Henry was missing!

Let's go through this quietly. We are asked to believe that the clerk didn't read the letter, because surely if he had he would never have filed it. Any clerk worth his wages would have passed it on to someone senior for action. What we can verify as fact is that Mr Newdigate wrote a second letter, and that it was not until 31 December 1888, which is seven weeks after the elusive William Norton is said to have collected young Henry, that the Homes secretary Mr Odling replied. He advised Mr Newdigate that transfers on purely religious grounds were not allowed under Homes rules. Whether they were allowed under the law of the land was not discussed. All of which had given William Norton, whoever he was and if he had ever existed, seven weeks to disappear into the far blue yonder, which was possibly, but far from verifiably, across the briny ocean to Canada. Mr Odling's letter seems to have been an attempt to brush Mr Newdigate away and hope he stayed away. He didn't go away and all hell broke loose!

If you think that is all there was to this fantastical story, read on. According to the teller of this tale, Norton had asked that there should be no contact with the Gossage family, or any possibility of them interfering, claiming that young Henry had gone through enough already at their hands. For that reason he didn't leave his address in Canada. It is jaw-dropping, but that was the tale that was told. Do we, for goodness' sake, believe a word of it? Our teller of the tale was, we now recall, the man who wrote all those wonderful stories for the *Children's Treasury* for so many years, so someone with a very inventive mind in this line of work. Do we believe a single word of all this, or is it, to use the politest word we can think of, a load of ancient rigmarole? My vote is for the rigmarole.

What we find we are discussing is a ten-year-old boy, who had previously been given away by his mother to an organ-grinder, that bit we know to be true, handed over to a man whose only credentials are a smart suit, a cultured voice, a good way with words, and a few letters which might very well have been forgeries. And he's been given seven weeks to disappear, without even leaving a forwarding address! And the teller of the tale, with all his experience of children in desperate and cruel circumstances, said that was what he agreed to.

The story continues that T. J. arranged with the elusive Norton that Henry should be collected on 14 November 1888. Whether he actually did or not is far from definite, though the last entry on the lad's file is 'disposed of by Director, 14..11..88'. It noticeably doesn't say that this was to Norton. The entry is in T. J.'s well-known handwriting, so he appears to have returned to work by that date. 'Disposed' does seem to treat the lad like some unwanted parcel, it really is an inelegant and undignified turn of phrase. It isn't what you would expect from someone who was into saving souls. And if that wasn't all, the picture of this little boy had been torn out of the records. That's where whoever did it missed something. You will recall that there were before and after pictures taken of all the children. Only one of those was torn out, the other one wasn't and is still in the modern Barnardo charity archives.

Mr Newdigate did not go away, and continued to represent the interests of Mary Gossage. In January 1889 a letter arrived, and while we cannot say that Mary Gossage composed it, it was not disputed that it was the genuine article. There are two stories about its origins. One is that she was illiterate and only capable of making her 'mark' in front of a witness, the other that she was capable of signing in full. The letter is now apparently lost with so much else in the chaos of the 1940 Blitz, so which of the two options this comes under cannot now be verified. This latest letter demanded the return of her son. Failure to oblige by Barnardo Homes resulted in March 1889 in a writ of *habeas corpus* being applied for in her name. Clearly this lady now had powerful backers willing to spend money. She didn't have any money to pursue the matter herself, and legal aid would not be available until decades into the future. It quickly transpired that she was now being represented by Leathley & Co., a firm of solicitors known to work for the Catholic Church and its causes. The writ demanded that young Henry be handed over forthwith! In response to this T. J. went to court and presented the defence that at the time of the writ young Henry was no longer in his care. There is no record of the personal opinion of the judge, but on this dubious technicality the judge, Mr Justice Matthew, felt that he had to throw out the writ. If it hadn't been for T. J.'s virulent blind spot when it came to Catholics, that is where the matter might have ended. A lot of lawyers were to make a lot of money out of his sectarianism as the months, indeed the years, rolled by.

*

We should now consider the remarkably similar case of Martha Ann Tye. The Family Records Office have been able to supply a birth certificate showing that she was born in Chelmsford, Essex, on 28 September 1875, the daughter of James and Margaret Tye. The mother's maiden name is shown as McLachlin. The father's trade is shown as lace maker, which seems to have been an error; that was Margaret's trade. We now move from Chelmsford to Tamworth, Staffordshire, where the census return shows the family, Martha now five and both parents twenty-three. Both parents are engaged in repairing china. The copperplate handwriting on the census return is the only thing nice about it. There are twenty-three people shown on the sheet, of whom six were of school age, eleven unemployed, so only eight had jobs. Because of a clerical slip by the enumerator the name of the street hasn't been given, but we are told it is in the parish of St Editha. Against the entry for Martha it gives place of birth as Chelmsford, so it all fits, we can be happy we have the right family.

The year after the census we have a death certificate for James Tye on 7 March 1882, age given as twenty-five, cause of death given as rheumatism of the viscera of the heart. Your favourite medical doctor might be asked to explain that in modern jargon, but it isn't relevant to our story. The deceased is described as a glass and china repairer, again it fits previous information. Quick calculation indicates that Martha was born when the couple were eighteen or nineteen years old. Tamworth is in what was then called the Potteries, where china, porcelain and glass were manufactured in enormous quantities. What a repairer would have been paid is difficult to discover, but the feeling is that if you were a mouse in search of crumbs to eat you would have moved next door.

A copy of a marriage certificate has been obtained from the Family Records Office which shows that on 19 September 1882 Margaret married Francis Ward Jnr, so poor James was only six months dead. We have the bride described as a widow aged twenty-four, so depending on her exact birthday that also agrees. Francis Ward is described as a bookbinder, and Margaret reverts to her earlier trade of lace maker. At that time lace making was very badly paid, but a bookbinder was an artisan, so marrying him seems to have been a minor step up for her.

All that description may seem to be terribly fussy, but these old documents from an age when not everyone could read and write are full of inconsistencies. One likes to be absolutely sure. For instance, on Martha's Chelmsford birth certificate her mother's maiden name is McLachlin. On the marriage certificate to Francis Ward her maiden name is shown as McLaughlan. On the death certificate we are told that James Tye died at Kings Head Yard. However the informant is his widow Margaret, living at Kings Head Court. Little slip-ups like this abound throughout the records. When we discussed much earlier the origins of the name Barnardo, one sees how easily through documents, not just dialects, names can change over the generations.

Bearing in mind the character we have ascertained in our hero T. J., this is where it gets interesting. The Margaret and Francis marriage was Catholic. Margaret's maiden name of McLaughlan sounds very Irish. We have already discovered that such a combination can cause the eyes to glaze and the gaskets to blow, and would we be discussing the story unless T. J. is going to become involved? It would appear that Martha's family were originally poor Irish Catholic, though we have a census record that Margaret was actually born in England, in the small town of Barton on Humber. As in the previous case with young Henry, there was to be a battle over the custody of little Martha Ann, and whatever the moral rights and wrongs, and there were plenty on both sides, all hell broke loose yet again!

George Muller had German origins somewhat similar to those of Papa Barnardo, except that he was never Jewish. He had founded an orphanage in Bristol and gained some minor fame. When still in Dublin and aged about seventeen, T. J. had entered into a short correspondence with him, asking for some advice. Careful reading of Muller's reply shows him non-committal with a young man he didn't know, but he did suggest that getting down to some serious Bible study was a good start.

That gives you the back story, let's now go into action mode at the gates of the Muller orphanage, where at some time in 1888 we find young Martha, aged about thirteen, in a terrible state of distress and begging to be taken in. The director of the orphanage was Dr Mayo, who found he really didn't have a permanent place for her. What he did was contact Barnardo Homes in London who agreed to accept her. The Barnardo record is in T. J.'s familiar handwriting, and it lays out what was known up to this juncture as related to him by Dr Mayo. Technically it's hearsay, but there's no reason to disbelieve any of it in general terms.

What we get from the Barnardo archives is that Martha Ann Tye came from a slum area of Bristol, so that means the family had moved from Tamworth. She had been clothed in rags and was complaining that she was being knocked about by her mother and stepfather. In particular she was being sent out to beg and she was thrashed if she came home with nothing. Now engage the mind with the thought of how old she was. Martha Ann was thirteen and was being sent out to beg. In this context define in your mind what was meant by the word beg. What would a man expect for his sixpence? Surprisingly in all the uproar that later ensued, this point was never discussed, which to us is surely amazing. However there are suggestions in the research that not only was Francis Ward enjoying conjugal rights with Margaret, he was beginning to force his attentions on Martha Ann. If these suggestions, which aren't more definite, were indeed true, they would explain her state of extreme distress at the gates of the orphanage. The one thing no one disputed was that initial extreme distress.

By the time that Barnardo wrote this into the child's records, research indicates that Ward had been taken before the Bristol magistrates, but again it's not possible to nail down exactly why.

A bit more definite is that Ward had at some time seen the inside of Worcester Gaol.

When Barnardo Homes accepted her, the records on her personal file had three particularly relevant comments. The mother had been contacted and had agreed to the admission, but with a special limitation of only two years. Quite why she wanted this limitation isn't known, normally admission to the Homes had no limitation at all. About this time T. J. had started his Canadian emigration project. Margaret Ward, as we must now call her, had specifically not agreed to allow Martha Ann to emigrate. The record ends with 'R.C' written in capital letters. So right from the very beginning T. J. knew full well that he was dealing with a Catholic family. It doesn't take an act of genius to work out that Martha Ann was running away from her stepfather, and had he managed to get her back there is a serious question as to whether she would have survived. Whether Margaret was a battered housewife herself we never definitely find out.

Under the 'children being treated as property' ethos, which is our reading of the situation at the time, the normal assumption was that children were labelled with the religion of their parents. The idea that the child had a choice never entered anyone's head. To a large extent that way of thinking still lingers in some places around the world. Given that Margaret McLaughlan Tye Ward was Catholic by lineage though not by behaviour, that probably means that James Tye was also a Catholic. It's impossible to know as their marriage certificate was never found. However, in the custom of the times, all this is sufficient to label the girl as a Catholic.

Let us just drop in another observation that never came into discussion during the ensuing uproar. To be a Catholic you need first to be a Christian. Was the way that Martha Ann was being treated Christian? Had T. J. thought about it he could have won his case hands down, no trouble at all. He didn't, and as has been said, all hell broke loose.

About ten days before Christmas 1888 a letter arrived at Stepney Causeway demanding that Martha be returned. Someone arrived to collect her and was told that they had wasted their time making the journey, the girl was staying where she was. This precipitated a letter from a solicitor, to which T. J. replied, demanding to have it confirmed that the mother was indeed married and who to, and that she could now properly support her daughter. This in turn evoked a reply which arrived 1 January 1889, which was dealt with as before. Martha wasn't going anywhere! The speed at which the Wards, whose whole previous history had been of dire poverty and life in the slums, could suddenly afford a solicitor is revealing. There arrived a further letter from the solicitor on 7 January 1889, this time threatening legal action. All this flurry of correspondence back and forth had only taken twenty-one days. If it does nothing else, it pays an enormous compliment to the postal service of those far-off days.

On the threat of legal action T. J. made a startling announcement – startling to his friends and opponents, not so startling to us as we have read the Gossage case. It was said that Martha Ann was no longer in England. It was declared by T. J. that she had been abroad and outside the jurisdiction of the British Courts since 22 December. Why this information wasn't given to the opposing legal team in response to the letter of 1 January is food for speculation. As in the case of young Henry Gossage it was T. J. against the world, and he was daring them to call him a liar. Are we surprised to find that the Ward legal team was headed up by Leathley & Co., who then proceeded to make an utter mull of the entire affair, precisely because they didn't call him a liar!

Indeed what we get here is a feeling of having been here before. Again there is a writ of *habeas corpus* and again we meet our friend Judge Matthew. Once again T. J. proves to be a man of wonderful imagination in the invention of romantic tales for children. He certainly rose to the occasion this time, and he told a beauty. The tale he told this time was that he had received a visit from the delightfully named Gertrude Romand. There's enough of the English in Gertrude and enough of the European in Romand to make her sound very exotic. We are told that she was a lady of considerable wealth who spent most of her time wandering luxuriously around Europe. She is implied to have been a long-time and generous supporter of the Homes. Again there is a question never asked. Could he prove it? Was she there on the receipts list he so meticulously maintained? What he was never asked he was never forced to prove.

Madame Romand, he claimed, had visited the Homes just before Christmas and had suggested that she would be happy to take three of his little girls on a prolonged tour around Europe. He agreed to her suggestion and one of the chosen three was Martha Ann. How remarkable that another miraculously opportune visitor should appear absolutely on cue, or at any rate on 21 December 1888, just like the Good Fairy in a pantomime, to whisk Martha Ann away from what the ultra-sectarian T. J. saw as a difficult situation. It inevitably came up before Mr Justice Matthew, who gave T. J. the benefit of the doubt and adjourned the case to allow T. J. some time to recover Martha Ann and bring her to court.

In the third week of May the hearing reconvened and letters were read out in court. The originals not being traced, we are indebted to a report in the archives of *The Times* of 24 May 1889. The first is from T. J. to Madame Romand and no one disputed he had written it. This is not paraphrased.

Dear Madame Romande

You will, I dare say, be surprised at the contents of this letter. You doubtless remember those three children I handed over to your care on 21st December last. It is the eldest of these Mary Ann Tye of whom I write. The wretched mother of this poor child has it appears lately married. However this man and woman have moved the High Court for a writ of *habeas corpus* to compel me to produce and give up the child. I frankly told the Judge I had given her over to the custody of a lady, not mentioning your name. I have done my best to protect the poor girl, but now in view of the writ being issued, it seems my very plain duty to ask you to enable me to comply with it, and to

cancel if you will the agreement I entered into with you, and to
return the child to me in time to produce her in Court on the day
named.

There are immediately sundry points to pick up. Martha Ann
is referred to as Mary Ann, and her records and her admission
photograph at Barnardo's are in the name of Ward, not Tye. The
copy marriage certificate obtained from the Family Records Office
shows that the Ward/Tye marriage had been on 19 September
1882. That means they had been married six years, not recently as
suggested. Was the agreement mentioned verbal or in writing, and
if in writing where was the Barnardo's office copy? The second
sentence says, 'You will doubtless remember those three children.'
Excuse me, but surely those three children are permanently with
her, she ought to be seeing them at breakfast, lunch and dinner!
What sort of phraseology is that? Nor does he ask about all three
girls, or hope that they are enjoying their holiday. He doesn't send
them a message telling them how grateful they have a duty to
be to such a kind and generous lady. It rings as loudly as a wet
sponge. And mentioning earlier the hash Leathley made of things,
there is no record of either they or the court asking to see the
letter.

Fine, he wrote the letter, so he says. According to T. J., who is
our only source, she got the letter. It would also appear that the
court never asked what the exact nature of the agreement was,
nor did it ask for sight of the file copy. Let's be polite and call it
a hypothetical agreement. This is very involved, as we discover
when T. J. reads out what he claimed was Gertrude Romand's
reply from Cannes.

Dear Dr Barnardo.
    Your letter does indeed surprise me and you must look on
me as one who is demented. I cannot understand you one bit. I
have read and read your letter and the oftener I read it the more
perplexed I am. That you, the protector and defender of little
children, the guardian of hundreds of little girls, should really

ask me to return to the wretches who so brutally treated the poor child Mary Ann passes my comprehension. However, of one thing you may be assured, I will not comply with such a request. I am leaving here tomorrow and am wandering about for a fortnight, but I shall hope to be in Brussels with my little maid on the eighteenth of next month, and if you write again will you address my letter to the Post Office, for I am not quite sure where I shall stop. On the subject of Mary Ann my mind is made up and my decision is irrevocable. Moreover I am very angry with you, and don't think I shall sign myself as very sincerely your friend

    Gertrude Romand.

We have here language couched in literate middle-class English. This certainly suits the Gertrude half of the name. It also suits a three-volume novel of the period in its idiom and emotion. The more one reads it the more one wonders if she ever existed. This is being presented as an item of evidence; again I ask, did anyone other than T. J. ever see it and did they ever compare its handwriting with a sample of his own? We notice that the other two 'little maids' have dropped out of the correspondence, remember she is alleged to have taken three. Did anyone check the Barnardo records for the other two? Martha is repeatedly called Mary, yet Madame Romand was supposed to be seeing all three girls over the breakfast cups every day, so surely she ought to have used the correct name. The copy of her birth certificate shows the name Martha quite clearly. It seems odd that both people in this exchange make exactly the same mistake, that is to say, if there were actually two people in it. But there is no record of anyone raising the point, or wanting to see and read the documents for themselves, which would have been interesting for anyone who knew T. J.'s handwriting. If he'd written to Leathley & Co., they would have a sample themselves.

    These are only the opening salvos. Leathley & Co were again involved, which meant that the Wards were clearly being used by powerful Catholic interests to attack someone they knew was anti-Catholic. Once the battle was joined neither side seemed to give a damn for the Wards, or even Martha Ann. This descended into a sectarian war being fought out in the English High Court. It soon transpired that far from wanting Martha Ann to return to her home with the Wards, which even they recognised was fraught with danger, Leathley & Co. and their backers wanted to put Martha Ann into a Catholic home run by nuns.

So here we go again, it is just like the Gossage case and the Catholic home they had in mind for him. The last thing that crossed the mind of any of the participants was what the children themselves might have wanted. We come again to the question of whether the children were people or property, and property to be passed around without reference, as suited the grown-ups. Of course they couldn't ask them because, according to T. J., they had gone missing. As Oscar Wilde might have said, to lose one child could be said to be unfortunate, but to lose two so completely inside a couple of days does sound like complete carelessness. That's if they were lost, of course.

There was a perfectly justifiable argument in saying that the appalling treatment Martha Ann had suffered was good reason for his utter determination not to send her back to the Wards. The question we are entitled to ask, from the safety of our hindsight and our generation's different attitudes, is whether T. J. could have argued that the girl having been so badly treated, then even under Victorian law the parental rights claimed by the Wards had reverted to the state, so it was now the duty of the court to act as custodian and make a direction as to her future care and upbringing. That really would have opened up a huge new can of worms, and a lot of lawyers would have made even more money than they did out of it.

The point is raised because essentially it is the situation we have today. The state invokes its reserve powers when parental care fails, and it is what happens when a child is 'put into care' in cruelty cases, as the Ward case obviously was at its beginning. The Ward and Gossage cases are where the philosophical osmosis started and the long journey towards the 1908 Children's Act began, and from that seminal piece of legislation we have come to have our present-day views.

However much the court may have sympathised with all that had it ever been presented, things had moved on. It wasn't the intention of the Catholic side to send Martha Ann back to the Wards, but to a Catholic establishment where she would be brought up as a good little Catholic. Opposing this idea was T. J., who wanted her brought up as a good little Protestant. That was the crux of the argument between the two sides. What was being argued by Leathley & Co. was that Margaret Ward, as the child's mother, could have been Lucretia Borgia or the Gorgon Medusa, but she nevertheless owned proprietary rights over Martha Ann. It was obvious that Margaret was merely a pawn in other people's power plays, that she was in no position to argue, and wouldn't have been listened to had she tried. From Martha Ann's point of view it would have been terrifying had she known about it. We can at least agree on one thing: just as well that T. J. had got her clear.

When the case was reconvened, Mr Justice Matthew had the assistance on the bench of Mr Justice Grantham. Judge Matthew was definitely not happy with T. J. and said that he was in contempt of court. He didn't send him to prison, which was an option, but he ordered that he must be ready to answer questions from the Ward lawyers as and when they were ready. Judge Grantham was vociferous in his condemnation. Speaking of T. J., he is reported as saying,

> He is quite unworthy to be entrusted with large sums of money for the maintenance of a charitable institution, quite unworthy to be entrusted with the care of such numbers of children, if he is capable of acting in such a way as he has acted in this case. He has not right to question the moral competence of the mother to have custody of her child, and even if he did so, he had no right to make himself the judge of so delicate a point.

This gives us a window on the thought processes of people like Grantham. Regarding the probity with which T. J. handled the money, that wasn't an issue and therefore wasn't admissible. Regarding his right to have a view on Margaret Ward's morals, if he thought that Martha Ann was in danger of being subjected to criminality if she stayed with the Wards, he had not merely rights but a duty. Where he went astray was in taking the law into his own hands, though the law available was so weighted against the child it was a near-impossible situation. Hence the view expressed that children were being treated by the law as possessions, not as citizens. The whole reason Martha Ann had come to the Homes via the George Muller Orphanage was that she was running away from just such criminality. Is Grantham saying that she had not right to run? What do you think? With such an ace in his hand, why didn't T. J. play it? The answer can only be that he was as much a bigoted idiot in his own way as Grantham was in his.

That the state has reserve powers never seems to have occurred to anyone, yet all states proclaim that they have them. Every state has the power and the duty to guard its citizens' rights. The citizen child Martha Ann had a right to an upbringing free from domestic moral and physical danger, diligently delivered. It takes two people to make a contract, and the other party in all this is the state. She had a clear contract with the state that it would protect her if things went wrong. There is a vast army of legal eagles who would be only too pleased to take your money if you wished to learn more about Victorian law on this subject, and how it might differ from what it is now. As you will gather from all this, the Homes lost.

To put it bluntly, the nation that was going around the world murdering populations in order to steal countries and calling it an empire didn't have what it took to protect one twelve-year-old girl! In other words, Grantham was to all appearances arguing that Margaret Ward had rights of possession over the life and liberty of her daughter, irrespective of the evidence. The counter argument, which T. J. never introduced, was that because of that evidence Margaret Ward had forfeited her rights, and her rights had to be taken up by the court, representing the state. As things turned out, no one involved in what became a huge case realised that such a line of discussion existed. In our modern times, that in a nutshell is what we have come to.

Of course all that begs the question of what motivated the opposing sides, and the answer is that it was sectarian war. In defence of Judge Grantham we have to bear in mind that he was a Victorian, very much a product of his age. He was dealing with this under Victorian law, Victorian social attitudes and all the legal baggage – or we might say the desperate lack of the right sort of legal baggage – that the subject carried. Grantham did, towards the end, grudgingly acknowledge that T. J. had done great work on behalf of destitute children, which was little concession in the context of his general tirade about his behaviour, some of which wasn't even relevant to the case before the court.

The Barnardo Trust Committee met to consider the position. Had John Sands or Lord Cairns still been alive everything would surely have been done differently. In the absence of their wise counsel the committee allowed T. J. to bully them into going along with what he was doing. They agreed that it was wrong to transfer children out of the Homes on purely religious grounds. The staying power of that position within the law then in force was very much an issue; it was really what much of the argument was about. What we might find incredible in the records of the meeting is T. J.'s remark that he was only seeking their opinion, it was down to him to take the final responsibility. By 1889, when all this was happening, T. J. had been a paid servant of the trust for about six years. It was the committee's responsibility – they were the legal entity, not him! It was on just this point that the Arbitration Court in 1879 had ruled that a Committee must be created. The reason for the ruling was to stop T. J. from running riot and to keep him in some sort of check.

We must again be grateful to *The Times* for an extract from their Law Reports columns of 16 May 1889. This was eight days before the hearing. This is a story which has to be classed as speculation, as the salient points were never proved, but the newspaper had a good reputation and wasn't often far wrong. By this time the Homes were boarding out many of their children with reliable supporters, a system we will explore in a later chapter. It was suggested that Martha Ann had been boarded out with a Mrs Grogan, probably the previous summer. The story was that Martha Ann, far from being sent on a luxurious excursion around Europe, had been sent instead to Canada as part of the institution's rapidly expanding emigration programme. Like so many things that T. J. got mixed up in, Mrs Grogan was never traced, and she may have been the proverbial red herring trying to put the hunters off the scent. Or she may have been transmuted by T. J.'s special brand of circumlocution, his magic with words, into the mysterious Gertrude Romand, who didn't turn up either.

*

Charles and William Baker were brothers and both barristers. By now Charles was the trust's lawyer, and when the committee agreed to let the Ward case go to appeal both brothers agreed to assist. A few weeks later the appeal was thrown out. The tipping point was not that the mother was being deprived of her child, but that Martha Ann had been put beyond the court's jurisdiction. What could annoy the court more? The defence that the child was beyond the jurisdiction of the court before the writ was issued was not acceptable. One can see that to have come to any other conclusion would have opened the floodgates to a thousand others, who unlike T. J. would have had criminal intent from the word go.

Shall we agree that all that is logical? The normal procedure was that the Homes entered into a written contract with the parents that they would take on the job of bringing up the child or children. There was nothing in these contracts which implied that the Homes were allowed to send them abroad without permission. Indeed in the case of Martha Ann there was a specific prohibition in respect to Canada. The whole deal implies that in each case the child would remain in Britain, within the jurisdiction of the British courts. In respect of these contracts there were three people, the Homes, the parents and so often forgotten by the lawyers, the child. These contracts were made in Britain, signed for in Britain, between people and institutions resident in Britain. The implication – do we really have to write it down in words of one syllable? – was that British law applied. There seems to be nothing in the agreement implying that the Homes had any right to move the child in an unrestricted way to third parties such as Norton or Romand, or without permission to move them outside the reach of British law. What T. J. did seems to be a complete breach of a written contract. This is yet another line of argument which never came up for discussion as the case proceeded.

When the court threw out the appeal it was inevitable that Leathley & Co. would go back to the Gossage case and in November 1889 there was another writ of *habeas corpus*. The money that was being spent on these legal wrangles could have kept several hundred children in the Homes for a year. As you can imagine, it was something that was said with rising anger among the supporters and donors. There was an unsuccessful campaign to raise money to pay for the legal fees, which fell with a dull thud. While people were still happy to support the Homes, they were outraged at being asked to support the lawyers in their mansions. Giving on the general account stalled but thankfully didn't go down, so costs for running the Homes could be met, but it didn't go up either.

But if the committee agreed to continue with the cases, the institution was liable and the lawyers expected to be paid. Advised by the Bakers, the committee agreed to contest the latest writ. The Bakers seeing themselves as interested parties, another solicitor was employed to help T. J. in the proceedings. By this time he had angina, he had always been short-sighted and he was now going deaf. There had been an upgrading of the status of the case, to the top man in the country no less. Presiding was Lord Esher, who as Master of the Rolls was the president of the Court of Appeal. So the judiciary were taking this very seriously.

In his usual way T. J. more or less took over, making a speech which took the best part of two days to deliver. Quite how much of it was scripted and how much unscripted we will never know, but his own edited version of it appeared in the house magazine *Night and Day* as a special booklet. One of the things he had to say drew him a great deal of sympathy, even from his most outspoken opponents. There had been an outbreak of diphtheria at the end of the previous year and his son Ken had died on 10 January 1890. These proceedings were about two weeks later.

While the writ referred now to the Gossage case, everything said in it should be read bearing in mind the case of Martha Ann Ward. These cases would become more and more inextricably linked. The main thrust of his argument, as we would expect, was an attack against what he alleged was the conduct of Mrs Gossage. She was depicted as the woman who had let little Henry down, hadn't cared for him and still didn't care for him. She wasn't a proper person to bring the boy up. Lord Esher rejected that as a proper line to take. From his perspective he said it wasn't envisaged that Mrs Gossage would be taking her son back home, but that another institution similar to Barnardo's would be doing it. Then he hit the nail of what we have been discussing squarely on the head. If T. J. had sent Henry to Canada he hadn't obtained the permission of the mother, and his reading of the law was that it was imperative that he should have done so. The judge, and they didn't come higher up the scale than Lord Esher, saw it as an argument between Barnardo's and St Vincent's, and the winner was the one Mrs Gossage backed. Breaking the law, even with the very best intentions, was still breaking the law, and on this point T. J. had broken the law.

Again it is worth making the point that the proposition of the citizen child was never introduced, let alone that the child had rights and the state had duties towards it. If your favourite legal eagle, having taken your money, tells you that there was no such thing as a citizen child at that point in the Victorian era, do not be surprised. However we are, as has been pointed out, in 1890, so in that they may be slightly off track. In the previous few months there had been an Act of Parliament by the long-winded title of *The Prevention of Cruelty to and the Better Protection of Children Act*. So the repeated proposition that the state had a duty was at least beginning to be recognised. Just the fact that it had that title, even if the content wasn't all that exciting, was progress. There had also been a new Poor Law Act, of which much the same might be said, not very good but better than what was before.

Although the Child Cruelty Act wasn't wonderful, it was obviously a matter of some importance that the situation had been changed by its passage into law during the course of the proceedings, and all parties would need to take those changes into account. It was also a matter of importance that T. J. couldn't avoid introducing comparisons with the Martha Ann Ward case, and the fact that he had lost it. Legal readings are largely based on precedent, where a precedent exists, and Lord Esher and his colleagues would be able to make use of the case in their view of this new Gossage writ. For this reason T. J. beat them to it by saying openly that he realised the two were linked. A man of great eloquence once he got going, he did very well, if a bit short of brilliance. He then summed up his case with a last well-aimed shot. We will dispense with the long-winded preamble, but for the sake of clarity this still has to be paraphrased.

> It is very remarkable that while the tide of public opinion and the action of the legislature are steadily proceeding towards the limitation of parents' rights and powers when parents do not perform their duties, that it is at this very juncture that the courts are disposed as illustrated in the Tye case and this, to extend the doctrine of *habeas corpus*, so as to enable parents of the very class contemplated in the Act I have quoted, to resume their powers over children whom they have grossly neglected. [Note he still calls Martha Ann the Tye case, not Ward.]

It was a well-phrased conclusion and is the source of why we have been discussing it. It didn't change the opinion of the Master of the Rolls, who ducked it completely and went back to what was for him far safer ground. It was, he insisted, merely an argument between two entrenched religious camps. He then delivered this short comment.

> It is much to be regretted that good people when animated by religious motives, would not act with that candour and openness which they display in any other circumstances. I cannot approve of such modes of conduct. I therefore think that the writ should be issued.

It was a delicately phrased way of telling T. J. that he thought he'd been too economical with the truth far too often, without coming to the point of calling him a liar. Had he done so then T. J. would have been up to his ears on a charge of perjury. In order to buy some time T. J. immediately launched an appeal to the House of Lords. He was shrewd enough to realise that he would almost certainly lose, but that the wheels of justice grind exceedingly small and exceedingly slowly. With ordinary good fortune the case wouldn't come to the top of the list for about two years, and maybe in that time it would have quietly faded away.

His greatest problem was that he was not fighting the Gossage and Ward backers, he was now fighting the system. As had been said by Lord Esher, even if he had broken the law with the best of intentions, he had nevertheless broken the law. The legal system intended to defend itself. The one thing he had on his side was the Cruelty to Children Act, which had yet to bed down in the law book. He could point to the fact that it had been his own agitation, along with the rest of the philanthropic world, that had achieved this change. His argument was that the legal position of children must henceforth be taken far more seriously. When the appeal finally came up in the Lords, it would be an ideal test case against which to measure the force of the new legislation.

*

And just to make sure that no one dozed off in the interim, he got himself embroiled in a third case, which we immediately realise springs from all too familiar origins: his fanatical anti-Catholic stance. Enter now John James Roddy, said to have been born in 1878 as the illegitimate son of Margaret Roddy. It is phrased like that because while the Family Records Centre have several Johns and a couple of Jameses, it was not possible to find a birth certificate for John James Roddy, though the records were searched all the way through from 1874 to 1884.

It is perfectly possible that Margaret Roddy may not have been able to bring herself to go to the registrar and say that her baby was illegitimate, which was a terrible stigma at the time. A great many such babies were kept close and never registered for this reason. No one honed hypocrisy to such a shine as the Victorians. In the case of John James Roddy he was certainly baptised. In fact rather oddly he was baptised twice, once as a Catholic, once as an Anglican. Whether she was in some way trying to make amends for her legal omission we will never know, but what she actually did was sow the seeds of a great deal of confusion.

In 1880 Margaret married a man called McHugh, about whom little is known, other than that he fell ill, lost his job and ended up in the workhouse. One does however note that it could just possibly be an Irish name, and a lot of Irish people were Catholics. There is nothing to suggest he was the boy's father, but everything to suggest that she was a poor judge of men. She, however, seems to have been a respectable and hard-working woman. Her main source of income was as a domestic cleaner, for which she earned 10 shillings (50p) a week. That wasn't much even in those days. Her rent was 3 shillings (15p) a week, which left her with a shilling a day to feed herself and her son. When we translate those figures into 2000 values it is about £24 a week. It could hardly keep a mouse in cheese, let alone Margaret and her growing boy. When John James was ten years old she finally admitted defeat and in 1888 she managed to get him admitted to the Barnardo Homes.

The case arose out of her desire for access rights. Here was a loving mother who wanted the best for her son, but she did need a hug every now and then. She appears to have written several letters, so we can appreciate the great advances in literacy over the previous decades and the availability of the Penny Post for their delivery. Matters came to a head in September 1889, when she wrote that she wanted to visit the Homes to see her son. To us it sounds perfectly reasonable, but it's where the spark lit the powder. She received what was on the face of it a nice enough reply, telling her that the boy was doing very well and any letters she wanted to write to him could be sent via the office. However she couldn't come to see him as he was living in the country. The letter gave her no more details than that. A few days later she was chatting to one of her nieces about how disappointed she was, and the niece was on the Catholic side of the family and was a regular churchgoer. Are we surprised that when the niece asked her priest for advice our friends Leathley & Co. appeared on the scene?

Before we start blaming the Barnardo Homes too quickly, let's stand back and consider one or two things. By this time there were over 3,500 children in residence, some within the Homes, a lot more being fostered out around the country. That for a start tells us how hugely successful Barnardo Homes had become. It appears that John James Roddy was one of the fostered children.

If we think about visiting day in a prison, the wives are allowed to visit their husbands, they can talk, there are several warders with oversight supervision all the time, or at least that's the theory. The aim is to end up with the same number of prisoners you started with. Now try organising that sort of thing when the children (in our case) are living all over the country. Just the travel would be a nightmare, the motor car had only been invented five years earlier and there were maybe fifty in the entire world. How do you do the logistics and guarantee that at the end of the day you end up with the same number of children you started with? What uproar would there be if someone who wasn't the real parent managed to gain access and there was an abduction? All hell would break loose and everyone would blame the Homes, none of them would blame themselves.

That was some of the thinking which was behind the Barnardo Homes policy. Add to that idea the fact that so many of these children had been rescued from a rotten family life, which was why they were in the Homes in the first place, and it would be a disaster for them if they went back. So we can see that the Homes had a legitimate point. The welfare of the child came first and they didn't want any upsets caused by family contacts, given that so many of the families were of an unsavoury nature. Margaret Roddy McHugh wasn't that sort of mother. That didn't quite make her an anomaly, but it did make her rather different. Trouble arrived with a strong wind behind it when T. J. and the office failed to appreciate that vital point.

Let us refer back to T. J.'s long address to the court in the Gossage case, and pick up on the remarks when he was talking about the new Child Cruelty Act. He used the phrase 'so as to enable parents of the very class contemplated in the Act'. The use of the word class in this case doesn't mean social class, what he means is type, the sort of person who would in this context be cruel to children. It was a middle-class teacher in an upper- and middle-class prep school who gave little Winston Churchill such a thrashing that his upper-class American mother removed him immediately. It wasn't just the working class who thrashed children.

Some of the problem may have been that the middle-class T. J. was dealing with a poverty-stricken working-class woman. Simply put, he would have had an ingrained sense of superiority born of the class gulf, which didn't recognise that Margaret Roddy McHugh was literate enough to be able to write letters, something that he in his ragged school had been working so energetically to make possible. There is a line from a Victorian hymn, 'the rich man in his castle, the poor man at his gate'. Poor Margaret was at his middle-class gate, so she had to fit certain preconceptions in his middle-class mind. Preconceptions he'd spent his lifetime as an educationalist trying to destroy, and he failed to realise that in her case he had succeeded.

Margaret Roddy McHugh comes over very much as a mother desperate for the welfare of her son, who had given him up reluctantly because he would have a better life in the Homes than she could give him. She hadn't seen him for a year and like any other good mother, she missed him. The husband never featured in the case, he was in the workhouse. One feels that if the niece hadn't been a churchgoing Catholic who asked her priest for advice, things would never have run out of control in the way that they did. The Homes had a perfectly understandable policy, which could be explained over a cup of tea in the office, and T. J. and Margaret could have worked something out between them. Here was a mum who wanted the evidence of her own eyes, and she wanted a hug. We can all like Margaret, she comes across as a nice lady. It all went wrong when religious sectarian antipathy stuck its ugly nose into the affair. Doesn't it always?

When he was served notice that the case was going to court, T. J. did in fact go a little way towards trying to do some sort of a deal. If Margaret would pull out of the case they could find a resolution between them. If she didn't he would go looking for any dirt he could find about her. If he found any it would be made public. It was probably this letter more than anything else that made her continue. She was insulted, and seems to have decided she no longer wanted John James kept in the care of someone who could write to her in such un-Christian terms.

The case went to court and we are by no means surprised to find Mr Justice Matthew, but this time sitting with Lord Chief Justice Coleridge. So last time it was the Master of the Rolls, now we have the head of the Criminal Bar. We cannot complain about the status of the judiciary who were taking an interest in this tangle. Was there now a hint that T. J. might be guilty of crimes rather than just civil misdemeanours which led Lord Coleridge to be there? Here we go again with a writ of *habeas corpus*, and both sides were given a week to present affidavits. Between them the two sides presented twenty. Much of the contents on the Barnardo side were reports written by agents investigating Margaret Roddy McHugh.

The next mistake T. J. made was trying to fool the court over his intake records. There had been the usual intake photograph, but he omitted it from his initial presentation. He told the tale of young John James arriving in the usual flea- and lice-infested condition and dressed in rags, the usual emaciated urchin. The truth which quickly emerged was that Margaret was a cleaner by both employment and habit, what little she had she kept clean and that included her son. In fact one of the people she cleaned for had given some decent if second-hand clothes for John James to wear when he went away to the Homes. That speaks well of her standing with her employers. It also emerged that while the boy wasn't overfed, he certainly wasn't half-starved either. When this emerged in the early stages of the evidence, the judges took the dimmest of dim views of T. J. and his story. Whether, on the other hand, these very middle-class Victorian gentlemen took very much notice of Margaret and her side of things is another matter. They were, as has been said before, products of their society and their era.

Habeas corpus means 'produce the body'. The difference was that in this case the body, that is to say John James, had been produced, and he was actually in the court building. The judges decided to go and have a chat with him and actually treat him as a person, not just a parcel to be passed around from hand to hand. Quite a concession in those days from a couple of high and mighty judges to make to a working-class eleven-year-old. What they found was a neat and tidy lad, obviously bright and intelligent, happy where he was living and who simply didn't know what the fuss was about. Whoever else was complaining, it definitely wasn't him. As for his relationship with his mother, he loved her very much, wouldn't think of complaining about her and she certainly had never neglected him.

Having had their face-to-face interview with the central subject of the whole affair, they returned to announce that they would adjourn the case until after Whitsun. It was to take a lot longer, because the judgement wasn't announced until 6 August. In it the judges came down angrily on T. J., accusing him of making a most scurrilous attack on Margaret Roddy McHugh, which they declared her son had, without any coaching from them, utterly refuted. They concluded by saying that in their view the best thing for John James was to leave him in the foster home that had been found for him, and where he was quite happy. They went on to say that T. J., by his behaviour, was in their view unfit to have the uncontrolled and absolute power he claimed over Mrs McHugh's child, and that Mrs McHugh was entitled to insist that her son be withdrawn from his influence.

It would seem that he had dragged defeat out of the jaws of victory in a fight that should never happened, and which he could so easily have avoided. It may seem incredible to us with the benefit of our hindsight, but T. J. appealed. Knowing him now as well as we do, it was some sort of knee-jerk reaction. However, knowing that his legal status was only as a paid employee of the trust, why did the committee allow it?

It is a fact of British law that appeals cannot go over all the same grounds again, they can only review points of law that the appellant disputes. An appeal is not a retrial. The quote from Lord Esher below makes that clear. Everyone involved in this tangle knew that the Gossage, Tye Ward and Roddy McHugh cases were similar tunes played on the same fiddle. The argument in all three cases wasn't that any of the children had been mistreated in Barnardo Homes. It was an argument over possession between the powerful Catholic interests and the openly declared Protestant stance T. J. had taken up and wouldn't shift from. This was a disreputable religious war and the judges were embarrassed and angry for having been dragged into it.

A new factor was brought into the Roddy McHugh affair, that of guardianship. Again we shake our modern heads in wonder. Margaret was still alive, and unless she was declared incompetent by reason of insanity, or she was shown to have criminally mistreated her son, she remained his legal guardian. Where it was agreed he would lodge and be educated was a different matter. In each of the other two cases the mothers had failed their children, so there was a case for taking their respective child away from them. That doesn't apply in any way to Margaret. She was quite plainly a poor but respectable working-class woman being used as a shuttlecock between two wealthy middle-class religious factions. She was being shouted down and her natural rights usurped. There was a Mr Walsh, about whom nothing is known but his name, who was the choice of the Catholics. He appears to have been an upright and worthy citizen of excellent reputation. A previous Lord Mayor of London, Alderman Sir Robert Fowler, was the nominee of Barnardo Homes.

As before T. J. argued his own case and tried to widen the scope of the discussion, which made the bench even more annoyed. Sitting for the appeal were Lord Esher, assisted by two other eminent judges, Lord Justice Lindley and Lord Justice Lopes. Once more we cannot complain about the seniority of the judiciary involved. Lord Esher was obliged to pull him up when T. J. was in full flow, and remind him that an appeal was not a retrial.

> What we have to do, as I have told you before, is to consider the law. Suppose you leave out all that about yourself and what the judges said about you. They also said that they were strongly of the opinion that Mrs McHugh was entitled to insist that her son should be withdrawn from your institution. Is that not so? We have now to consider whether the judgement is according to the law or not. This is all we have to do.

It is really to nobody's surprise that the appeal was lost, and with our usual use of hindsight it's a good question to ask why it was ever launched. The trouble was that T. J. insisted on representing himself, and he had a fool for a client! Lord Justice Lopes summed up by saying that it came down to an argument as to which of two competing institutions John James should go to, and whether Margaret Roddy McHugh as the boy's mother had the right to decide that. In what is a clear nod towards the new atmosphere, where it was beginning to be accepted that children were people, not just property, he also said that the interests of the child were central and should be protected. He said that he joined with his colleagues in dismissing the appeal, but he doubted if a change of surroundings would in fact be entirely aimed by those involved at John James's welfare. One feels that he was a man who was getting used to the change in the wind, but still liked to wear his old coat.

Lord Esher summed up his views by laying bare all the bones of the dispute in no uncertain fashion. 'It is a fight over the soul, not the body of the child.' Well said my Lord, well said indeed! Lord Lindley was of a similar view to his colleagues, and said in equally plain terms that the case should never have come up. He sided with his colleagues and found in favour of the mother. As in the Gossage case, plain damned awkward and never one to admit he was wrong, T. J. took his case to the House of Lords, where in July 1891 it was thrown out again. At that point he was obliged to hand the boy over. If he hadn't appealed, the sentiment of the remarks made in the original court leaves one to feel John James may well have been left in his original foster home.

As a footnote on the other two cases in this vast tangle, modern computerisation of archives is becoming a greater and greater help to researchers. More things can now be found by those who know which buttons to press than it was possible to find even in the last decade of the twentieth century. More and more data is being freely milled through internet search engines. Research done with the assistance of people in Canada has found no trace of Henry Gossage entering Canada. If as T. J. claimed he went over early in 1890, he should have been on the census of 1891 or at least 1901. As matters transpired he was never traced, nor has he ever come up in that name on any British census. The same remarks apply to Martha Ann Tye Ward. In whichever part of that choice of names she chose to use, she also has never been traced.

I will therefore run an idea, trying to understand T. J. and how he thought, because first and foremost he was acknowledged as being devoted to all the thousands of children he helped. Without a shred of evidence in support, might it have been that neither child left the country, and, as has already been suggested, William Norton and Gertrude Romand were figments of his fertile imagination?

Consider Britain at the time. It had big cities such as London, Birmingham and so forth, it had country towns and it had lots and lots of villages. Most of the fostering families were in the country villages. The fostering families were country folk who still looked on a visit to the county town as a bit of an adventure, and if they ever went to London it was enough to talk about for the next year. No motor cars, no telephones or television, no twenty-four-hour worldwide news, but a pastoral setting, local squire, church and pub either side of the village green. Take a child from one village setting and move it 100 miles to another village setting, and who would know? Small children are always called by their first names, their surnames aren't really important to them. Tell them that with the move they will be using a new one. And don't tell the new family there is anything odd going on.

My view is that T. J. at his most eloquent could not only think it up, he possessed the barefaced effrontery to pull it off. No one ever quite came to the point of calling him a liar, but one finds it difficult to look on his conduct in any other way in these three cases. And in the countryside of Britain in the 1890s he could get away with it. As I say, there isn't a shred of proof, but when one thinks it through, a man who from a standing start twenty years earlier had built up the Homes from nothing to the national institution it had then become, was capable of a very great deal which would be beyond ordinary folk like us. I am aware of a claim, made in a mid-twentieth-century book on the general subject of our hero and the Homes, that at some later time T. J. did make contact with Henry Gossage. The claim does not extend to Martha Ann Tye Ward. The claim, which is said to be in a book I have only heard about and not traced so not read, appears to trace back to T. J. himself. Given the back-story and my opinion as stated, I retain my doubts. There is nothing reliable which records how John James fared in his change of circumstances. We can only hope that they came to no harm and all fared well. My suggestions are perhaps more hopeful for them than some of the other possibilities.

Without the help of friends and supporters T. J. would have been personally bankrupt. The committee had been established to stop him being so stupid and doing things like this, and was a total failure in its duty. He was the subject of a great deal of unpopularity, and any vague hope he might have harboured of some official recognition, some minor order or even a knighthood, died in the ashes, never to rise again. He had offended too many influential people by his conduct. Appeals for help for his legal bills fell on deaf ears, even though most people continued to support the Homes. Financially it was costly and had diverted time and huge sums of money from the original cause of helping the children.

Morally it was something else entirely. As the old proverb says, it's an ill wind that blows no good. The two sides had been hammering away at each other in a stinking sweat of bigotry. One effect of this, which neither antagonist had calculated, was to stir up the muddy subject of children and their rights, even asking if children had any rights! It is no coincidence that the Child Cruelty Act and another, the Custody of Children Act, were both in their own ways direct and beneficial outcomes of the great publicity the tangle of wrangles attracted. It is no coincidence either that the highest-ranking judiciary took personal interest in it all. Things were brought to the public notice from the bottom to the top of society that they had never thought about before, and they were shocked. To that extent it advanced the status as well as the care of children.

The nastiness of the conduct of the antagonists, both protesting their Christianity, was at the expense of their own dignity. It was an argument about which brand of religious manure produced the better Christian turnip. Children are children, they aren't turnips. How many residential and boarded-out places at the Homes could have been provided by the money involved is of course a very good question. I do not want to create the impression that my main concern is to criticise T. J. and in any way to denigrate the work he was doing. No one is perfect. Much to the surprise of all my friends and family, that even includes me. In my mind T. J. was very much like Matilda in the famous poem. When he was good he was very, very good, but when he was bad he was horrid. This has been the chapter of his horrid period. Behind all this horridness he was still doing a brilliant job of leading his wonderful team of East Enders on the crusade to better the conditions they were living in. That never stopped, it grew and grew and made more and more of a difference to their lives.

The Homes did recover ground in the eyes of the general public, and after a bit of a plateau in giving, cash flow did improve. In 1889 they pulled in £106,000, and reached £198,000 in 1906, the year after our hero died. These translate in 2000 values to just over £8 million and just over £14 million respectively. It sounds a lot if you say it quickly, but it was a drop in the bucket compared with the amount needed. Matters have progressed on into our own era, and these days the state fully accepts the child citizen concept, and that the state has a responsibility towards all children.

EIGHT

Emigration and its Many Problems: 1886–1896

The way a mountain lake maintains its natural depth is that in compensation for all the streams that flow into it, there is at least one of sufficient size that flows out of it. So it is with any system, there has to be some sort of outflow to stop the thing from becoming clogged up and stopping. The same natural order of things was needed with Barnardo Homes. They had a wide variety of streams of children flowing in to use their facilities, but they didn't have infinite resources of supplies, money, property or staff. While the older lads and girls steadily left, as they were educated, trained up and were found jobs, even then they often needed lodgings, which were found for them at an affordable rent, until the young person had been established in the world of work. It was a good system, but it was often suffering from serious overload. In addition there was the problem that we were discussing when looking at Barkingside, where the Village was accepting girls who because of severe learning and other difficulties could never be allowed back out into the general community. There was a need for a regular and reliable outlet to relieve the pressure which was being imposed by a long list of problems.

The first line of relief was boarding out. It allowed for far more children to be brought under the protection of the institution at a reasonable cost, and did not require the space, the beds, supplies and so forth at Stepney Causeway and all their other addresses. More on this in our next chapter. What we will be discussing now is the thorny subject of emigration, and just how thorny may come as quite a surprise. We will start by paraphrasing from the *Memoirs* one of Thomas John Barnardo's long and wonderfully wordy quotes.

Well planned and wisely conducted child emigration, especially to Canada, contains at its heart the truest solution of some of the Mother Country's most perplexing problems, and the supply of our colony's most urgent needs. First it relieves the overcrowded centres of city life and the congested labour markets at home, while at the same time it lessens in a remarkable manner the burdens of taxation. Second it supplies what the colony is most in want of, an increase in the English-speaking population. Third it confers upon the children themselves some great advantages. The change at the young and formative period of their lives, gives to each child whose character is good and who is successfully absorbed into the colonial population, an immediate prospect of an independent existence at a higher level than anyone would have thought possible. I regard with amazement the unwillingness of a great administrative department of government to sanction a small expenditure for the maintenance of its child clients in one of our colonies, at half the annual rate that is already being incurred in maintain the same children in England. In all probability this small annual expenditure, if carried out in the colonies, would only continue for a very short period, say about three years, compared with the length of time over which the charge must extend if such children are retained in England.

All of which sounds wonderful until we start digging deeper. In this passage there are some telling comments on the period and on the mindset of even such a nice chap as our hero. We are all the products of the times in which we live, and he was no different. Canada had been fought over by the British and the French, who in their imperial ways had ignored the rightful owners, the First Nation tribes. In the Seven Years' War of 1756–63 the French lost the vital Battle of the Plains of Abraham near Quebec. Both the opposing generals died, the British lost Wolfe and the French lost Montcalm. This paved the way for Canada becoming a British colony. Victorious in arms, what it left in peace was a very large number of French-speaking Canadians in the Quebec area. To this day a large percentage of the population are Québécois, retaining French as their first language.

The repetitive reference to colonies is part of the linguistic colour of Victorian Britain. The empire was enormous and still growing, while on the frock-coat covering that fat imperial belly there was an ever-growing stain of home-grown poverty and exploitation. Some were beginning to be ashamed of it, but even in the 1880s translating that shame out of hypocrisy and into action had some way to go. The main concern for T. J. was the East End of London, and he had growing difficulties that needed solutions.

He wrote in the plural, but his concentration was on Canada. That was where virtually all his emigration efforts were to be directed up until his death in 1905. Geographically it was the nearest large colony that he could easily reach. As he says in his quote, emigration was a way of expanding the English-speaking population, which in Canada would reinforce English as the main official language at the expense of French. France was still seen as an imperial rival and in Britain at the time this was a popular thing to say.

There are various things we can think about on his mention of money. It seems to have been a plea to the government, quite which department he had in mind is not exactly clear, to come up with some support for the programme. Keeping children in a workhouse, even at a low subsistence rate, was an expense. Sending them to Canada ought to be a cheaper option. He also seems to be touting for some support for them, at least for the first three years after they arrived. He makes a great deal out of his suggestion that emigration seems to be a cheaper option. If this was the case, then anything that costs less and gives a better result is surely music to a politician's ears. If you don't agree, answers on a postcard! Whether at the Canadian end the ultimate expense would have been less is a question with a great many complications. At this long distance of time we aren't really qualified to discuss it.

Up to 1884 emigration played only a small part in the affairs of the institution. There are various comments in the records suggesting that it had occurred to him as an idea in the very early days, but other things had been more urgent. The *Memoirs* provide us with figures for emigration from 1869 up to 1906, the year after he died. For the eighteen years up to 1883 this was a mere trickle averaging about sixty-nine a year. This shot up as the programme greatly increased from 1884 onwards, and by 1906 the yearly figure was substantially above 1,000 a year. In the same thirty-seven-year period the emigration to other colonies and dominions was a mere 473 altogether. Of the very few who went out to Australia, the star Barnardo boy was Big Jim Paige. Australia changed from being a colony to a self-governing dominion in 1901. Jim Paige became a Member of the House of Representatives for Queensland and was a leading light in Australian politics for several years.

Australia had been relieved of the dubious distinction of being the dumping ground for Britain's criminal throw-outs when the Transportation system was terminated. Begun in 1788, it ended in 1868. It had behind it a theme we have touched on already, sending English-speaking people to fill up a great big empty land. Or, shall we say, empty if you ignore the Aborigines, which, with imperial frock-coat duly stained, they did. Once transported, a small proportion did return, the most famous of these being the Tolpuddle Martyrs, half a dozen farm labourers convicted of what was then considered a heinous crime, trying to form a trade union. Transportation had previously been tried in early attempts to populate North America for the same English-language reason prior to 1776, but at that time it seems to have been something Canada managed to avoid. After the end of Transportation to Australia this was to change, and Canada was to be on the receiving end of a wave of immigration. While the immigration was in their case voluntary, the Canadians didn't always like what landed among them.

Under the impetus of J. A. Macdonald and other leading Canadian politicians, the concept of the self-governing dominion, rather than that of a colony, was developed. Conveniently right at the beginning of our period, in 1867 the Dominion of Canada was created, with Macdonald as its first Prime Minister. This was a revolution of immense importance in the politics of how to run an empire, and was to benefit other colonies as the century changed from the nineteenth to the twentieth.

Canada is a vast country, stretching from east to west 100° of latitude from Newfoundland to British Columbia. From the American border, latitude 49°, it goes northwards most of the way to the North Pole. In those Victorian days Canada was viewed as being virtually unoccupied, so long as they ignored, as they always did, the First Nation tribes, and the Inuit, also known as the Eskimos. It is still possible to this day to view Canada as being underpopulated, considering its vastness. The Inuit are the people of the far north, living in a land from which only they know how to make a living. The incorrectly named Red Indians, who were neither red nor Indian, were present but in nowhere near the numbers of the tribes of the American plains. Estimates of their numbers in Canada were about 100,000 in the late nineteenth century. By then they were already heavily outnumbered by the immigrants from Europe, who were estimated to number close to 5 million. Mostly still in the eastern provinces, Europeans were steadily expanding westwards.

To line up the geography of Canada, first of all, find your map. As the second-biggest country on the planet, slightly bigger than China but considerably smaller than Russia, it's a bit difficult to miss. Along the border with America are the Great Lakes, and north of those is the huge inlet of Hudson's Bay. After the world's four great oceans, Hudson's Bay is the world's eighth-largest sea. So Canada is seriously enormous. Trace a line westwards from the Great Lakes along the line of latitude 50°, so a degree north of the American border, and you will find Winnipeg, capital of Manitoba province. Further west but still just in Manitoba is the town of Russell, on the Shell River.

When we are discussing what was called the Barnardo Industrial Farm, that's where it was. Again it was big, about 15 square miles, what in America would be called a sizeable ranch. The reason for buying it was to use it as a training centre for farming and other skills. It was far too big therefore far too unwieldy, never lived up to the hopes placed in it, and in 1908 was sold off, much to the relief of all those involved with it. When locating other centres, find the St Lawrence and its vast estuary, along which you will find Quebec and Montreal. The estuary is to the east of the Lakes. The Canadian capital of Ottawa is on the Ottawa River, a tributary of the St Lawrence. The town of Peterborough lies just north of Lake Ontario, one of the Great Lakes, and was an important Barnardo base in Canada.

*

This was a time when the newly created Dominion of Canada was flexing its muscles and getting used to its independence. By the time we have reached in our discussions, it was being realised in some quarters that the country was being used as a bit of a dump, not everyone arriving was the sort of person they wanted. Comparisons were made with Australia. Some Transportees may have been harshly done by when they were deported around the world, but the majority were criminals rightly convicted and, under the harsh laws of the day, lucky not to hang.

Did Canada want Britain's roughs and scruffs? The answer was no. In the second half of the Victorian reign, Canada was an increasingly popular destination where Britain could offload its young and destitute. It was T. J.'s ambition to instil into the minds of the Canadian public that his young people were different. Because of their time in the institution they had become highly respectable and hard-working, could be trusted and would be a credit to the new country. The *Memoirs* trumpet this claim, but with regret the claim doesn't totally hold up under close scrutiny. The Canadian venture was fraught with deficiencies, and one of those quite clearly was that T. J. wasn't running it himself. The people he hired to do it for him weren't up to the standard, and a lot of things went pear-shaped. Most of it worked out reasonably well, inevitably there were some star successes, but at the other end of the scale there were far too many sad endings.

There were two redoubtable Victorian spinster ladies, Miss Maria Rye, of whom not so much is heard, and more importantly Miss Annie Macpherson of Stratford, East London. Annie Macpherson was someone T. J. knew quite well. She ran her home for orphans and waifs and in his early days in London he helped her, going there to lead the boys in drill exercises. In the imperial mindset of the era, with an empire to hold on to, army-type drills were very popular. Miss Macpherson was a leading light in the juvenile emigration programme, and by 1870 she had sent several hundred young people over to Canada. Until T. J. set up his own programme he made use of her organisation. The first small party of Barnardo boys went across under her care as early as 1870, and the archives indicate that in 1871 Jim Jarvis was in the next group to leave.

Some of the impetus for developing the programme was that only a quarter of the children were orphans. There was always the danger that among the majority who still had traceable family, attempts would be made to reclaim one of them, and many of these families were so disreputable this would have been disastrous. T. J. did quite blatantly get children out of the country where there was known criminality in the family attempting to reclaim the child. In addition to that perfectly good reason there was also T. J.'s unfortunate sectarianism. It is a fact that he many times flirted with the rough edges of the law, and he wasn't allowed to get away with it every time without a struggle, as the cases we have reviewed make very plain. However, his central claim was that he was there to save the children, to educate and train them to be respectable citizens and make them fit for honest work. Emigration was initially a side issue, it would be at least a decade before it became a serious part of his programme of good works.

To be fair to the authorities on both sides of the Atlantic, as early as 1873 some worries were being expressed. There was by then an increasing and piecemeal emigration especially of small children, some as young as six and seven years old. The archives show that probably the youngest Barnardo child to be sent across was only four years old, which would seem to us to be startlingly out of order. The law in Britain gave the Boards of Guardians responsibility for children in workhouses. As the continuing demands of the evangelistic wing of society began to have effect, conditions were slowly improving in that environment, and an improving sense of responsibility was emerging. In 1874 Andrew Doyle, a Senior Inspector of Workhouses, was sent across to consult with Canadian government agencies and make a thorough investigation into how the children were coping on that side of the Atlantic. He was in Canada for three months and on his return his report should have sounded a clear warning to all. It is unfortunate that little heed was taken of it by most of those involved, T. J. being one of them.

While there were some who had been found comfortable homes, this was not the general case. Writing about the majority, Doyle reported, 'To send them as emigrants can be regarded, not as a way of improving their positions, but simply getting rid of them at a cheap rate.'

That it was cheaper was of course what T. J. had been pointing out in his own comments on the subject which have been quoted above, though he never saw it as a dumping exercise. Doyle's conclusions, and remember this was early in 1874, were against allowing any more workhouse children to emigrate until the Canadians had set up a system of inspections themselves, so as to fully safeguard the children. As a result emigration of workhouse children was stopped and did not start again until ten years later. The hole through the middle of this report was that it only applied to workhouse children. It did not affect the charities such as the Annie Macpherson organisation, who continued to send parties across. How good the Canadian system of inspectors had become by 1884, which is when the workhouses resumed their interest, is an open question. What is not an open question is that childcare in British workhouses was still pretty bad, though getting slightly better as the years passed.

The driving force remained the selfish mindset of the rich and the fecundity of the poor, who went on producing such a tsunami of children. To relieve both the pressure and the consciences of those in charge, let's not temporise about it, Canada would be used as a dump for the overflow for as long as Canada allowed Britain to get away with it. On the face of it Canada seems to have established a strict system of record and inspection, beginning in Britain and followed up in Canada. As the story unfolds we will see that while it weeded out some of the more obvious cases of those who shouldn't travel, any system is only as good as the people who run it. Most problems were not met at this initial stage, most of them were what happened to the children afterwards.

By 1882 emigration was looming larger in T. J.'s plans. The Methodist-run Children's Home was in Bonner Road, also in the East End, near what is at the time of writing the London Chest Hospital. This was run on similar lines to Barnardo Homes in many respects and it was under the supervision of Dr Stephenson, another of those people T. J. knew quite well. Bonner Road evolved over the years into what became the National Children's Homes. Stephenson had already established a Canadian base in Hamilton, Ontario and was happy to work with T. J. and make these facilities available.

In August 1882 a party of fifty-one Barnardo boys left on the good ship *Parisian* from Liverpool for Canada. They were under the charge of the senior manager at Stepney Causeway, Frederick Fielder and his wife. The lads were between fourteen and seventeen years of age, of whom five were thought to have fathers though only one of these had been traced, five had grandparents, eleven had absolutely no traceable relatives. The rest had some sort of family, but not parents. With the aid of the facilities in

Hamilton, within two weeks of arrival all these lads had been found situations.

From general reports in later years it is believed that all of them succeeded in establishing themselves. The important thing to notice with this first party is that they were teenagers, not tiny children. Later on in this story it becomes apparent how important that fact was, and just how pear-shaped things went when this initial rule wasn't followed.

The generally rosy picture that T. J. painted on how well things were going for the children, and which the *Memoirs* continued to promote, does not stand up to close inspection in later years. Obviously he wanted to promote stories of his successes, so we are regaled with the story of Frank. We are never told his surname but apparently Frank was a street acrobat, entertaining the crowds for pennies that might be thrown into his hat. Flea-bitten and filthy he might be, but at least he was fit. Accepted into the Homes he was cleaned up, proved intelligent, learned how to read and at one time wanted to join the band. When the chance came to go to Canada he jumped at it. The story concludes as one of almost fairy-tale promise. In Canada he was found a job in the home of a Member of Parliament. He did so well that a friend of his employer who was a lawyer took him on as a trainee in his legal firm. The story ends there, but we are led to expect him to go to greater things, gain his qualifications and then who knows what successes might have come his way? One swallow doesn't make a summer, and by a very long way one success like Frank doesn't make a universal triumph.

We've all heard the question, 'Do you want the good news or the bad news?' What happened to Frank was good news, and for a large percentage of the young immigrants the news was reasonable. Again we must not lose sight of the good and only think about what went wrong, because a very great deal of all this ended up as successes. It is regrettably true however, that for an unacceptably large number the news was far from good. There were three great differences between Canada and Britain. In winter snowdrifts can be 30 feet high, and the icy blast comes straight down from the Arctic across the vast plains. The country is over 3.8 million square miles, which means distances can be vast. Even in modern times Canada does not have a huge population, and back then it averaged barely two people per square mile. In a lot of it there were no people per square mile, not even the Inuit lived there.

Add to that the distance from home base at Stepney Causeway. Across the Atlantic was 3,000 miles, to which add once you had landed another 1,000 miles to Manitoba. It wasn't yet possible just to pick up a telephone and talk, electronics hadn't been invented. Things T. J. could supervise and keep under close control in Britain he had to entrust to people he engaged over there, but he couldn't supervise the quality of the service delivered. Optimism is no substitute for reality, and he put too much faith in their efforts right up to the day he died. It must be emphasised that most of the staff did a good job, but a number didn't deliver as they should. Andrew Doyle was to be proved absolutely right in his assessment, but with regret his warnings were almost totally ignored, at great cost to the children who weren't as lucky as Frank.

With regret there exist on the files and the records a large number of sad and desperate cases where things went wrong. These include one possible case of manslaughter, though the case was never proved in court. It is not intended to go into the small print and dig out individual details here. All this happened over 100 years ago, and there are in many cases descendants still living in Canada who would not want their family history raked over. The general conclusion one can draw is that only about a quarter of the children got off to a really good start and about half had a hard time but managed to cope. It is with the final quarter that things, by varying degrees, went pear-shaped.

There were reports coming across, and T. J. should have heeded the warnings, but strangely he didn't. This wasn't a case of hindsight, Inspector Doyle had issued his warnings right at the outset, when Barnardo Homes was barely contributing to the flow. We have to wonder why he had such a blind spot, when he was usually so sharp in matters that involved children.

*

What sort of set-up did he establish? By 1883 he had engaged as his agent in Canada a man by the name of Alfred de Brissac Owen. It was his job to set up the Canadian side of the enterprise, and he had to work in co-operation with the immigration departments of the Canadian national and provincial governments. In later years it emerged that he had employed one or two of the immigrant girls as rather more than housemaids, much to the understandable fury of his wife. However it would appear that before these distractions, in the early years, he did a good job. By June 1883 a further party of 100 lads were shipped across. Under the close chaperonage of Miss Emilie Moorcroft, another of those dedicated and redoubtable Victorian spinsters, a party of girls went across in the July. To accommodate these arrivals Owen had found premises at Farley Avenue in Toronto for use as a distribution centre.

In 1884 T. J. went across to Canada on the *Parisian* to do a tour of his growing interests. As an idea of his impression of what he saw, we can quote a sentence, and it is all only one sentence, from a much longer quote.

> Shortly after landing I made my way to Peterborough (Ontario) and there found myself at home at Hazelbrae, the charming house situated a little outside the town, upon a hillside commanding a view of the country round about and standing in its own grounds of some six acres, the whole of which had been the generous gift of the Hon. and Mrs George Cox of that town.

George Cox was a self-made millionaire railway magnate who was also a senator in the Canadian Parliament, which is what earned him the prefix Honourable. This means that T. J. was already adding a list of well-known and influential Canadians to his banner. Hazelbrae was made available on a long-term free loan.

The idea of acquiring a site for an industrial farm was already being investigated. The name may seem a bit odd, but it was intended as the main training centre and it would specialise in agricultural skills. When the final arrangements for the site at Russell were negotiated, both the Canadian government and the provincial Manitoba government came up with grants which covered a great deal of the cost.

This first tour proved to be very extensive and took him to Winnipeg in the central provinces and then out west to the Pacific coast of British Columbia. Quite how many of the children he actually saw in these distant locations is unclear, as most of them were still in the east. What does emerge is that his contact with George Cox was very useful, the railway magnate arranging free travel for most of his journey. On his return T. J. said that he had met several people from the East End who knew him through having been involved with the Edinburgh Castle Mission. The *Memoirs* also provide a revealing note, somewhat outside his general remit, of a visit he made to Toronto prison.

> One is impressed with the sense of humanity which is manifested everywhere. The prisoners are treated as men and women, not as automata. Guilty men and women to be sure, deserving punishment, but having human sympathies, hopes and fears through which they may be reached and benefited. They are not treated like mere machines, as is so often the case with us. On Sunday there is a Sunday school at most of the prisons. Fancy that, a Sunday school for prisoners!

For the late Victorian era that was a very progressive regime. One might of course say that with what was still a very small population and vast acres, maybe crime wasn't the pressing problem it was back in Britain, though inevitably there was some. Another thing he commented on was the very low rate of excessive drinking, a matter close to his temperance heart. Those who drank at all, he assures us, did so in moderation. The French in particular have a long tradition of taking their wine thus, and the Québécois were substantially French by descent. As opposed to the French, a large number of the English speakers were Scots, descendants of victims of the Highland Clearances of the eighteenth and early nineteenth centuries. The Scots were split between the Calvinistic abstainers and those who had a liking for a wee dram or several. We can make of the references to general sobriety what we may wish. It was, one feels, only natural that he was being guided on his tour by people who would instinctively prefer him not to see the unpleasant corners of their society.

By comparison, and again somewhat outside his general remit, he also visited the United States, passing through Chicago, New York and Boston. In each of these cities he persuaded the local police to take him on a tour of their slums. His views of Chicago are really colourful: 'Some cases of social and city life are particularly bad. Of course, being a much smaller place, there was not so much of it as in New York, but what it lacked in quantity and diffuseness it had in quality and concentration of badness.'

One must make a note of the date. Chicago was at the time recovering from the effects of a massive fire. As we know, it has very much caught up in size with New York since the late nineteenth century. Even after these condemnations he continues by saying that he found it a wonderful city, and that he very much admired the pushing enterprise of its citizens.

He was ever the optimist, and one feels his own high morality and his belief in the ultimate good nature of people was at times unrealistic and went too far. As characterised by Dickens, Mr Wilkins Micawber was always hoping that something would turn up. The trouble with T. J. at times was that he deluded himself into the belief that something indeed had turned up, when it had not. He hoped that things would eventually work out all right, but he was often taking monumental risks with the lives of the children. With regret things didn't always work out all right; sometimes they worked out disastrously wrong.

He put in place some very sensible regulations, and if everyone in every branch of the institution had delivered on them 100 per cent, then things would have worked out well. Human nature being what it is, very far from perfect, not everyone was up to the standard required. The *Memoirs* give us his full list of the principles he laid down for the Canadian venture, which seem at first reading to be really good. On second reading there are one or two red warning lights. This again is a paraphrase, in order to sort out his archaic style and vast multi-clause sentences.

1 No child shall be sent who manifests criminal or violent tendencies.

2 Children must be healthy at the time of departure without any tendency to disease.

3 All such children, except the very young ones who go out for adoption, must have had a period of careful training, not only in industrial trades, but also of a moral and religious nature.

4 Of the children who meet these three conditions, only the flower of our flock shall go to Canada.

5 On reaching Canada, all children are to come under the care of properly qualified persons connected with our Institution on the Canadian side, by whom they are to be distributed carefully into well selected homes. Even then our work is not to be considered complete, and regular communication must be maintained with these children by personal visits of experienced assistants, and by a system of written reports from the child and its employer. Careful statistics must be kept showing frequent reports of their whereabouts, progress and general welfare, until they are old enough not to need our supervision.

6 If despite all these safeguards the child, after being placed out in Canada, becomes immoral or criminal, then every effort is to be made to repossess the child and bring it back to Britain.

Well what's wrong with that? The answer is several things, and probably the most important is that T. J. wasn't over there to make sure it ran properly. His genius for leadership was 3,000–4,000 miles to the east, and he was having to rely on others, many of them untested and therefore unknown quantities. The principles look pretty comprehensive so long as that sort of tight supervision backed them up to the high standards needed. That wasn't always there with sufficient force. There are a couple of gaping holes, and a lot of trouble fell through them.

Firstly, this was a child emigration scheme not a family scheme. Lone children, many of them not yet teens, without parents or adult relatives or any other grown-ups they knew. Had they all been sixteen- or seventeen-year-olds who could stand up for themselves, a lot of those troubles would not have happened. There was about it all the pious hope that these children would be adopted into loving Christian families. In the real world that just didn't happen all that often. He very soon stopped sending very small children, as we discover from this paraphrased quote: 'Our mortality rate during the seventeen months that this experiment was tried, of emigrating infants under five, *rose to a rate of 20 per cent per annum.* Alarmed by this I resolved not in future to favour emigration of *children under six* [my italics].'

He is losing 20 children per 100 to death, and he doesn't stop the whole programme and find out what on earth is going on before he sends any more. All he does is tinker with it, by raising the minimum age to six years. What we have to recall is that in an era when 20 per cent of children died before the age of five, and by his own efforts the institution had their own figures down to 6 per cent, he was used to infant mortality. One can even say he was inured to it, he expected it! It horrifies us, when even one child dying would cause uproar. He was a Victorian, and it makes a huge difference. We have to think with his brain, not ours.

The other gaping hole is clause five. One of the main safeguards installed locally was that each intending host family would be endorsed by a local clergyman, and at least one other reference of known respectability. That's something else that sounds good until you try it. How well do most pastors know their flock, and who guaranteed the other references? Might it have been the clergyman? One is reminded of the references allegedly possessed by the nebulous William Norton.

More and more children were being poured into the scheme before it had been road-tested to make sure it worked. Where it did that was fine, but too often it didn't! Clause five simply didn't work well enough in practice, which caused too many cases of heartache and several of real tragedy. It was a doubled-headed fact that Canada, at least initially, didn't have the necessary laws on its Statute Book that this flood of immigration demanded. Consequently it didn't have the experienced officers and officials to see, at the local level, that all these children were being properly protected.

Another onion in the stew we can discuss by looking at our modern experience. We have mentioned the Tolpuddle Martyrs a couple of times. They were where trade unions began, and as a result of all that has happened in that field since, Britain now enjoys a comparatively high standard of living. In our generation, if immigrants willing to work for less arrive, it causes dissension. If manufacturing gets sent abroad because things can be made cheaper in other countries, there are even more grumbles. It isn't a new grumble, the poor freemen in Ancient Rome grumbled that they were being undercut by the slaves.

In a small way the same thing happened at times in Canada. Whether a child or an adult, an immigrant was often prepared to work for less and accept lower working conditions than the local established people. It isn't an exact analogy, but it is an appropriate thing to mention, and it happened when my own immigrant grandparents arrived from Eastern Europe. In the East End where everyone was poor, they were poorer, until enough time went by and they were established, then they were entitled to grumble in their own turn a generation later. There was therefore an undercurrent which could briefly surface every now and then. You can wash the child, but you can't polish the accent or change the ripe choice of words in an instant, it takes years. Children from the East End were not necessarily welcomed with open arms, even if they came under the Barnardo banner. One has to remember that even if sixteen is, at the time of writing, the minimum school-leaving age in Britain, at the time being written about it was ten. The thinking was that at ten years old a child from a poor family was old enough to start work.

Another drive to the urgency we see in all this is the sheer volume of numbers. For every bed the Homes could find there could be another 100 destitute children out there in need. Ideally the Homes should have kept all the children they accepted until they were about sixteen, so that they were fully trained and ready for the labour market. There is no question that all those sent to Canada should have been at this age and up to a high standard of training. In fact the Homes were having to get them into employment by twelve or thirteen, and it helps us to understand the pressures they were under. Every bed that could be emptied could be immediately refilled from the streets, so let's not be too hard on them. What T. J. was doing is one of the foundation stones of our present-day quality of life and our attitude to the poor. We have hindsight, he had the problem.

Lone immigrants, children and young teens, were being poured into Canada by Barnardo and other organisations. There was no serious control on numbers, no great check on the suitability of skills and experience. The children were not always being adopted into kindly Christian family homes. All that sweetness and light and all those pious hopes fell on some very icy ground.

The system used by the majority of them was an apprenticeship, which was a working contract, and they were being employed by small farmers. The complaint soon being heard was that it was disrupting the Canadian labour market in agriculture. Under the terms of the apprenticeship the lads had to be clothed, housed and fed and supplied with such tools as the job required. In return they had to work all the hours demanded at whatever job had to be done at the time. Stepney Causeway was 4,000 miles away if they wanted to complain. Wages might be as little as 50 Canadian dollars a year, but could be as much as 80 or 90. Cases came to light where the pay was as low as $25, and just to repeat, that was for a year. Shades of the Ancient Romans complaining about the slaves!

Any hope that their education would continue in such circumstances was a non-starter, other than what a back-breaking, hard job farming was in the age before the invention of the tractor and the combine harvester. The young people simply had to stick it out until they were twenty-one and legally adults. Not every case was so black, indeed not even the majority, but enough were for it to be a bad system, without enough controls and supervision. If it was possible for them to make friends that helped, but the next farm could be 5 or 10 miles away, so the chances outside the immediate farm were slim.

The real killer, and that is meant literally, was the Canadian winter. The children came from city slums with childhoods of malnutrition and bad health, and while being cleaned up, cured of their diseases and cared for counted for a lot, it didn't do much for a poor constitution. Kept in England they had time to recover from that sort of childhood. Thrown into the unrelenting harshness of a Canadian prairie winter, far too many of them succumbed very quickly. We have had the story of John Summers, known as Carrots, who died in a barrel on a cold winter's night in Billingsgate. On the Canadian prairie that would have been warm for that time of year.

It is true that the Barnardo organisation made a huge effort to get the Canadian operation to work. As in Britain their own inspectors were employed and detailed records were maintained. The boarding of children was subsidised by $5 a month in many cases, and generally the best of British experience was transferred across. In the end the enterprise was employing a considerable staff and not all results were bad. That still leaves us those that were. Records are all very well, but how sound was the training of the inspectors so as to ensure the best standard of inspection?

Some of the staff were employed in providing a home for those among the girls who had, to use the euphemism of the time, fallen by the wayside. No matter how good the training, the numbers involved meant that this problem would inevitably arise. To be fair this part of the enterprise, when the need arose, seems to have worked very well.

Annie Macpherson had family resident in Canada who ran that end of the operation for her, and they seem to have been excellent. It was kept small and within bounds of what they regarded as sensible and manageable. Without her advantages, T. J. allowed the operation to get far too big and unwieldy. We go back to the fact that he wasn't there to supervise it himself. He was a fantastic and inspiring leader, but not from the other side of a huge ocean.

Canada was still a young country, and rather new to the independence of being a self-governing dominion, but it was quickly moving forward. In 1884 Ontario passed an Act which was based on the Barnardo principles. That took things a long way forward in the field of immigration regulations as they applied to children and young people. However it would not be until 1924 that immigration of lone children under the age of fourteen was banned. Barnardo Homes ceased their Canadian operation ten years later, though until 1967 very small numbers were still occasionally sent to Australia.

My own experience of emigration was the 40 or so miles I went in 1940 as a completely bewildered five-year-old, from London to Bedfordshire, where I remained for the duration of the Second World War. I had two billets, one for six months I hated, one for the remainder I sort of got on with. But at least I knew there was some family around, and I was never asked to hand-milk 100 cows in a freezing cold barn at six in the morning. Kids not long out of the East End slums, with a bit of cleaning up, were being thrown into that sort of situation, without a mate of their own age as a point of reference. It must have been awful for some of them, and that they got through it makes you feel proud of them. Why more use wasn't made of the farm at Russell is a mystery, but a couple of years there to acclimatise and learn the job would have probably saved a lot of the heartache and quite a few lives.

All that having been discussed, it is unfair to paint the Canadian enterprise completely in black. Its principles and ambitions were wonderful, its delivery sadly flawed. What you don't try you can't learn from. All told T. J. did five tours, and by the last one there were many young people he met who were proving this to be true. The majority managed to tough it out and survive and become the ancestors of the current generation. Their genes are ingrained in the modern Canadian personality, and all things considered those genes seem to be serving that great country well.

NINE

Fostering Out: 1886–1896

And talking of the evacuation of children from the big cities in the Second World War, one of the reasons it all worked so well from an organisational point of view was the work done half a century before by Barnardo Homes. Ever since 1887 the Barnardo organisation had been rescuing children from the city slums and fostering them out with families in the countryside. The horrors of the Spanish Civil War in 1937 demonstrated what the advent of bomber aircraft had done to warfare. Should a war ever break out involving Britain, the government made plans to get the children away from the big cities in case of a repeat performance. The rest, as they say, is history. Barnardo's were there to offer advice, but they do not seem to have been specially consulted or particularly asked to help, even though at that time they were still running residential homes and were fostering out. The government seems to have managed in its own Whitehall way, though the idea that such a programme was possible was by then embedded in the national experience.

Even more embedded in the national experience was the system used by the Scots, who had been fostering out for centuries. There is a Scottish Act of 1579, when Scotland was still a separate country in the reign of James VI, cousin of and eventually successor to Elizabeth I. We find in the *Memoirs* a paragraph from a much longer piece, written in old Scots dialect, which is a direct quote from the law.

> Gif any Beggars Bairne, being above the age of five years and within fourteen, male or female, sal be liked of be ony subject of the Realm of honest estait, the said person sal have the Bairne be the order and direction of the said Provost and Baillies within the Burgh, or the judge of every Parochin to Landwart, gif he be a male child to the age of twenty four years, and gif she be a woman child, to the age of twenty two years. And gif they depart or be intised from the maisters or mistresses service, the maisters or mistresses to have like action or remidie as for their hired servants or prentises, as well as against the Bairne as against the taker or intiser thereof.

A translation into modern English is fairly straightforward. Read the word 'be' as normal where it fits, or as by, as in 'by any subject', where that makes more sense. Therefore if an established beggar, the English equivalent would be pauper, had a child which was liked by anyone of honest estate, that is respectable and with an income, who was prepared to take in the beggar's child, the authorities could authorise it. In the towns this would be the provost, in those days roughly equivalent to the mayor. In the countryside there is the archaic word parochin, related to the word parochial and in practice meaning the Scottish version of the parish, with probably also a nod from the local laird. Quite why the child of destitute parents cannot join the scheme below the age of five or if they are above fourteen seems very odd. What the thinking was behind those limitations is baffling. In fact the kindness of strangers is a powerful thing, and one can be sure that many a wee bairn was taken in, though not covered by such a technicality, and the authorities knew and turned a blind eye. Once accepted the boys were to stay in their situation until the age of twenty-four, girls until twenty-two. The section covering enticement or taking away of these bairns makes it evident that in return for the kindness of giving them a home, bed, board and clothes they were expected to work. They were not allowed to leave the household without express permission, and the masters and mistresses had legal rights over them. The same rules applied to them as were the legal rights they had over their hired staff.

While the bairn was given bed, board and clothes, there is nothing to suggest that there was any requirement that they be paid, hence the comparison with the specifically paid hired staff. Further reading, though not here quoted, indicates that should the master or mistress die, the charity bairn had no automatic rights of inheritance. They would always be a charity case unless there was a legacy in a will. They would be, to use the old phrase, back on the parish, with no money and living in the hope that someone, maybe even the same family, would take them in on the same terms.

If they were old enough they might be sent out to work, and if they had been well treated and well taught would be able to earn a living. However, whereas twenty-one was the usual age of majority, the women would be held an extra year and the men an extra three. There are several other questions you might like to ask your favourite legal eagle or historian, should your funds be sufficient to cover their fees. Let us say that systems like this work well when there is good faith, and are a mess when there is not. The general feeling is that there was, and the Scots made it work well for over three centuries. Such goodwill was the benefit and when absent it was also the problem, wherever we have been discussing poor children in the Victorian era.

After a variety of systems operated in England, some with outdoor relief and some not, we come to the 1834 Poor Law Amendment Act, which was in force for almost all the period we have been discussing. Effectively it stopped outdoor relief and brought it all indoors. In order to do that it needed the doors, which is to say it needed the building and the staffing of the workhouses, places the Scots didn't need. Just as a note here, Ireland did have them.

In Scotland, as far as it related to children, wherever possible their care was based on fostering out. This helped to avoid the generational poverty loop, where the children of paupers became paupers themselves. Not 100 per cent successful, but far more than the system in England. The burgh and the parochin didn't get this for nothing, the carers received a small subsidy.

We can look again at the *Memoirs* with an extract from a much longer piece. It originates from the Sessions Clerk of Rothsay on Bute, an island in the Firth of Clyde south-west of Glasgow. It is undated but is thought to be about 1880, and seems to be slightly different from the more normal family fostering situation, however there is a clear similarity.

> In general there is only one child from the children of the same family boarded in the same house, except in the case of Miss Craig's house, who commenced an Institution about twelve months ago for the care of orphans, and who has several females to superintend the different departments of it. In that Institution they have a child from each of two families. There they pay for one child two shillings and for the other two shillings and sixpence, the latter being the elder. Witness and others of the Elders call to see the orphans are properly taken care of. He considers that Miss Craig pays very great attention to the orphans. He has not seen anything equal to it in this part of the country. She pays very great attention to the education of the children, and takes them regularly to church with her.

From which we gather that the fact that there is no such thing as a free lunch was just as true with Miss Craig as it is with us. Whatever funds she may have been receiving from other sources is not discussed in the quote, but if the parish wanted her services they had to supply a subsidy. By the details given, especially that there were several staff besides herself, it would not have been cheap, but she was giving good value. Likewise in England, as the Barnardo organisation developed and grew, it qualified for public subsidies and grants.

In the case of Miss Craig, the translation of subsidies to 2000 values shows £7.80 per week for the younger child mentioned and £9.75 for the elder. Given that this was rural Scotland and cities are always more expensive to live in than the countryside, possibly that's a bit conservative. Even so it looks as if the parish was getting a bargain, and surely there was other income as well. From the quote it would seem that, unlike T. J., our good lady in Rothsay was actually running an orphanage, though one can be an orphan and still have extended family. One imagines that in her case the families involved, if they existed, were not sufficiently prosperous to rally round and care for the children themselves. Mention of the elders brings out the very Christian nature of Victorian Scotland. There would be little going on anywhere that the kirk didn't know about, and in which they would take a definite interest. While this lovely lady operated in slightly different circumstances, she is a good example of other and better public attitudes and legal possibilities in Scotland than operated in England.

Clearly the system, though operating well, was being updated from time to time. In 1875 Scottish records indicate that about two-thirds of registered orphans and pauper children were being boarded out. In 1903 this was up to just under 90 per cent. Set that against the English experience, which is just about the direct reverse. In 1905 only 13 per cent of those registered in England were boarded out. Note the use of the word registered, and it allows us to wonder how many who were in that sort of need had not been registered.

In respect of children, as early as 1870 a committee of the House of Commons was hearing evidence about the superiority of the Scottish system over the English Poor Law workhouses. One or two Poor Law Unions were using boarding out, but very oddly it was being done slowly and grudgingly and over a very long period of time. A quarter of a century later in 1895 only a quarter of them had adopted it as an option. Some of the problem may have been lack of money. The English have a long tradition of joking about the Scots being mean. They aren't, and their joking reply is that they can only spend what the English let them hang on to.

In this case the Scots were noticeably more generous in what they spent on the children. As an example, for the year 1903 Glasgow spent £18 per head on its pauper children. The English spending varied between £10 and £13 on each of their children. Glasgow organised a special study into the effectiveness of its methods over a ten-year period. During that time they looked at 772 case histories and found only one conviction for felony. That is another very impressive statistic, strongly in favour of the Scots in this field of welfare.

We have now reached the point where the differences in values with 2000 have become difficult to justify. From now on we will dispense with them. We now live in such a different world, where wages and salaries bear little relationship to those at the end of the Victorian era, and two-thirds of the things we have in the shops hadn't been invented yet.

In 1887 T. J. was giving fostering out serious thought and he travelled up to Glasgow to investigate. He attended a conference in Glasgow, where the Lord Provost claimed that pauperism had over recent years declined from 4 per cent to 2.5 per cent. That sounds wonderful until you realise that in as big a city as Glasgow had then become, 25 adult and child paupers per 1,000 of the population was an appallingly high number. The Scots were better at how they dealt with it, but it was still a shocking number to have to deal with. While we are playing with numbers and recalling the mention of generational pauperism, it was calculated that one in seven boys and one in four girls left English workhouses to become paupers like their parents. Clearly there had to be a change in the mindset throughout society.

*

What T. J. brought to the problem was a different attitude. Before a child was boarded out, very detailed research was done into the character of the candidate foster family. The criteria began with the accommodation, which had to be an unshared cottage, no lodgers, no extended family. There had to be enough rooms, there would be no sharing a bedroom with a member of the family, other than a baby in a cot. The foster children themselves could share, but no more than two in a bedroom. If a double bed was being shared it was strictly same-sex only. In those days single beds were not all that common, so sometimes the institution would supply a single. A particular requirement which set them apart from the others was the demand for good sanitary arrangements, and they were way ahead on hygiene and cleanliness. The foster father had to be in full-time employment with a decent wage coming in, so that the family were not relying on the Barnardo subsidy for their income. The money was for the upkeep of the child, not the family.

Once a village had been chosen as a suitable location a local committee was formed. This normally included the vicar, the squire and his wife and other willing local worthies. Impeccable references were required from the foster parent's employers as well as from other respectable and reputable local people. What was wanted was a stable and respectable working-class family, where the husband was steady and working, and the wife stayed home to raise the family. It was logical to insist on the working class, they would be looking after working-class children. If an earl had asked to be considered he would have been turned down. These children came from the labouring poor, and none of this is as stuffy as it may sound. The earl would have passed on all the work to his staff, but taken all the credit among his friends. These kids had been born with a tough start, that sort of condescending, patronising attitude they could well do without.

In 1887 the scheme got underway. The statistics tables in the *Memoirs* tell us that the pilot scheme during that year distributed 330 children between the ages of five and nine to foster families. This figure registers with us the sheer number of children available in that age group that Barnardo Homes were caring for. Some of these were doubles and without the details we can only assume it was to keep brothers and sisters together. An important innovation was the appointment of that newest invention on the social scene, a lady doctor. To act as the inspector we have Dr Jane Walker MD. She it was who developed the system of random visits, never less frequent than once in three months, to check on the health and well-being of each child. The odd scratch and bump is normal in any child, but severe bruising or any other symptoms of neglect were off limits, and the child left with her there and then. The word soon got round that no one argued with Dr Walker. She was a lady that T. J. greatly respected and listened to.

As always T. J. formulated his principles, in this case in a contract. Along the lines of the Scottish system there was a weekly subsidy for each child fostered. The foster parents had to sign a detailed agreement, which we get from the *Memoirs*. The Barnardo letter heading was followed by the expected preamble of names and references, then the contract clauses.

> In consideration of receiving the sum of ... shillings per week for the lodging, maintenance, washing, school fees, clothing and care of the above named child, ... do hereby undertake
>
> 1 To bring up the said child carefully, kindly, and in all respects as one of my own family.
> 2 To provide the said child with proper food, clothing, washing, lodging and school fees.
> 3 To endeavour to train the said child in habits of truthfulness, obedience, personal cleanliness and industry.
> 4 To take care that the said child shall attend duly at church or chapel, and shall be taught the habit of daily prayer.
> 5 To take care that the said child, when of suitable age, shall attend regularly at a public elementary school, unless prevented by sickness or other urgent causes.
> 6 To communicate with the lady or gentleman who has charge of the children in the district upon all matters affecting the welfare of the said child, and in the case of the said child's illness to report it *immediately* to the Director, and to the lady or gentleman who has charge of the children in the district, and if necessary at once to call in the assistance of a medical man.
> 7 To forward to the director for inspection all letters which may be received from relatives or friends of the said child before

allowing the same to be opened, and to do likewise with all letters written by or for the said child, not permitting them to be sent direct to the persons to whom they are addressed, and not to enter into any correspondence myself with any person who may claim to have a relationship to, or interest in the said child.

8 At all times to permit the child to be visited by any person appointed by the Director, and to permit no visit from *relatives or friends* without the Director's authorisation.

9 To restore the said child to any person sent by the Director to receive it, on getting one fortnight's notice of removal, or equivalent payment.

Note the very clear language with an absence of legal technicalities. The first-person singular is in frequent use throughout, emphasising that this is a personal commitment. The Homes put the financial arrangements first, and originally this was 5 shillings a week, a reasonable sum in that era. The whole arrangement was intended to be child-centred, the said child was the little person it was all about. Carefully and kindly are the words used in clause one, and start as you mean to go from there. Clauses two and three are pretty much as we would expect, but note that while there were by then publicly funded schools, there was still the need to pay for various things. Ask anyone who belongs to a PTA and they will assure you that bit hasn't changed much, except that they are too shy to call them fees these days.

Clause four required a Christian upbringing, and we have already discussed the very Protestant Christian stance upon which the spiritual ethos of the Homes was based. Clause five reinforces the priority of ensuring that the child received a good education, because an educated child stood a better chance in the labour market.

Clause six goes into health factors, bearing in mind that most of the children had grown up in an unhealthy environment. There had to be regular contact with the local worthy overseeing the village, and through them with the local committee. In days long before the National Health Service, doctors had to be paid directly. If medical help was needed then one must be called, and the director was to be informed right away. With an organisation the size of Barnardo's, payment of the bill was guaranteed. Note the use of the phrase 'medical man'. Dr Jane Walker was a rarity, most doctors were men.

Clauses seven and eight between them absolutely forbid any family contact other than through the director, who might give special permission but in fact almost never did. If one reads through the smoke it seems that John James Roddy was being boarded out, and that the whole furore in his case came from a far too rigid invoking of this rule. Clause nine takes a little thought, but has perfectly good logic. It maintains the Homes' hold over the child, after all they are helping to pay for its keep. What it doesn't do is share that logic with the foster family, which in some cases did cause a lot of upset. There were children and families who had grown very fond of each other, then suddenly the child was called back. Note the use of the word director. As we have already discussed he was by this time a paid employee of the trust, but only T. J. could make these decisions, which we will agree is very revealing.

Very sensibly, the number fostered out in a district did not exceed twenty, which aimed to avoid them becoming a noticeable intrusion in the local community. The number of children fostered out with any family was limited to three. Given that many country cottages in those days were small, there were limitations built into the programme which excluded perfectly worthy families for want of space. An odd thing became apparent quite early on. The Barnardo standards of cleanliness weren't universal in the countryside. This meant that when the Barnardo children mixed with the others in school, it was the kids from the city slums who were catching the local fleas and bugs, not the other way around. It became noticeable that standards actually began to rise, with local mothers not wanting to be shown up by all these charity children. The literature and the records indicate that most fostered children enjoyed a very happy stay in the countryside, and a great affection grew up between them and their foster families.

So successful was the programme that it was steadily expanded and in five years had reached 2,000. By the time T. J. died that figure had doubled. What also comes out of a study of the *Memoirs'* vast treasure trove of statistics is that between 1893 and 1899 there was a national financial squeeze and considerable inflation, which hit the entire organisation hard. Numbers fell and it was not until the year 1900 that they recovered to 1892 levels. When one adds that the Trust Committee allowed the director to get them involved in expensive litigation, it makes the point that pressure was coming from more than one direction.

None of that reflected on the excellence of the programme itself. The obvious benefit of fostering out was that it made more room in Stepney Causeway and all the other addresses for the unending stream of other children in desperate need. It also cost less, even when including the salaries paid to Dr Walker and her small team. The calculations are that fostering out was costing per child about £14 10s a year in direct subsidy and administration charges. The cost of keeping children 'in house' was at least £16 and at the Girls Village about £18 a head.

Victorian Britain was a very stratified society. There were the landed gentry and the aristocrats, who might live in country houses with 200 servants. The well-to-do middle class might make do with a couple of dozen servants, and even a prosperous shopkeeper might have a live-in maid. Part of the Barnardo 5 shillings subsidy was intended for clothes. There were cases where the local committees grabbed a shilling of the weekly subsidy and claimed that they were buying wisely, using the economies of scale. The result was that all the charity children in their district would be clothed exactly the same. It was never intended to be what it became in those districts, a social class uniform. The charity children were being marked out and never allowed to forget that they were socially inferior. The fact that their hair was cleaner, their manners often better, and they were often brighter than the local children didn't mean anything. They were charity children and they had to be kept in their place, which was right at the bottom. It was always the intention that the foster parents should have the money directly and buy the children's clothes themselves. In the majority of cases this happened, the result being that those children blended into their background community very quickly.

Despite all the problems that T. J. and people like him in the field of philanthropy encountered, there was a growing change in the attitudes shown throughout society, including those which up to then had been the main causes of all the deprivation and poverty. Not only were the evangelical Christians such as T. J. and his friends in the fight, they now had the support of that new phenomenon, the Socialists and the trade unions, as well as other liberal political movements. Successive governments were being made more and more aware of the need for change.

Referring particularly to T. J. we have a *Memoirs* quote from A. J. Mundella MP, who in 1895 was chairman of an enquiry into Poor Law Schools in London. This is a little paraphrased.

> I can only say without in the least flattering Dr Barnardo, that at the conclusion of our enquiry I came to the conclusion, which was shared I think by most of my colleagues, that we could wish that in the Local Government Board there was a Department for the Poor Law Children, and that we had Dr Barnardo at the head of it.

From what we have heard about our hero in our discussions, we would have to shake our heads at the thought, and be thankful that this volatile, workaholic, one-man-band sort of individual never became anything like it. He would have been a disaster. It is enough that he was the wonderfully warm-hearted champion of children and he did things his way. If the social horrors he fought against hadn't been there he wouldn't have had to fight for them in the way that he did. He definitely had a heart of gold, but he was also a religious bigot and a far from totally honest litigant on far too many occasions, and at far too great a financial cost to his organisation. Let's say you cannot blame a leopard for being spotty and leave it there.

One bull he took by the horns was the predicament of the mothers of illegitimate babies. The full beam of Victorian hypocrisy glared down on them, ignoring the fact that these things take two people. The attitude towards the men was that they had only been sowing a few wild oats, and what was wrong with that? Let's say everything! There was a lot of shrewd thinking behind T. J.'s idea, which was, where it proved possible, to attach the man to the cost of bringing up the child, using the Victorian version of a maintenance order. He then found the baby a foster home and the mother a suitable job nearby. That kept her and the baby in full contact, involved her in bringing it up, and meant she could make a contribution towards the costs.

This was of course the complete opposite of the no-contact rule in place for all the other children, but here the circumstances were totally different. One can well understand the second rule, which was that if it happened a second time she was out on her ear! It was a bit of social thinking half a century ahead of its time, but he had a fight on his hands with the more censorious and self-righteous half of the nation. Girls have been getting into trouble since Eve developed a liking for apples! It isn't right, but the one person you cannot blame is the baby, and the baby should always be at the centre of the need to sort it out. As a certain rather famous preacher and teller of wise tales once said, 'Only he who is without sin may cast the first stone.' The trouble is that if people have decided to throw verbal stones at those they think can't answer back, they will go right ahead and throw them. In the situations discussed, T. J. took action which was very effective.

*

If we were to try and compare what was achieved in Britain with what was achieved in Canada, it soon becomes apparent that we are not comparing like with like. The systems being operated in the two countries were not the same. In Britain the children were being placed with carefully vetted working-class village families, with a backup local committee in a settled social situation. In Canada so many of the children were being placed out on apprenticeships, without a clear definition of what an apprenticeship was as understood by the farmer, let alone the youngster. One thing we can understand is that an apprenticeship is a job, the youngster was expected to work, and there doesn't seem to have been a clear, mutually understood definition of the terms. The British model didn't call for that, the child wasn't expected to work at all. Relatively few children in Canada were being fostered out on the British model.

The country was different, the terrain was different, the society was different, and certainly the weather in winter was different. The strength of the organisation and the supervision wasn't up to the needs, hard-working though most of the staff were. In Britain it was under very tight control, with T. J. backed up by Dr Walker and her dedicated team. The Canadian programme was not geared up for a foster care situation with a loving family, where the child would go to school every day and church on Sunday.

And with regret that was T. J.'s fault, because he failed to set it up properly. He did not find out enough about Canada before he went charging in full throttle, and he allowed himself to be deluded by the hope that it was all teething troubles, and it would come out right in the end. Let us not damn the entire enterprise, because for up to three-quarters of those that went across things did work out, with varying degrees of success. However for about a quarter of them it didn't and we've already mentioned the appalling death rate among the very young. That is the point being made. In Britain he knew what he was doing and did it brilliantly. Across the water he was not personally in charge, and there is no way around that central fact.

*

Not that everything was perfect in Britain, and that was down to a failure of communication. Children who may have been with a foster family for several years were suddenly 'recovered', and had to go to Stepney Causeway, which was an almighty shock to the child and to the family in too many cases. It was like a bolt from the blue and they didn't understand it, and the problem seems to have been that it wasn't explained to them. The foster family wasn't asked, the child wasn't asked, the order came from on high, two weeks' contractual notice was given; pack up the child's things, the child and their belongings will be collected on such and such a day. Was it some perceived fault, the families asked themselves? If so, what was it? If people have things explained to them and can see the sense behind it, they will usually go along with it. It would appear that though not a universal fault, it was a frequent occurrence and in such cases it caused a great deal of upset.

Yet there was a perfectly good explanation. The countryside was a wonderful place for the children to be brought up in. It was in fact positively idealistic in many respects except one. The countryside was a desperately difficult place to live if you were looking for a job. Most of the families, if this had been explained, would have agreed immediately. For more than 100 years previously the countryside had been losing population to the towns for just this reason. People weren't leaving the countryside for the towns for better jobs and conditions, in fact often the wages were lower and the conditions far worse.

Farming and all other countryside trades had radically changed. The Enclosure Acts had a huge effect on land tenure and rights to common grazing. If you had a patch of ground you could at least grow some vegetables for your family, but now even that wasn't guaranteed. And above all that there were the huge families, in an era that either hadn't heard of birth control, or had been brought up to condemn it as some sort of immoral crime against nature. Put into that equation all these kids from the slums and finding the answer isn't difficult. Such jobs as there were would be going to the locally born youngsters, and the townies would be so far to the back of the queue that it wasn't worth joining it. Therefore it was necessary, when the children were old enough, to call them back to London and get them trained up for a job. And by then the Barnardo organisation was proving very good at finding them jobs in the town environment.

With the luxury of hindsight we can understand all that. At the time there were many placings where a genuine love had developed between the parties. That is the gold-star standard that was being achieved. When such cases were badly dealt with and the reasons not fully explained, the result was that the foster families had a deep sense of hurt, and would never volunteer to take in another child.

Maybe we should have another look at T. J. and his character. We have to realise that it wasn't his fault that he had been born prosperous middle-class, had been brought up prosperous middle-class, and that every now and then he had a blind spot. A man of outstanding intellect, possibly classifiable in his special subject as a genius, it never quite registered with him that some things which seemed blindingly obvious to him needed to be explained to very loving but not well-educated villagers, who had given from their hearts what they couldn't give from their purses.

TEN

Tying Up the Loose Ends:
1896–1906

It is now time to draw together all the threads and gather up all the loose ends. Time doesn't stand still, and even in the forty years that T. J. was operating a great deal had changed, both in Britain and around the world. Throughout Europe, and that of course includes Britain, there was an old aristocratic order which either lived in denial or in total ignorance, it is difficult now to decide which. Queen Victoria died in January 1901 still mourning her beloved Albert, and the new century had dawned with growing imperial rivalries threatening the peace, and new inventions making war potentially more terrible.

In British imperial matters, in 1898 Britain agreed with China on a ninety-nine-year lease on Kowloon near Hong Kong. When that fell due in 1997, Kowloon and Hong Kong were all handed back to China. The British Empire reached its zenith with the loss of life and the hollow victory over the Boers in South Africa. This was fought more because of the greed of Cecil Rhodes and his cronies than any other logical reason, there being both diamonds and gold found at Kimberley, which was in Boer-held land not far from what is now Johannesburg. In 1912 the hollowness of the victory was made plain when South Africa was made a dominion, effectively handing it all back to the Boers, including Cape Colony, which previously they hadn't held. The way the war was conducted, which included the invention of concentration camps, gave a clear warning just how incompetent and out of date the British Army, and especially its senior officer corps, was becoming. This warning was ignored to everyone's great cost less than a generation later.

Young Winston Churchill was in South Africa as a journalist. He made a name for himself by escaping from the Boers after capture. In 1913 Victoria's grandson the Kaiser was welcomed on a visit of friendship, or that was the public pose. One of his side trips was to St Mary's church, used by the East End German community, to whom he gave an inscribed Bible. A year later the safety curtain came loose from its moorings and crashed down onto the stage of the European theatre, killing four empires and a cast of 10 million. They called it the First World War.

In politics, in 1892 James Keir Hardie was the first Socialist Member of Parliament to be elected. This was to be a signal of profound change in the whole political scene; the only surprising thing about it was the speed at which that change happened. At the other end of the political spectrum that lad Winston popped up again. This maverick grandson of a duke was elected as the Conservative Member for the very working-class constituency of Oldham, on the fringe of Manchester. He switched allegiance to the Liberals and gained office. Not happy there, he soon switched back to the Conservatives.

Moving pictures became an entertainment phenomenon, attracting crowds and creating the cinema industry. In America Henry Ford gave up bicycles for building what he called automobiles, powered by petrol engines. Having such engines allowed Wilbur and Orville Wright to finally get an aeroplane off the ground, for a first flight of about 60 yards. Electricity continued to grow as an industry, with the American Edison still arguing with the Englishman Swann over who first invented the filament light-bulb. Sad to note and also in America, President McKinley was assassinated, which brought his deputy, the ebullient 'teddy bear' Theodore Roosevelt to the White House.

*

Meanwhile, back in the East End there had been a looming financial crisis ever since those vastly expensive court cases. Additional to those we have discussed, there had been several others which were not as famous or spectacular, but no lawyer works for nothing and they had cost a lot of money. Quite apart from our hero's expensive hobby of being virulently sectarian, other financial worries were created. Whenever he saw a problem for which he could see a solution, in he went. It was very difficult to get into his head that this was a famous but financially modest charity, and these were problems that needed the resources of the government.

More of Stepney Causeway had been acquired, pulled down and rebuilt, and the Children's Hospital created, and against his original publicly stated determination to live within his income this rebuilding had been done on borrowed money. Some of the creditors started to get restless. In the decade 1889 to 1899 income went up 50 per cent. In that time work trebled and expenses went through the roof. There had been a Golden Jubilee appeal which had raised a little, but every other charity had their own so the competition was fierce. The same had to be said about the Diamond Jubilee appeal, only a similar small amount for similar reasons.

While T. J. was a dynamic figure and very popular with the general public, he had offended a lot of influential people, the sort that had deep pockets. These were the ones who either turned to other charities, or who limited their giving because of his character. Add to that the fact that the decade experienced a considerable business slump and one can see why someone as controversial as T. J., despite his acknowledged golden-hearted genius, sometimes didn't stand out from the crowd as everyone's first choice.

The decade was not the time for expensive new projects without guaranteed support, but telling him he wasn't the Chancellor of the Exchequer didn't always register. As for legally being a servant of the trust and subject to the authority of the Committee of

Trustees, this never really stuck in his mind either. It is wonderful that he had a heart of gold where the needs of the children were concerned, but that wasn't gold in the bank account. Either the committee put the brakes on or the place would go bust.

Increasingly the committee had to insist that they had the right to say no and they said it more often. Even then they didn't always succeed. On behalf of the children he would always try to bully them around to his way of thinking. The Baker brothers, who were now the legal team, tried to keep him in check, and there were several other members skilled in finance who somehow managed to keep an increasingly leaky ship afloat. One particular creditor was a bank owed £18,000, which is about £1.5 million in 2000 values, but as the value conversions on property become trickier by this time, maybe an awful lot more. The bank was in possession of property deeds to cover the liability, and had they foreclosed it would have been the end. The organisation was seriously overstretched in every direction.

In 1888 the Earl of Meath agreed to become President of the Trust. One of his first actions was to call for a full audit, which to us sounds very sensible. A committee member was fool enough to say that if he wanted one he would have to pay for it himself, and it doesn't surprise us that he walked out. This had the effect of waking everyone up to the need to have one, as no one by then had a clear idea what the real situation was. When the report came in they all went a sickly shade of grey. If word ever got out to the general public they would go out of business, they were to all intents and purposes bankrupt. The response was a huge effort and brilliant fund-raising ideas; the worst of the holes were plugged, but it was a close-run thing. Despite protests from T. J. some retrenchment was made, eventually including the closing of the Deaconess House in Bow. A range of other economies were made, staff numbers were trimmed, everything that could be nailed down was mortgaged and everything that couldn't be nailed down was used until it fell apart. There were inevitably more loud cries of protest from T. J., but the real world had to win the argument. He came under a great deal of internal criticism which they all made sure never became public, but the committee was now taking a lot more control.

In 1903 he was a passenger in a train which was in an accident near Liverpool, which left him badly shaken but otherwise all right. One increasing problem was his personal health. He had always been short-sighted, he was increasingly deaf and was suffering from what we now call angina. There was a medical clinic in the German city of Nauheim which he began to visit when things got really bad. The committee never quite had the courage to fire him, but the bankers were saying in private that he was a luxury they would prefer not to afford, if a nice way of getting him to retire could be found.

An audit when he died showed liabilities of just under £250,000. With our now very fluid idea of what that converts to, the figure is certainly not less that £18 million and more likely £25 million. Donations in 1906, the year after he died, were just under £200,000, so they owed in 1906 terms 1¼ times gross income. Out of those receipts they had to pay the running costs before they could look at debt repayments. A well-run commercial company with a good product to sell can cope with figures like that for a short time. For a charity like Barnardo's it was dangerously near the edge. One can understand how a Chancellor of the Exchequer feels on Budget Day.

The good news was that the organisation thus far was continuing to do its good works, the soup and sympathy was still being dished out. Yet more figures come from the goldmine of statistics that the *Memoirs* offer. In the thirty years up to 1905 over 750,000 free meals had been given out and 250,000 free lodgings. Just in the last decade of that period 600,000 garments had been given to the needy. To which add, complementary to the Girls Village, they had started up a Boys Village. To which add the training and welfare work. Sam Smith had in mind a home for waifs and strays. What this sounds like is a welfare state in miniature. The only limit was the availability of resources.

The trick that many of these Victorian philanthropic organisations were able to pull was to spend less than they received and build up an income from investments. Sometimes they were left profitable legacies. The most famous of these was when J. M. Barrie left the Great Ormond Street Children's Hospital the copyright of Peter Pan. Just before the century turned there was an attempt to start such a fund but it never got off the ground, the demands on all income were too pressing.

The one trick they did have up their sleeve was the lawyer William Baker. He gave up what was a lucrative legal practice to devote himself full time to the organisation. The state they were in called for determined and at times ruthless measures. Not a penny was to be spent unless he said yes, and he often had to say no. It was to take him about twelve years, but in the end he hauled them out of trouble and finally managed to balance the books.

There have been a lot of figures banded about, but we all know that the oil that lets the wheels of commerce turn is money. In the forty years that we have been reviewing, the total collected from all sources and recorded in *Memoirs* is £3,513,825 up to the end of 1906. We have been agreeing that the best guesses of the Office of National Statistics, valuable as they are as a guide, are just that, best guesses as they openly declare. One could possibly convert that total to about £300,000,000 in 2000 values. Compared with what was needed it was chickenfeed. When our hero died the aristocracy still ruled and old mindsets aren't changed in an afternoon. The welfare state didn't arrive until after the Second World War forty years later. When we consider what the state spends these days on these services it gets it into perspective, especially as things are a lot better socially now than they were then.

The Duke of Wellington is on record as having famously remarked, while still fighting Napoleon, that the British soldier was the scum of the earth. People like him said things like that at the beginning of the nineteenth century. Men like Shaftesbury realised that they had been born into a privileged society, and that saying things like that to the poor was wrong for two good reasons. Firstly it is rude, and secondly scum is the stuff that floats on the top. Wellington was at the top, so what did that make him? Shaftesbury and T. J. were never quite the friends that T. J. at times tried to suggest, his Lordship steered clear of him after a while. Lord Cairns was totally different, because he could see through the exterior façade and realised the value of the man inside.

After several moves the family finally ended up in Surbiton, the archetypal London suburb as the name is intended to suggest. In 1905 he was definitely a sick man, worn out by work and responsibility, perhaps disappointed that he had never received any official recognition or honour. He went again to Germany, had a bad attack of angina in Cologne but after some rest was able to make it as far as the clinic. After ten days there he felt well enough to return home by easy stages. On 19 September he was catching up on correspondence, his only concession being that he worked from home. He and Syrie had tea, but about six in the evening he complained of feeling unwell, collapsed on his wife's shoulder and died within minutes. He was sixty.

*

It has been my purpose to try and get inside the character of a great man, and also inside the character of the East End and society at large in the second half of the nineteenth century. He was a very great and fondly remembered man in the East End that I grew up and went to school in, just after the Second World War. It hasn't been possible to ignore his faults, but the people who never get some things wrong never do anything. He did far more that was right than he got wrong, so let us say that loud and clear. For every criticism there were 10,000 people that he helped. For each niggle there were children that he took off the streets and fed soup and sympathy. He was a bloke who got off his backside and did things, and while he wasn't perfect he still managed to be marvellous.

We have been looking at the character and attitudes of the very different and heavily stratified society of Victorian imperial Britain. When I went to school we still had an empire and a peer of the realm wasn't the commonplace they are now. My own grandparents were part of the respectable working poor of that era and lived a five-minute walk from Stepney Causeway. They may well have passed several of the people named in the street. I knew the area in the forties and fifties very well and still have relatives living in the area. The East End is part of my heritage.

Having read this far, I don't want anyone to feel that I have been so fascinated with figures and technicalities and the problems of character he had that I am somehow throwing out the baby with the bathwater. With the help of hindsight we can all have a go at the upper classes, that's the easy bit. They had a shameful attitude towards the poor, which is where much of the poverty started. Shaftesbury and the evangelicals were the exception, and people of inspiration like T. J. mobilised that feeling and steadily got those attitudes to change. His lifetime achievements were huge, but we keep coming back to my opening question. In the world's greatest empire, in the world's richest nation, why were there so many destitute people? Why did Carrots freeze to death in a barrel at the age of ten? Our hero was a towering personality wrapped up in a 160 cm frame. Much of modern practice in respect of not only children but also adults with problems started with him and the other late Victorian crusaders for social justice around him.

Barnardo's as an organisation still exists, and is involved in the welfare needs of many thousands of children and young people, continuing to make a valuable contribution to society. There are many other agencies in the field as well. Even the government can't do everything, and it uses Barnardo's in its modern style to pick up some of the load. It continues to be one of the largest charities in the field. Things have radically changed, and the organisation works in a way which suits the modern world. Among other things the welfare state has changed the legal framework, which excludes it from things it once did as core activities. For instance, it no longer has children in residence.

The idea that modern prosperity has cured the problem of poor children, battered and exploited children, doesn't stand up to even the briefest examination. Let us not waste our brain cells on statistics, there is only one figure that matters. Each child is 100 per cent of that child, and that child needs a 100 per cent careful and loving upbringing. That's the only statistic that matters, just as it mattered to our hero way back then. It's what he said and he put it into clause one of the fostering-out agreement.

Stepney Causeway is now ancient history. The headquarters of the organisation is now in Barkingside, on part of the site that was the Girls Village. The old apple orchard was grubbed out to make way for the new head office building. Its 1970s architecture leaves it sadly marooned in its decade but the dedicated people who work there continue in the spirit they inherited from their founder. It is work they know with regret will never be finished. But let me leave you with a thought about kids: the world's best sticking plaster is a hug.

Acknowledgements,
Bibliography & Thanks

Acknowledgements

It is not the mission of this book to look at the ongoing work of the organisation after 19 September 1905 and the death of its founder. There are several books on that subject and I would like to pick out four. They are listed in the bibliography that follows.

Gillian Wagner was Chairman of the Executive and Finance Committee at the time she was writing. Her book *Barnardo* ends roughly where this one does, early in the twentieth century. It was her job to be part of the decisions which led to the closures of the residential part of the enterprise, and the era that closed with them. This meant the end of Stepney Causeway and moving the centre of operations to Barkingside, when vacated by the last of the children. June Rose was writing *For the Sake of the Children* shortly afterwards. She included the early Dublin days, and was able to go on into the early 1980s period. Both ladies illuminate their take on the story with some excellent descriptive writing, though they use a more academic style. While I have leaned heavily on their research, my historical canvas is wider. I have found some new archive material, and any views expressed herein are my own.

Commissioned by the organisation, the *Memoirs* are an absolute goldmine of original material; our hero seems to have collected and saved every scrap of paper and was a fanatic about statistics. However, as we might expect, the book does take a biased view in his favour. Material which might lead to criticism was left out. Recent researches have driven several large coaches pulled by a great many horses through some of its claims about the Barnardo family origins. By all means read the book, but if you do it would be wise to cross-reference with later material.

A strong recommendation is the 2005 book *Keeping the Mission Alive*, written by council member Winston Fletcher. This was commissioned to mark the centenary of T. J.'s death, and takes the story forward into the first year or so of the new millennium. It is in large-format paperback, has lots of pictures, many in colour, and the text is very readable. For those who want an insider's update, this would be your port of call. Using Barnardo's as it now exists as his starting point, he offers an extensive and knowledgeable view of how modern charities tick, what happens in children's work these days, social changes and so forth. He also discusses where the money comes from and how it is spent, and is able to comment on the place of government in all this. The key phrase is 'Third Sector Work' when referring to voluntary agencies these days. It is an easy-to-read book written by someone who has done it for real.

I also benefited from various nineteenth-century Ordnance Survey maps, published by Alan Godfrey Maps. These helped to give a picture of where various places were in relation to each other, and where they would have been if they were still there today.

The Office of National Statistics kindly supplied me with Leaflet RP51, which is a guide to inflation in the period discussed. Written prominently on it is the statement that all nineteenth-century details are educated guesses.

Bibliography

Memoirs of the Late Dr Barnardo, by James Marchant and Mrs
    Barnardo (Hodder & Stoughton, 1907). This is by the widow
    and her ghost-writer. See acknowledgements.
Barnardo, by Gillian Wagner (Weidenfeld & Nicolson, 1979). See
    acknowledgements.
For the Sake of the Children, by June Rose (Hodder & Stoughton,
    1987). See acknowledgements.
Keeping the Vision Alive, by Winston Fletcher (Barnardo's, 2005).
    See acknowledgements.
The Times, 24 May 1889.

Thanks

Staff at the Family Records Office and also at Redhill Library.

Anglo–German Family History Society, in particular Peter
Towey, with whose assistance leads were found which led to
various puzzles being solved.

Pastor Christoph Hellmich of St Mary's Lutheran church and
Steve Pilcher of the Historic Chapels Trust. Helpful pointers on
research into German church communities of the period.

Staff at Barnardo's at Barkingside for encouragement and help.

Sean Solan, a genial genealogist in Dublin, who found all sorts
of things in the archives. Bearing in mind that in 1922 the Central
Records Office in Dublin burned down, he did a great job. Irish
details for this reason can often be difficult to find.

Mike Lindley for his great assistance.

Amberley Publishing, especially Nicola Gale for that essential
encouragement that all authors need.

Particular thanks to Dr David Barnardo and his sister Mrs
Priscilla Harvey, great-grandchildren of George, one of T. J.'s elder
brothers. Their help included not only general encouragement,
but also access to the family archives. The help of Sean Solan and
his researches has allowed us to verify a few more facts and to add
that archive.

Index

Also available from Amberley Publishing

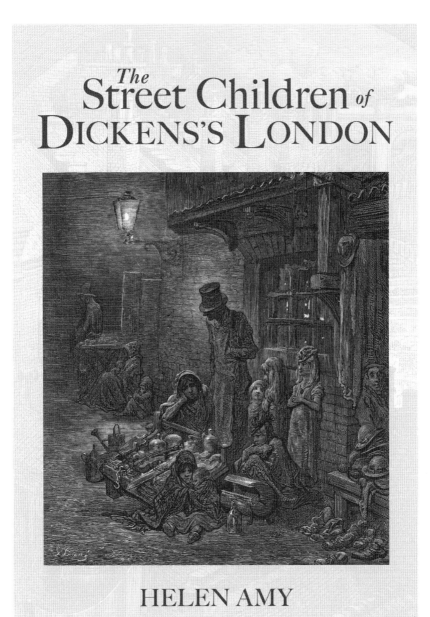

The
Street Children *of*
DICKENS'S LONDON

HELEN AMY

Available from all good bookshops or to order direct
Please call **01453–847–800**
www.amberleybooks.com